THE COMPLETE SAMOYED

"The White Dog with the Smiling Face"

THE COMPLETE

Samoyed

by

ROBERT H. and DOLLY WARD

1971

HOWELL BOOK HOUSE INC.
845 Third Avenue
New York, N.Y. 10022

Lindy and future Ch. Starchak's Witangomote.

Raising a dog is like raising a child, except that the dog is never independent of you.

We dedicate this book to our two daughters, Lindy and Mardee. Because our girls were raised with Samoyeds, loved them then, and love them now, our families will always have Sams. Our children have Sammies of their own, for themselves and for their children, because Samoyeds are the ideal dog for children.

Contents

7

PART III
Breeding, Care and Training

Frontispiece drawing, p. 2, by D. K. Dennis. Drawings on Pages 17 and 170 by Dr. Art Smith. Drawings on Page 169 are by G. M. Adams. Drawings of rights and wrongs in conformation of the Samoyed on Pages 162, 171, 172, 173, 174, 175, 176, 177 and 178 are by Mrs. Mel Fishback.

Foreword

IT is with great pleasure that I write the foreword to "The Complete Samoyed."

Books are important for the background and education they impart to owners of purebred dogs. This book, and its treasure of pictures of memorable dogs, admirably serves such a purpose for those interested in the Samoyed. It not only traces the establishment of the breed and its year-by-year development in America, but provides a richer understanding of the breed's outstanding qualities and character.

I have known Bob and Dolly Ward for over 25 years. They are most qualified to write this book, and fortunately have taken the responsibility of it seriously. Their quarter-century experience as breeders, exhibitors, trainers, and judges has provided an excellent background, and their experience as educators has helped them in the extensive and thorough research the work has required.

They have served the Samoyed Club of America in various offices since 1943, including membership on the Breed Standard Committee that rewrote the official standard in 1956. Dolly served as the club's president in the early 1960's, and Bob in 1969 and 1970.

My own acquaintanceship with the Samoyed goes well back, too. I have judged them at the shows since 1937, including two parent club Specialties, and have witnessed their steady increase in number. It is good to note that despite this growth, consistency of type and quality is seen. And it will, I hope, continue to be seen.

—Major B. Godsol

(Mr. Godsol's sudden death in December 1970 took from the dog sport one of its ablest and most admired leaders. We are very proud of what he had written in foreword to our book, and deeply grateful for having known him as a friend.—*The Authors*)

9

Intriguing for Samoyed owners is the dog portrayed in "The Morning Walk," painted by Thomas Gainsborough in 1785, more than a hundred years before the expedition dogs were brought to England by the Kilburn-Scotts.—*National Gallery, London.*

Preface

IN the comparatively short span of eighty years, the Samoyed has risen from an almost extinct breed to one of the most popular.

The tribes of the Samoyed people, from whom the dogs were obtained by the early explorers, have been dispersed by the Russians, and their mode of living altered by industrialization. It is fortunate for us that the handful of dogs released in the period of 1890 to 1912 were handled so skilfully that the breed was preserved. With wars and political upheaval, not more than a half dozen were obtained from Russia in the 1920s, and since then the door has been closed.

Because the Samoyed is one of the breeds most nearly akin to the prehistoric or natural canine, it has been one of the easier breeds to duplicate. The erect ears, the smiling face, the buff to white coat, the plumed tail—all come naturally. The disputes that there have been over proper size for a Samoyed are a problem created by humans, and not by nature. We would indeed be more successful as breeders if we would trust nature more. As it is, we have been quite fortunate, for Samoyeds have no coat color problem, no docking, no cropping, and no trimming. In man's desire to "improve" the breed, he did concentrate upon the black points—the eye rims, the nose, and the lips. While this contrast of black against the white face is very pleasing, records show that the pink or Dudley (pink with black) noses were natural.

Research reveals that the black, black and white, and even brown and white dogs which existed in the sled packs along with the white Bjelkiers were Laika and Ostiak dogs from around Archangel, and were of a different ancestry. The Bjelkiers were from a thousand

11

miles east of Archangel, in the area east of the Yenisei River stretching to the Olenek River, where the Samoyed tribes of the Tungunese and Yakuts lived. If this difference in the dogs was not so, we Samoyed breeders have found a way to refute the Mendelian theory, for there have been no mixed colors in England or America plaguing the registrations for the past fifty years.

—*Bob and Dolly Ward*

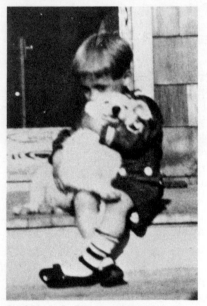

Author Bob Ward exhibited interest in Samoyeds at an early age.

Acknowledgments

MUCH of the information in this book has been gleaned from early club bulletins, old books, and countless rewarding days in the library. But an especially valuable source for us has been the contact with people who had seen the original imports to England and the United States. We are especially appreciative of the cooperation we have received from Mrs. Enid Brownson and Mrs. Ivy Kilburn-Morris, daughters of the English pioneers in the breed—Mr. and Mrs. E. Kilburn-Scott.

In assembling the facts for the period 1922 to the present, we have been fortunate to have had the cooperation of Samoyed enthusiasts everywhere—from all sections of the United States, from Canada, from Australia, and from England.

Special thanks go to Mrs. Serena A. Bridges, sister of the late Mrs. Catharine Self Quereaux, for permission to use her sister's vast files and notes of breed history.

For their cooperation and help with articles, drawings or information, we are indebted to Mrs. Trudie McIlnea-Westwood (England), Mrs. Helen Harris, Mr. Miles Vernon, Mrs. Agnes Mason, Mrs. Aljean Mason Larson, Dr. William Ivens, Dr. Joan Sheets, Mrs. Eileen Whitlock, Mrs. Borghild Ulfeng, Mrs. Bernice B. Ashdown, Mr. Charles L. Rollins, Mrs. Gertrude Adams, Mrs. Jean Baer, Mrs. Lila Weir, Mrs. Joyce Cain, Mrs. Bernice Helinski, Mr. Warren Stevens, Mrs. Vera Messier, Mrs. Ethel Stefanik, Mrs. Jan Kauzlarich, Mrs. Lenora Sprock, Mrs. Mel Fishback, and Dr. Arthur Smith, Daniel Winn, Margaret Schlichting, Susan M. North and Ab Sidewater. For assistance in design and typing we thank Miss Wilda Reese, Mrs. Margi Tuttle, and D. K. Dennis.

To the many who have cooperated in the request for pictures, we hope that their reproduction here will give you as much pleasure as they give us, and are sure to give future owners.

PART I
History

The photograph above of a typical northern scene is included with permission of Beech-Nut, Inc. The Samoyeds pictured are Ch. Yate-Sea Arctic King, Eskimo and Yate-Sea Alaska Dawn, owned by Walter Yates.

The Name:

The correct pronunciation of Samoyed is
SAM-A-YED
(Accent on the last syllable.)

The name was chosen by E. Kilburn-Scott, English pioneer of the breed, and honors the Samoyed tribes of Siberia from whom the founding stock was obtained.

In both England and America, the breed was originally written as *Samoyede.* The final "e" was dropped by the English in 1923, and by the American Kennel Club in 1947, and the simplified spelling is now used in reference to either the people or the breed.

The word *samoyed* is literally translated as "living off themselves." Some reporters have interpreted this as implying cannibalism, but we believe the truer implication is one of self-sufficiency—a nomadic people who managed to live off the land by their moving about.

The Russians sometimes called the dogs *Voinaika,* which can be translated to mean either carriage, lead or direction dogs, or guard, hunting and war dogs. But the natives themselves called the dogs *Bjelkiers,* "white dogs that breed white."

17

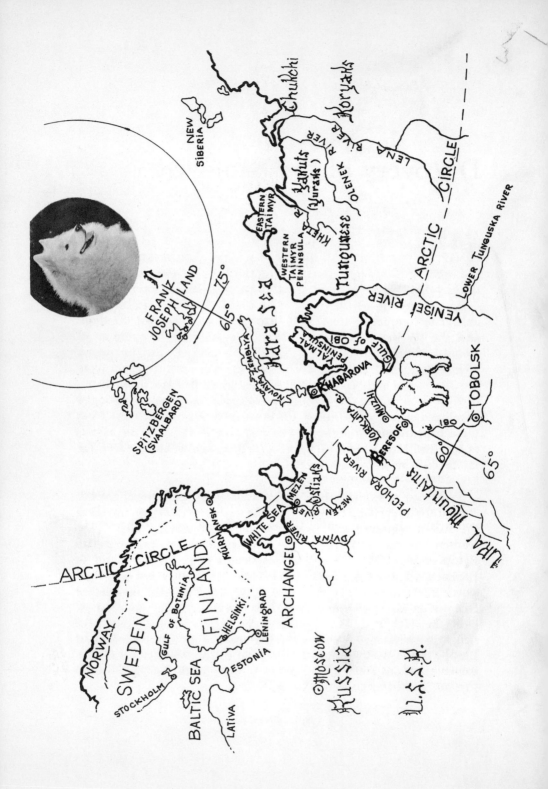

Discovery of the Samoyed

THE white dog with the smiling face, the dog we know as the Samoyed, was brought to the attention of Western civilization through Dr. Fridtjof Nansen, the noted Norwegian explorer.

Dr. Nansen firmly believed that sledging with dogs was the answer to conquering the Arctic wastes. He recommended the dogs, and the services of his dog broker, Alexander I. Trontheim of Tobolsk, Siberia, to many explorers. This proved most fortunate. The majority of the dogs used in their expeditions thus came from the same area and, because the natives' dogs had not been inter-bred with outsiders for thousands of years, were of a strongly-developed strain. As we shall see later in detail, it was dogs from these expeditions—brought to England largely through the efforts of Mr. and Mrs. Ernest Kilburn-Scott—that became the nucleus for the breed as we know it today.

Tribes of the Siberian Tundras and the Eskimos of North America had early discovered that the safest method for traveling the frozen regions was the sledge, usually drawn by dogs. (Dr. Nansen, in his book *Northern Mists,* quotes the explorer Ibn Batuta (1302–1377): "Four dogs to sledges going to the 'Land of Darkness'—dogs or guides, a leader who has been there before is worth 1,000 dinars.") But it was in Siberia that this method of locomotion was first applied to polar exploration.

In the 17th and 18th centuries the Russians made extensive sledge journeys and charted the Siberian coast from the borders of Europe to the Bering Strait. Baron Wrangell wrote of traveling the barren wastes of Siberia with sledge teams, and of their use by the "Yassak" men (tax collectors for the Czar).

19

The Russians usually traveled with many dogs and few men. The early English explorers, in contrast, used many men and few dogs. Dr. Nansen's research, and the experience of a trip across Greenland on skis in 1888, convinced him of the wisdom of using dogs in overwhelming ratio to men.

In preparing his expedition toward the North Pole in 1894, Nansen asked his friend, Russian explorer Baron Edward von Toll, to procure good sledge dogs from Siberia. The Baron had used these on his trip to the Arctic.

Baron von Toll engaged Alexander Trontheim to purchase thirty dogs. When he heard that Trontheim was preparing to purchase Ostiak dogs, he asked that the dogs be purchased instead in eastern Siberia from the Tungunese branch of the Samoyed people, whose draught dogs were better than the Ostiaks.

Trontheim headed toward the Petchora district to obtain the dogs. Hearing of a disease raging in that area among the dogs, he turned instead to Berezof, which is located n. 64° latitude and e. 64.5° longitude, and here purchased 40 sledge dogs. Trontheim hired a native named Terentieff, who used a herd of 450 reindeer and sledges to convey him, the 40 dogs, and 9600 pounds of food for the dogs to the coast at Khabarova. This, a distance of 400 miles, was the arranged meeting place where Fridtjof Nansen was to pick up the dogs. The trip took three months.

Dr. Nansen's account of his first meeting with the dogs reads: "Many of them appeared to be well-bred animals, longhaired, snow-white, with up-standing ears and pointed muzzles. With their gentle, good-natured-looking faces, they at once ingratiated themselves into the affections. Some of them resembled a fox, and had shorter coats, while others were black or spotted. Evidently they were of different races, and some of them betrayed by their drooping ears, a strong admixture of European blood."

What Nansen saw as a difference in the dogs stemmed from a difference in the people that owned them. There were two types of Samoyed tribes—one nomadic, the other pastoral—and each had their own kind of dog.

The nomadic Samoyed tribes had the all-white *Bjelkier* dogs, who served as hunting and draught dogs for their owners. *Bjelkier* means "white dog that breeds white." In native usage, the term was also applied to the ermine, the white fox, and the white bear.

The pastoral tribes had dogs of the Renvall-Hund or Elkhound type. Some were white, some black and white, and some brown and white.

The books *Dogs of All Nations* by Count Henry de Blyforte, *The Voyage of the Vega* by Dr. Otto Nordenskiolds, and *In Northern Mists* by Fridtjof Nansen, all repeat this classification of the nomads with white hunting dogs and the reindeer-pastoral tribes with their smaller Renvall-Hund type, which were white, black and white, and brown and white, weighing thirty to fifty pounds.

In reports by explorers and expeditions sent out by the Smithsonian Institute, the Peabody Fund, and the British Zoological Society, accounts have been given of the various dogs in the Siberian area. One account told of white sled dogs hitched four abreast being used to pull barges on the Yenisei River. The Yenisei River is 200 miles east of the town of Berezof where Trontheim procured Nansen's dogs. The Smithsonian Institute Report of 1898 quotes from *Die Tungusen* by Dr. B. Langkavel, who in 1872 said: "The tent-living Samoyeds use only reindeer as draught animals and have the dogs for herding, but the remainder of the Samoyeds and Yakuts use dogs and indeed each one can pull two to three and one half *pud* [a pud is 32 pounds]."

Another German explorer, in 1892, told of the people in the area of the Sameanda. He declared there were two types of tribes: the dog people who had no reindeer and the reindeer people who had no dogs. The two classes of natives were continually battling because the dogs would kill the reindeer and the reindeer people would then kill the dogs. These dogs were described as pure white, quite gentle, but terrific hunters. Their speed deeply impressed the expedition.

Thus we had tribes of similar peoples with fairly similar dogs, yet there were distinct differences. The question arises, "Did these tribesmen have a breeding program?" When we read accounts of the devious means used by the Europeans to obtain the dogs which the natives refused to sell, we know that the natives prized their dogs highly. Small wonder, for the natives' total existence depended upon their possessing good dogs. They must have felt the same intense personal pride in their strains that breeders exhibit today.

21

Explorers and Expeditions Influencing the Breed

The great age of polar exploration, from 1870 to 1912, brought all Arctic dogs to notice. However, we shall confine ourselves here to the explorers of note who used the Bjelkier, now known as the Samoyed.

Fridtjof Nansen. Dr. Nansen, a professor in seven chairs or departments at the University of Norway, designed his own ship for his expedition. *The Fram* was so well-built and excellent in its design that it was used for five expeditions over a period of 35 years.

Nansen did considerable research in making his selection of the dogs for the sledging phase of his expedition. The cataloguing of the weights of the 28 dogs selected for the final journey toward the North Pole, recorded after nearly a year and a half of living and working in the Arctic regions, shows that the 19 males averaged 58.7 pounds, and the 9 bitches averaged 50.5 pounds.

The weights of Nansen's dogs (in pounds) :

Males:

Storraeven, 70	Barrabas, 59.5
Kaifas, 69	Kapperslangen, 59.5
Sultan, 68	Lilleraeven, 59
Pan, 65	Blok, 59
Perpetuum, 63	Russen, 58
Gulen, 60.5	Potifar, 57
Flint, 61.5	Narrifas, 46
Isbjon, 61.5	Barnet, 39
Haren, 61.5	Livjaegeren, 38.5
Baro, 60.5	

Bitches:

Kvik (Nansen's own from Greenland) , 78
Ulenka, 57
Freia, 50
Suggen, 61.5
Barbara, 49.5
Katta, 45.5
Sjoliget, 40
Bjelki, 38
Kvindfolket, 37

Nansen's theory for sledging was a disastrous one for the dogs. He and partner Frederic Johansen set out with many dogs, but planned

Fridtjof Nansen's drawing of himself and Frederic Johansen en route to Franz Joseph Land in kayaks, lashed together by their dog sleds.

Borchgrevink and dogs on an ice ledge in the Antarctic.

that as they ran out of food, the weaker dogs would be fed to the stronger ones. The trip over the ice packs eliminated all the dogs but two, their lead dogs Kaifas and Suggen. And even these two had to be sacrificed when they arrived at open water, for the men were cautious about taking them in their kayaks.

After selecting the draught dogs of the Samoyed people for his attempt at the Pole, Dr. Nansen recommended them to other explorers. He sent an all-white Samoyed bitch, named Grasso, to the Duc d'Abruzzi as a good example of a sled dog.

Jackson-Harmsworth Expedition. Major Frederick G. Jackson led this English expedition to Franz Josef Land, above the Arctic Circle. Here they met Nansen and Johansen, returning from their 18-month journey by sledge and kayak, and brought them home. Major Jackson was also very interested in the Samoyed, and returned some to England. He presented his best dog, Jacko, to Queen Alexandra. Jacko was all-white, and the get of Nimrod out of Jenny. Dr. Kotelitz, a physician with the expedition, brought the bitch Kvik back with him, and she is found in early pedigrees. Eight other dogs brought back by Major Jackson went to Mr. Kilburn-Scott's kennels in 1899.

The Duc d'Abruzzi, or Luigi Amadeo, the distinguished Italian adventurer, aimed for the North Pole, and sought the counsel of Fridtjof Nansen. Upon advice, he ordered 120 dogs from Alexander Trontheim in July, 1898. Not many explorers have given detailed comment on their use of dogs, but the Duc left the following: "Although born in an intensely cold country, they were not insensible to temperatures below a −30° centigrade. When it was very cold they were often seen to raise their paws out of the snow from time to time, and to go about looking for straw or wood to lie upon . . ."

The Duc's account of the harnessing of the dogs is very interesting to sled drivers because he was the first to use the double tandem hitch. He wrote:

> While Trontheim showed us how Nansen had harnessed the dogs abreast by separate traces attached to the sledge [fan hitch], as was done by the Samoyeds and Esquimaux to allow them more liberty in their movements and to utilize all their strength, it had great disadvantages. The traces became all mixed up and required much con-

tinual, tiresome labor. To avoid this inconvenience I decided when at Christiana to follow this method used by the Yakuts of the Lower Lena River who make use of a single long trace, to each side of which the dogs are harnessed by shorter traces attached to the central trace. The dogs showed strength and endurance and I felt more confidence in them after a four-day trip of 70 miles. Rings were fixed on the central trace on a level with the dogs' heads when they were pulling, and to which they were hooked by short chain, which also served to tie them up during the night. Our dog harness, like that made by other explorers, consisted of three or four layers of canvas, two lines of which passed between the animals' forelegs and two along its back, where they were all united to the trace.

Most interesting is the Duc's description of his best lead dog, an all-white Bjelkier named Messicano.

> We are decidedly rivaling not only Nansen, but also Wrangell, who was celebrated for the rapidity of his marches. We are able to accomplish these remarkable stages now, partly because we have only four sledges, and partly on account of the tracks which Messicano, the leading dog, was able to follow again today, even where they had been almost entirely effaced by the wind. It is a small white dog, with thick hair, and very intelligent eyes. It is so called Messicano on account of the abundance of hair which fringes its legs, resembling trousers which widen at the feet. Ever since our departure from Templitz Bay, it has held the first place of the first sledge, because it followed the man at the head of the convoy better than the others. Has followed obediently from the outset, being the most obedient to the word of command. Although not as big as some of his companions he always pulls, and falls upon the dogs of the other sledges which try to pass it. One would say that it feels all the importance of its position, and is proud of it. Messicano gallops like a dwosky horse with its nose always down in the snow. Sometimes it loses the track and then goes more slowly. Messicano shows its anxiety, it whines and runs up and down with its tongue out until it finds the track again. Then he darts off in the right direction, often for long stretches where it is utterly impossible for us to see a trace of our former passage.

One Samoyed male from the Abruzzi expedition was returned to England. This dog was Houdin. Houdin was shown and used at stud, and left a good mark upon the breed. Russ, another dog that had been purchased in Tobolsk by Trontheim for this expedition, also eventually made his way to England, and is in early Samoyed pedigrees.

Carsten E. Borchgrevink, a Norwegian who lived in Australia, led an English expedition to the Antarctic in 1904. He had over 100 Samoyeds with him at the start of the trip. While he did not write much about the breed, two dogs from his pack had tremendous impact upon the breed. The greatest was Antarctic Buck, left in the Sidney Zoo after the expedition, and in 1908 imported to England by Mr. and Mrs. Kilburn-Scott. The other dog was Trip, who ended up on the Ernest Shackleton expedition, and was returned to England by Lieutenant Charles Adams. Borchgrevink handed over 27 of his dogs to Dr. Douglas Mawson in 1911 for another Australian expedition.

Sir Ernest Shackleton, on his 1907–1909 Antarctic expedition, had a few teams of dogs from other expeditions that had been left in Australia. He was a strong advocate of the use of ponies for sledge-work in the Antarctic, but the problems created by their weight and the need to provide food for them made it necessary to destroy all of them.

Captain Robert Falcon Scott followed in the pattern of Shackleton, and used many men and ponies, with but few dogs, for his expedition in 1911. Why he did not use dogs as a main plan in dashing to the South Pole is not clearly known. Perhaps he did not care to use them in the customary cannibalistic way of the other explorers, or he may not have trusted them. This is particularly puzzling in that he was the brother of E. Kilburn-Scott, who did so much to establish the Samoyed breed in England. In fact, E. K. Scott gave his brother the dog Olaf, a son of Antarctic Buck, to take on the expedition. Captain Scott did take several teams of dogs with him to the Antarctic, but planned to rely upon ponies and men to pull the sledges. The ponies broke through the snow, sweated, and froze, and eventually all became snowblind. The freezing of the ponies was due to the fact that they sweat through their hides, while dogs sweat through their tongues and pads of their feet. Someone docked the tails of one team of Scott's dogs, and they died of pneumonia within three weeks because of the lack of the thick bushy tail, which is a great protection to the dogs while sleeping.

Scott made his dash to the South Pole with six men laboriously pulling the sleds. From his diary, found after his death, we have

Members of the Shackleton Expedition returning on the "Nimrod." The
Samoyed "Trip" was brought to England and Mrs. Kilburn-Scott
by Lt. Adams of this expedition.

Dogs of the Borchgrevink Expedition.

27

Samoyed across the South Pole with the Roald Amundsen Expedition.

ETAH, lead dog of the Amundsen expedition, pictured at 11 years of age. In his later years, ETAH was a pet of the Princess de Montyglon.

learned that he did reach the pole, only to find it covered with paw prints of dogs and a note from Roald Amundsen giving him greetings dated a month before.

Roald Amundsen, first to reach the South Pole (planting the Norwegian flag there on December 14, 1911), was the most successful "dog man" of all the explorers. His accounts of the training and selection of his sledge dogs are outstanding. He acquired 97 dogs for his expedition, and after much training used 52 of them and four sledges for the dash to the pole. As planned, they returned with the four men, one sledge, and 12 surviving dogs. The round-trip covered 1,860 miles in 99 days, and the first animal over the pole was an all-white Samoyed lead dog. Twenty-seven of Amundsen's dogs were given to Douglas Mawson for an Australian expedition in 1911, and the rest returned as pets of the crew.

The points made by Luigi Amadeo had been proven. He had written, "Dogs are undeniably the most useful animals for man in his expeditions with sledges over the ice of the Polar Sea. They have this advantage, too, that unlike horses or reindeer, they readily eat their fellows. Their weight is small, and they can be easily carried on light boats or ice floes. Their loss represents but a small diminution of motive power in comparison with that which results from the death of a horse or reindeer."

On each of these expeditions, except the ill-fated Scott expedition, the Samoyed played a major part. Almost all Samoyeds today can be traced back to expedition dogs.

Although the utility of the dogs was the main concern, the warmth of their personalities was frequently noted by the explorers. Samoyed admirers of today will recognize their dogs in such comments as: "and the white dogs crowded around to be petted" (by Fridtjof Nansen); "At night we could tell the white dogs, as they poked us with their noses to get attention" (by James Murray, biologist for Shackleton); and "We found that at night the best way to thaw our sleeping bags was to spread them out, for the white dogs would jump right on them" (by Roald Amundsen). In his book *First on the Antarctic Continent,* C. E. Borchgrevink wrote: "It was curious to watch the marked difference in the habits and manners of the Greenland dogs to that of their brethren from

29

Dogs of the Borchgrevink Expedition, from which came Antarctic Buck.

Siberia. The former were much more wild and seldom or never mixed with the other dogs, nor did they attach themselves as much to man as the Siberian dogs did."

While not an explorer in the sense of the polar expeditions, **W. B. Vanderlip** in 1898 made a two-year trip through Siberia, and left us a detailed account of travel by dog sled. Frequent references to the Tungoos, Uraks, and Koraks show us that he covered much of the land where Trontheim collected dogs for the explorers. From the book *In Search of a Siberian Klondike* we quote:

> The reader may well ask how the natives can use both dogs and reindeer if the very sight of a deer has such a maddening effect on the dogs. The explanation is simple. The two never go together. There is the dog country and the deer country, and the two do not impinge upon each other. Even among the same tribe there may be a clear division. For instance, there are the Deer Koraks, and the Dog Koraks. In some of the villages of the former, there may occasionally be seen a few low-bred curs which are not used for sledging and have been trained not to worry deer.

Need we ponder further on the background of our beautiful breed? Were our Samoyeds hunters, draught dogs, or reindeer herders? No matter, for they all had the common faculty of being the "right hands" of their masters, and the means of survival in that cold bleak land.

One common reference weaves a thread through all the accounts of travel in Siberia—note of a white dog that breeds white. This dog is always living inside the *chooms* or *combes,* the houses, with his master. He is continually referred to as a friendly likeable dog, very unlike the wild creatures.

Thus, while the true origin of our breed is lost in antiquity, we *do* know that the Samoyed came from a general area east of the Urals, near the Arctic Circle, and we *do* know that the generic dogs which were combined were selected from Bjelkiers, the white animals that breed white. We know, too, that any black spots or markings have been a disqualification in the breed in England and the United States for the past 70 years. Nature must be telling us that fallible humans have allowed the one true dominant strain to come through loud and clear.

31

Ernest Kilburn-Scott with Prince Zouroff, one of the dogs from the litter pictured below.

A 1902 litter, by Jacko ex Olgalene, bred by Mrs. Kilburn-Scott. A dog of this litter was presented to Queen Alexandra.

Beginnings in England

O F the first dogs of the breed in England, only a few came from western Siberia. Later imports were from the Ural Mountains and the Island of Novaya Zemblaya and were likewise limited in number. Most numerous of the original dogs, and most influential in the establishment of the breed in England, were the dogs from the expeditions, which Alexander Trontheim had originally obtained from the area east of the Yenisei River, stretching to the Olenek. All of these were imported prior to 1914. A very few were brought to England in the mid-1920s, and since then—none.

The first importers, and establishers of the breed in England, were Mr. and Mrs. Ernest Kilburn-Scott. Mr. Kilburn-Scott was a member of the Royal Zoological Society, and in its cause had made a trip to the Archangel in 1889, from which he had brought back a dog. This was Sabarka ("the fat one" in Russian) and he was chocolate-brown in color.

Sabarka was not from the same district in Siberia as Fridtjof Nansen's dogs. He came from at least 900 miles west of the Olenek River. Mr. Kilburn-Scott had sympathetically bought Sabarka to save the young puppy from providing the natives a "feast." He was said to be typical in many good points of the breed such as head, stand-off coat, curled tail, and good carriage.

Soon after this, Mr. Kilburn-Scott brought in the famous cream-colored bitch, Whity Pechora. The mating of Sabarka and Whity Pechora produced a daughter Neva, who went to Lady Sitwell, newly interested in the breed.

Earliest mention of the breed seems to be an advertisement placed by Mr. Kilburn-Scott in 1891, under the *Foreign Dogs and Various* classification in the English papers. It read:

33

Ch. Pearlene, bred in 1901 of dogs of the Jackson-Harmsworth Expedition (Russ ex Kvik). Pearlene introduced the pure white and thicker type of plush coat, rounder tips to ears, and very black eyes and nose.

Nansen, bred in 1901 by Mrs. Kilburn-Scott. Nansen, who lived to be 16 years of age, was of the Musti-Whity Petchora breeding that was the beginning of the pure white Samoyed in England.

Lovely white Russian (Samoyed) sledge dog pups, like small polar bears, most gentle and affectionate. Splendid coats and tails. Very rare. Parents imported.

Samoyeds were first shown at the Leeds show in 1893 in the Foreign Dog class.

Lady Sitwell later imported a snow-white dog named Musti from northern Russia. When Musti was mated with Whity Pechora in 1901, the white proved dominant, and the litter was the beginning of the all-white Samoyeds in England. It included the famous dog Nansen, who swept the shows in 1903, and the great bitch Olgalene. A third dog, Rex Albus, did not affect the breed as much.

The mating of Musti and Neva produced Ch. Olaf Oussa, important behind pedigrees of today.

When the Kilburn-Scotts wanted more stock, they went through Alexander Trontheim, who had obtained Nansen's dogs in 1894. In 1899, while selecting dogs for the Duc d'Abruzzi, Trontheim chose Russ for the Scotts. This dog was bred to Kvik, the bitch brought back by Dr. Kotelitz when he was the physician on the Jackson-Harmsworth expedition in 1897. This breeding produced Ch. Pearlene, famous for her beautiful head and ears, and for her progeny.

Major F. G. Jackson, who brought back many dogs in 1897, had given seven to Kilburn-Scott, and one (the male, Jacko) to Queen Alexandra. Major Jackson and Mr. Kilburn-Scott worked together in the early years, and joined in the proposal of a standard for the Samoyed. (Both judged the breed in England until the mid-1920s).

Jacko, the Queen's dog, was shown in the first class solely for Samoyeds, in 1902. Six dogs were judged by Mr. Kilburn-Scott: Jacko was Winners, defeating among others the Honorable Mrs. McLaren Morrison's Peter the Great, bred by the Scotts. Queen Alexandra had other Samoyeds, notably Sandringham Pearl.

Nansen bred to Ch. Pearlene produced Kviklene in 1902, carrying on the whites for her grandmother Kvik of the Jackson-Harmsworth Expedition.

When Antarctic Buck was released from quarantine in 1909, he was bred to Kviklene and Olgalene. Olgalene's mating with Buck produced Kaifas and Kirchie, both whites. When bred to Jacko, Olgalene produced Ivanoff, a fine biscuit specimen.

But it was the all-male litter resultant of the breeding of Antarctic Buck with Kviklene that was to have the profoundest influence on the breed. In that one litter, Kviklene produced Southern

Cross, South Pole, Fang, and Olaf. This was the same Olaf that Captain Robert Scott took to the South Pole in 1911. And without Southern Cross and South Pole, there would not be many show Samoyeds today.

Antarctic Buck was a dazzling white dog standing 21½″ (measured at the shoulder, rather than at the withers), and 35″ long from tip of his nose to tip of his tail. He died in 1909, at ten years of age, having contracted distemper after being shown at Redhill, England. From this epidemic, only seven of his famous puppies survived.

Trip, another dog originally from the Borchgrevink Expedition, made his way to England in 1911. He was brought there by Lieutenant Adams of the Shackleton Expedition. Trip appears in some pedigrees, but not in as many as Houdin from the Abruzzi Expedition.

Mrs. Helen Harris, whose Snowland Kennels was so prominent on the American scene in the 1930s, once summed up the early Siberian imports:

> "There are twelve dogs of importance to the pedigrees of American Samoyeds: the Kilburn-Scotts' *Sabarka, Whity Pechora, Russ, Houdin* and *Antarctic Buck;* Lady Sitwell's *Kvik;* Queen Alexandra's *Jacko; Trip; Ayesha* (brought in in 1910 by Gordon Colman, and sold to Mrs. Cammack); and from Russia in 1925, *Pelle of Halfway* and *Yugor of Halfway,* imported by Mrs. Grey-Landsberg."

Mrs. Kilburn-Scott had refused to buy Ayesha because she did not like the "Spitz-like face, a faulty foreface, and slightly prominent round eyes."

Mrs. Harris concluded her summation with:

> "The credit really goes to the bitches for launching this breed, and the most influential bitches were Kvik and Whity Pechora."

The breed received some wide attention in 1911 as a result of the Glasgow Exposition. As part of the show, a group of Lapplanders were on display with their tents and reindeer. Spectators began asking, "How do you herd your reindeer?" Of course, the Scots used the Collie for their sheep, and expected to see some type of work dog. But the Lapplanders had not brought the smaller Renvall-type dogs which they used.

When the director of the Exposition discussed this with Mr. Kilburn-Scott, the latter offered some of his Samoyeds to be put on

Antarctic Buck, imported to England by the Kilburn-
Scotts from the Borchgrevink South Pole expedition.

Houdin, imported to England by the Kilburn-Scotts
from the Duc d'Abruzzi's North Pole expedition.

display as reindeer herders with the Lapplanders. Many of the English newspapers photographed the dogs and publicized them as reindeer herders.

Mr. Will Hally, a long-time dog columnist and Samoyed breeder and judge, questioned the Lapplanders as to the similarity of the white Samoyed to their herd dogs, and they were most emphatic in stating that there was no resemblance. But *reindeer herder* would not be an altogether wrong classification for the Samoyed, for they are indeed an all-purpose dog. Basically, the Samoyed was a hunting and guard dog for the family, but where occasion demanded he became a herd and draught dog for certain tribes. Joe Stetson, writing in *Field and Stream*, once summed it up "The Samoyed is a three-H Dog . . . Hunting, Herding and Hauling."

Initially the Samoyed was shown in the Foreign Dog class in England, and labeled Samozia Sledge Dogs. But by 1909, Mr. Kilburn-Scott's choice of name for the breed, the Samoyede, had become the established designation, the Samoyede Club had been founded, and a standard formulated. Beginning in 1912 the Kennel Club ruled that Samoyedes should be classified separately.

The Samoyede Club as originally formed had excluded women, so in 1912 the Ladies Samoyede Association was founded. In this same year, the Samoyed and the Laika were combined for show purposes, but only the dominant white was to survive as a breed and type.

The year 1912 also saw the coming on the scene of a breeder who was to become one of the legendary figures in the development of the Samoyed. Miss J. V. Thomson-Glover acquired her first Samoyed, Snow Cloud, from the Kilburn-Scotts. Miss Thomson-Glover was a strong influence in guarding the quality of the Samoyed for many years, and was particularly influential in maintaining the typical smiling expression in the breed. She played an important part in the founding of the Samoyed Association of Britain, which absorbed the earlier Samoyede Club and the Ladies Samoyede Association in 1920.

With importation halted by the cessation of the expeditions and the rumblings of World War I, the breeders of England took over on their own.

Scotland contributed mightily to the breed when in 1915 Miss E. Marker bred Antarctic Bru (by Southern Cross out of Zembla). She followed with Mustan of Farningham, a great sire.

But the greatest was yet to come. Ch. Kara Sea, by Mustan of Farningham out of Ch. Zahrina (later to become Ch. Zahrina of

The immortal Eng. Ch. Kara Sea.

It is interesting to compare this picture of a 1966 champion with that of Ch. Kara Sea above.

An interesting head-study
of Eng. Ch. Kara Sea.

Norka in the United States), was whelped on February 7, 1924.
Kara Sea was bred by Mrs. D. Edwards. He was shown to a fabulous
record that included 21 Challenge Certificates.

But even more than for his extensive winning over a long period,
attention must be paid to Ch. Kara Sea for his importance in the
concentration upon all-white dogs by certain breeders. His first
generation descendants included: English and American Champion Tiger Boy of Norka, Eng. Ch. Kara Queen of the Arctic, Eng.
Ch. Leader of the Arctic, and Am. Ch. Siberian Nansen of Farningham of Snowland. Second generation offspring of note included:
English Champions White Fang of Kobe, Ice Crystal, Surf, Riga, and
Greta of the Arctic; Kosca of Kobe; and Am. Ch. Moguiski.

Another Scottish breeder, Mrs. Simon, bred the winning Polar
Light of Farningham (Polar Sea out of Ch. Snowy) in 1923. This
dog, owned by Mrs. Kilburn-Scott, not only won Best of Breed at
Crufts Dog Show for five years, 1925 through 1929, but also contributed greatly as a sire.

Climaxing all of the activity in breeding and showing was the first
Samoyed Club show in England in 1923. In the same year, the
Samoyed Club of America was formed across the Atlantic.

Because the end concern of this book is with the development of
the Samoyed in America, from this point on only the English dogs
who were exported to the United States, and were of influence here,
will be noted in detail. Suffice it to say here that these exportations
were to be many and of the greatest importance in the progress of
the breed in this country.

In closing out the story of these beginning years, we think all
Samoyed owners and breeders will find interest in the observations

40

Eng. Ch. Polar Light of Farningham.

on size, type, and consistency over the first forty years of the breed, expressed by Mr. Will Hally in this 1934 commentary:

> The first fact is that we have not made the Samoyed bigger. I saw every one of the original importations, and I saw all the dogs which were secured from the polar expeditions. Now that takes me back to the first days of the 1890s, to the very, very beginning of Samoyeds in this country (England), and I say emphatically that Samoyed size has not altered in the very least during all that period.
>
> Then, too, in my travels as a young man, I saw the genuine Spitz in various countries, and no one who really knew the two breeds could possibly say that they were one and the same. The true Samoyed (and I am not writing of the white dogs, and dogs which have not been white, that have been paraded as Samoyeds) is radically and fundamentally different from the Spitz. The Samoyed is a product of the Samoyed people, and this is corroborated by every traveler and explorer who has gone into the matter deeply and intimately.

A statement such as this is very reassuring to Samoyed breeders today, for few owners of other breeds can look at pictures of their breed of 70 years ago, and see in them present-day show winners.

41

An historic win. Sweet Missy of Sammar, puppy bitch from the classes, winning the first all-breed Best in Show by a Samoyed in the United States, at Toledo Kennel Club, April 10, 1949. The judge was Mrs. Marie Meyer, and handling was breeder-owner Mrs. Joseph J. Marshall.

The Samoyed
in the United States

1907–1923

FROM origins steeped in mystery in the frozen far reaches of north central Siberia, the Samoyed was brought to the attention of Western civilization by a Nobel Prize winner (Fridtjof Nansen) and a king's cousin (the Duc d'Abruzzi), and supported in England by their Highnesses, Queen Alexandra and King Edward VII. It was only fitting then that it should be introduced into America by royalty, and this it was through the Princess de Montyglyon.

Mercy d'Argenteau, a Belgian countess and the daughter of a royal favorite of the Court of Napoleon II, was also a hereditary princess of the Holy Roman Empire. The Princess was one of the great beauties of her day. Her world was what today would be termed "cafe society." Despite her upbringing and contacts with royalty, she met and married Captain John Bonavita, a well-known lion tamer. Captain Bonavita was to be written up more fully in the story of Lillian Russell's life than in the Princess' own autobiography.

Princess de Montyglyon had the first Samoyed registered in the American Kennel Club Stud Book (December 1906). The dog was the Russian Champion Moustan of Argenteau, #102896. Moustan was obtained in 1902 in St. Petersburg, Russia, from the Grand Duke Nicholas, brother to the Czar.

The reported story of how the Princess became the owner of Moustan is quite a romantic one.

43

At the time, the Princess owned Collies and Chows, and exhibited them quite often throughout Europe. In St. Petersburg, as she was leaving the show grounds for refreshments, she found at her heels one of the string of Samoyeds being shown by the Grand Duke. In her book she describes the dog as being a big, square-headed, good-tempered beast dragging his chain. The Princess took his chain and led him back to the bench. Next day she paid a visit to the bench to see the dog, and he followed her again. This time the Grand Duke was there as she returned him and said, "You seem to like Moustan very much." She replied, "I would give anything in the world to have him, but I hear none of this breed can be obtained. I well know that this one is not for sale."

Nicholas replied, "Oh, surely not for sale—but to give anything in the world for him? Is it not a reckless offer? I must think it over." All this with a smile and a drawl so filled with meaning that the Princess hastily dropped the subject.

The next few days and nights were filled with parties and court balls. As her departure approached, the Grand Duke asked her the date of leaving. When the Princess arrived at the station, she saw one of the Imperial Coaches on the train. She was informed that the Grand Duke had put his private car at her disposal. In the drawing room, she found a huge basket heaped with roses and orchids. When she began to remove them, there emerged the shaggy white head of the Russian Champion Moustan, with a card from the Grand Duke tied to his collar. "Moustan is not for sale," it read, "no price could buy him, but it will be a favor to him and me if you will graciously accept him."

The Princess came to America in 1904, two years after obtaining Moustan. She brought with her four Samoyeds, two Collies, and two Chow Chows—all of which she exhibited in the shows of the day (as remembered and related to us by the dean of American judges, Alva Rosenberg).

Moustan has at various times been rumored to be from the Fridtjof Nansen Expedition (1894–1897). This would have made him 10 to 12 years old when he began siring litters. Some books have attributed Moustan to Antarctic Buck of the Borchgrevink Expedition, but Moustan's own son, Ch. de Witte of Argenteau, was born in 1904—the date of the expedition.

Even without known parentage, Moustan's name appears behind many of our Samoyeds of today. A few people survive who remember him, and one describes him as being "a large powerful dog and of sturdier build than many of the breed seen today".

Moustan's son, Ch. de Witte of Argenteau, whose dam Sora of Argenteau was also of unknown ancestry, became the first American champion Samoyed of record in 1907.

Of the four Samoyeds that the Princess had brought to America, only Martyska of Argenteau had known parentage. She was by Houdin out of Olgalene. Moustan, Sora, and Siberia of Argenteau were all shown as unknown. Siberia became an American Kennel Club champion in 1908.

Another almost unknown dog of the Princess' was the dog ETAH, which was given to her in 1913 by a member of the Amundsen Expedition. ETAH was one of the Samoyed lead dogs of the expedition. The Princess dedicated her autobiography to ETAH, and a picture of him at 11 years of age is included in it.

The only get by Moustan of note and impact on the breed was Czarevitch, who was out of Martyska. Czarevitch and a grandson of Moustan, Ch. Zuroff, won constantly in the early days, but were shown largely against their kennelmates.

Early competition for the Argenteau dogs was provided by the Greenacre Kennels of Mrs. Ada Van Heusen, who (as Mrs. E. E. Lincoln) had imported the two full sisters Volga and Tamara, along with Soho and Katinka—son and daughter of Southern Cross, in 1912. Tamara became the first bitch of the breed to win American championship.

The mating of Czarevitch and Tamara produced Zuroff. Czarevitch also sired Ch. Greenacre Kieff and Evalo. Ch. Greenacre Kieff was the grandsire of Champions Zanoza, Kazan of Yurak and Fang of Yurak, dogs found in the pedigrees today.

New owners and exhibitors were appearing upon the scene. However, we must bear in mind that they faced problems that the great advances of veterinary medicine have pretty much erased. Many dog owners of this era, and indeed up until the mid-thirties, would not exhibit because of the distemper problem.

In 1908, Miss Elizabeth Hudson obtained her first Samoyeds, Togo and litter sister, Alice, acquired from Mrs. King Wainwright of Bryn Mawr, Pennsylvania. Twenty and thirty years later Miss Hudson was to import two great ones, but we'll talk of them in their time cycles.

Mrs. Sidney Borg and her sister Mrs. Cahn imported Samoyeds from Mrs. Cammack and Mr. Common of England, to compete at the shows with the Princess and Mrs. Van Heusen.

As could and does happen (even today), with the large kennels importing dogs to improve the breed, an individual bitch brought

45

in as a gift to a schoolgirl by her father had some of the greatest impact upon the early dogs. Miss Ruth Nichols was given the bitch Wiemur in 1914, which was registered in 1918. Mated to Czarevitch, Wiemur produced the Champions Malschick and Shut Balackeror, as well as the uncrowned Boris. (Shut Balackeror, born on April Fools' day, was named after the last Court Jester to the Czar.)

Ch. Malschick was the sire of the bitches Otiska and Theda, who were later mated to descendants of the French import, Pompey, imported in 1915 by Mrs. F. S. Mills of Fairfield, Connecticut.

Ch. Shut Balackeror became a prominent stud in the beginnings of the Yurak Kennels, owned by Mrs. Frank Romer.

Thomas Girvan imported a bitch Trixie #267252 from Scotland in 1919. Trixie was sold to Ruth Nichols' Top O' The World Kennels in 1920, and her name was changed to Vera. Trixie, Vera, or Trixie-Vera in some pedigrees, was bred to Ch. Malschick to produce the bitch Otiska. Through Otiska, who was quite small and had a curly coat, Trixie-Vera had descendants in many early pedigrees.

There were other imports at this time but they had almost no effect upon the breed. An example were the litter brothers Sergovitch and Mustiruss, by Kosko out of Koona, bred by Mrs. Cammack. The dogs Mr. Pepp and Beauty were brought in from China, but had no progeny.

As we look back, these early days were discouraging, for type and quality were rather ignored. Beauty to the eye of the individual was the sole criterion. There was great discrepancy in size and a standardized type had not really been-settled upon. Few dogs survived in pedigrees. But isn't this true of other breeds as well? Many early dogs have been lost in oblivion after brief show careers, and the breeds have been carried on by just a few.

In all, from 1906 through 1920, exactly 40 dogs had been registered with the American Kennel Club. There had been 15 imports with well-authenticated English pedigrees traced by Catharine Quereaux, plus two imports from China, three from Russia, and one from France. The breed had seven champions of record (see Appendix, page 301) .

The end of World War I was a turning point in breeding in both England and America.

This new era got its start on this side of the ocean with the import of Tobolsk by the Yurak Kennels of Mrs. Frank Romer. Tobolsk was obtained by the handler-broker, Percy Roberts, now a distinguished all-breed judge.

Tobolsk was heralded as the greatest Samoyed of all time in America, and at the same time condemned as leggy and ungainly. No matter, for Champion Tobolsk #285263 proved to be a magnificent dog and a good sire. He produced the constancy of size needed in the breed, and together with later imports Ch. Donerna's Barin and Ch. Yukon-Mit was vital in giving America back the type of dog from which Trontheim had made selections for the expeditions.

Ch. Tobolsk, himself by Fang ex Vilna, when mated with Otiska, sired a great line of winners including Ch. Toby of Yurak II, Nanook II, and Nanook of Donerna. (Ch. Toby of Yurak II won until he was 12 years of age, and in fact was Best of Breed at Westminster at that age.) Tobolsk mated with Sunny Ridge Pavlova produced Champions Fang of Yurak and Kazan of Yurak. (Kazan, who had difficulty making his championship because he was 26″ tall, was a large heavily-boned dog who was shown from 1922 to 1927. He was owned by Mrs. John Earnshaw of Rhode Island.)

Many daughters of Tobolsk were excellent specimens and good producers. They included: Queen Marie, Queen Zita, Ch. Patricia Obi, Donerna's Nara, and Champions Valeska, Semstra, and Snow Cloud of Yurak.

Ch. Draga, litter sister to Tobolsk and imported at the same time, was bred to Shut Balackeror and Zev of Yurak, and produced Ch. Kritelka of Yurak, Boy Yurak and Toby of Yurak.

The Frank Romers were active in the breed for 21 years until 1937, when their Yurak Kennels was transferred to Eddie Barbeau. The Romers (and Barbeau too) were active sledding enthusiasts.

Returning to 1920, we note the importation by Miss Mildred Trevor Sheridan of Hasova #292683, a seven-year-old dog from Russia, bred by Davelaari, Tula, Russia and Loree #294040, a bitch from England. They are best remembered as the sire and dam of Lady Olga, #320651, born 1920. Lady Olga was the dam of Ch. Icy King, who became the sire of such big winners of the 1930s as the litter brothers, Ch. Icy King Jr., Siberian Icy King Duplicate, CD, and Ch. Prince Kofski. Miss Sheridan, now Mrs. Mildred Sheridan Davis of Park-Cliffe Kennels, is still producing champions fifty years later. Hers is the oldest Samoyed kennel still in operation.

Two notable kennels were added in 1921. The F. L. Vintons' Obi Kennel continues through the Obi suffix found in today's pedigrees. The other was Mr. and Mrs. Harry Reid's Norka Kennels. In 1929 the Reids were to give great impetus to the breed with their importation of Ch. Tiger Boy.

In this continued period of imports, the years 1922 and 1923 brought the Romers' Yurak Kennels the great bitch Olga of Farningham (by Antarctic Bru, a grandson of Antarctic Buck, out of Oka, a granddaughter of Buck) ; Trip of Farningham (by Antarctic Bru out of Miss Muffet) ; and Yurak's Fox Laika—all from Mrs. Kilburn-Scott. To Yurak also came Donerna's Kolya of Farningham, from Mrs. Wharton Duff; and Donerna's Tsilma, a litter sister to Donerna's Barin, from Mrs. Pitchford. To Louis Smirnow came Nico of Farningham, who was on the small side, as were his progeny. Miss Grafton of England sent Polas of Farningham to the W. B. Donahues. Mr. and Mrs. James L. Hubbard of Howardsville, Maryland, imported Olaf of Farningham, another son of Antarctic Bru out of Nish Nish (thus the grandfather was again Mezenett of Antarctic Buck's famous litter) .

The second of the three pillars of the American Samoyed was imported at this time by Mr. and Mrs. Alfred Seeley for their Donerna Kennels at the foot of the George Washington Bridge in New York. He was Ch. Donerna's Barin, a son of Eng. Ch. Kieff out of Ivanofva, bred by Mr. Pitchford of England.

It is interesting to note that Barin was sent to this country in place of Snow Crest when the American Kennel Club waived the three generation rule for Ch. Tobolsk. Barin, you see, went back to the expedition import, Antarctic Buck in just two generations. He was himself an able sled dog and proved a great worker in the sled teams of the Donerna Kennels.

Ch. Donerna's Barin had 120 registered sons and daughters. Therefore, by sheer numbers, he had great influence on the breed, an influence that was especially positive for size and coat. Barin was a measured 22″ and 60 lbs. Some of his get were larger, but judging from the picture of him in this book at his tenth birthday, he reproduced his size. Some of Barin's outstanding daughters were Donerna's Nona, Donerna's Zoe, Donerna's Czarina, Donerna's Dagmar, Laika's Donerna, Laika's Illinishna, and Naida of Donerna.

Donerna's Kolya was influential because 60 of his progeny soon

Eng. Ch. Kieff, sire of Ch. Donerna's Barin and Ch. Donerna's Tsilma. Kieff was noted for throwing good coat to his progeny.

Ch. Donerna's Barin (center) celebrating his ninth birthday in 1929. On his left are the bitches Ch. Ilinishna, Ch. Laika Natiya, and Laika Narrifas. On his right are his sons, Laika Trail Breaker, Laika's Lucky Day and Laika's Grim.—*Photo, courtesy, G. Adams.*

Snow Fairy (1921–1933), by Ch. Kieff ex Ch. Nada, bred by Miss J. V. Thomson-Glover, and owned by Miss Elizabeth Hudson.

appeared in the Stud Book, mostly bred in the Midwestern States. Bred to Polas of Farningham, Kolya produced Pollyanna and Princess Illeana. Pollyanna, who died in 1940 was the dam of Ch. Duke of Norka and the great winner Ch. Norka's Lubiney.

The 42 Samoyeds registered in 1922 equalled the total registration of the previous 15 years of American Samoyed history. In this last year before the formation of the parent club there were five large kennels: Donerna, Yurak, Top O' The World, Obi and Park-Cliffe.

It was a year of turmoil for Samoyed owners, breeders and exhibitors. Some dogs, both registered and unregistered, imported and homebred, were being denied ribbons or being excused from the rings because of their inferior quality and discrepancies in size and type. Lack of a standard and lack of any uniformity in the classes caused further loss of status to the breed. In Cleveland, the show committee had provided for the Samoyeds in the Miscellaneous Class, with the designation of dogs of 25 pounds or over. Still in 1922, judge J. Muss-Arnolt had a very nice entry of 12, and placed Nico of Farningham to Winners Dog, and Kazan of Yurak as Reserve. Both dogs had been refused ribbons at earlier shows.

1923–1944

The Samoyed Club of America was formed on February 14, 1923. But even with so auspicious an event, the day was a shocker for Samoyed exhibitors. At the Westminster Kennel Club show of the same day, the judge, J. Willoughby Mitchell of London, England, provided a skyrocket sendoff. He withheld the awards for Reserve Winners in both dogs and bitches. Mr. Mitchell declared they were apparently not true Samoyeds because of their small size and flattish lay-down coats. Three of the animals involved were newly imported from the kennels of Mrs. Kilburn-Scott in England.

Catharine Quereaux later wrote "Whether this was a backhanded slap at English breeders or indigestion, it assuredly was decidedly in error, and even today we speak of the wrath of the 1923 Westminster!"

Will Hally, veteran Samoyed columnist for the English publication *Our Dogs* wrote:

That remark of the London judge has created a lot of indignation amongst the Samoyed's supporters in the States, and with reason, I think. While I am not able to speak of all the exhibits at New

50

York, the authenticated British pedigrees of most of them are the surest proof that Mr. Mitchell is mistaken. I noticed that Mr. Smirnow refers to the New York Winners dog, Billy Boy of Yurak, as a flat-coated dog of good character, and perhaps it is that flat coat which led to Mr. Mitchell's criticism. Such a coat is faulty, but it by no means indicates a Collie influence. The American fanciers, from what I know of the stock they now own, are on the right road, and if they breed to the standard, they need not worry over what one or two judges say of their exhibits.

Nevertheless, following the judging at the Westminster show, the serious exhibitors and breeders of the Samoyed met in the club rooms of the Madison Square Garden of the day, and organized the Samoyed Club of America. The club's stated purposes were to promote the breeding of purebred Samoyeds; to urge adoption of this type of breeders, judges, dog show committees, etc., and to bring to the notice of the general public the wonderful characteristics and affectionate dispositions of these superlative dogs.

They adopted the English breed standard, adding the words "black or black spots to disqualify" and a description of disposition. This standard was adopted as the sole standard for excellence in breeding and awarding prizes of merit to Samoyeds by the American Kennel Club when it approved the Samoyed Club of America for membership in the AKC on May 15, 1923.

Thus the Samoyed Club of America was formed out of an emotional realization of the concrete need for a parent club to guide and standardize the breed beyond all doubt.

In 1923, there were less than 300 Samoyeds in the United States, and at least half of these were in just five kennels. The Samoyeds were being shown in the Non-Sporting Group with the Collies, Doberman Pinschers, French Bulldogs, Great Danes, Maltese, Old English Sheepdogs, Boston Terriers, German Shepherd Dogs, St. Bernards, Toy Poodles and Yorkshire Terriers. Registrations in the 1923 Stud Book were the heaviest yet, with 74 recorded.

The breed was beginning to move across the United States. Princess Montyglyon had moved to La Jolla, California, and new owners were showing elsewhere in that state. At the Los Angeles Kennel Club show, judge Mrs. N. A. Pabst placed Trotsky, Winners Dog (owned by Mr. and Mrs. F. W. Ward) and Whitecloud, Reserve Dog (owned by Mr. and Mrs. A. Thompson).

New bloodlines were added when Miss Elizabeth Hudson imported Snow Fairy (by Ch. Kieff out of Nada) from England, and the Frank Romers brought in Tsilma (bred to the English Ch.

H. N. Pinkham with the Laika Kennels' team at South Poland, Me. in 1929:

	Right point: Ch. Ilinesha	Right swing: Narifas	Right wheel: Grim
At lead: Trail Breaker			
	Left point: Ch. Natiya	Left swing: Lucky	Left wheel: Ch. Donerna's Barin

Proving that while styles may change, Samoyeds stay constant. Miss Katherine Morey, who later became Mrs. H. N. Pinkham (Laika Kennels), in this 1929 picture is seen wearing a suit made of Samoyed combings. The dog at left is Ch. Donerna's Barin, at ten years of age.

Zahra), who produced the outstanding bitch Ch. Donerna's Ilinishna.

Two new Samoyed owners appeared in 1924 that have stayed with the breed ever since. Miss Ruth Kilbourn and Mrs. Irene Confer have been pioneers and ardent promoters of the breed. Miss Kilbourn's first Samoyed was Sasha of Donerna (by Donerna's Barin out of Donerna's Day Dawn), obtained from Mr. Seeley. She is still a strong and active member in the Chicago area, and has attended more parent club Specialties than any other owner. Mrs. Confer spent many years as publicity director and editor of dog bulletins in the Midwest.

Additional publicity for the breed was provided by A. H. Seeley when he wrote a feature article for the *American Kennel Gazette*, February 1925. This article was entitled, "Dogs that See the Midnight Sun," and gave a history of the breed and a plea for research to aid in gathering more facts. As he stated, "The breed history was indeed lost in antiquity." Mr. Seeley was killed in an automobile accident shortly thereafter while moving his kennels to a new location.

Many of Mr. Seeley's dogs were acquired by Mr. and Mrs. H. N. Pinkham for their Laika Kennels in Ipswich, Mass. Among them was the famous Ch. Donerna's Barin. Mr. Seeley had been a sledding enthusiast, and Mr. Pinkham too was an avid believer in the working ability of the dogs. He wrote three feature articles for the *American Kennel Gazette:* July 1930, "The Dog Nobody Improved"; a series article in November and December 1930, "The Gamest Dogs In the World"; and in February 1932, "The Real Way to Raise Dogs."

Mr. Pinkham kept his dogs in the north woods and gave them immense runs of twenty acres. He retained the desired disposition in his dogs, and they were able to run together. The Laika Kennels' winter home was twenty miles from a traveled road and all supplies were transported by dog team. These desired traits were passed to California in 1935 when Mrs. Agnes Mason of Sacramento, California went to the Pinkhams for Dasha of Laika, with aim of breeding dogs with sledding ability, conformation, and good Samoyed dispositions. Both the Pinkhams and Masons bred for show dogs that could work.

The present dean of breeder-specialist judges, Miles Vernon, began with a Barin-sired dog called Cham, out of Pollyanna, who was from the fine old stock of Tobolsk and White Fang strains.

Cham was 24″ tall and weighed 80 pounds. In 1925, he became one of the outstanding dogs of the breed. It was unfortunate that he never finished his championship, as he had fourteen points before an automobile accident left him with a permanent limp. Mr. Vernon has held every office in the parent club from president to American Kennel Club delegate, and has been approved as a breed judge since 1930.

The most influential import in 1925 was Yukon Mit. He passed on his style and true Samoyed type to his get. Yukon Mit's dominance in producing style, Barin's in improving coat and gait and Tobolsk's in establishing size, gave America back Samoyeds of the type of the original expedition strains.

The mating of Yukon Mit to Barin's daughter, Nona of Donerna, produced the great Ch. Gorka. Gorka was the pet of Mrs. Horace Mann, who was urged to "support" a show with her eight-year-old dog. She walked off with the wins, including Best of Breed and the Working Group at Trenton. Ch. Gorka ideally fulfilled the dual role of pet and show dog. Yukon Mit, mated to another Barin daughter, Nanci, owned by Catharine Quereaux, produced Ch. Mitboi, who belonged to Dr. and Mrs. William Bridges of Maryland, and Tarquin (who sired Ch. Tarquin II), owned by the Very Reverend Monsignor Robert F. Keegan.

A West Coast import was Jason, a son of Osten and litter brother of Donerna's Barin. Jason was sent on a sailing ship around the Horn to Miss Alma Bennett in California. His best known son was Ch. Jack Frost of Sacramento, owned by the Jack McClearys, who won the 1937 Specialty at Cleveland, beating seven of the top winning Eastern champions.

In 1927, at the 1st annual show at Culver City, California, Ray Bennett's Yuratado of Snow View was Best of Breed. This dog was to become the first Samoyed champion in California.

Dr. Allen Dunton of Cincinnati, Ohio, who had obtained others of the Donerna Kennel dogs upon the death of Mr. Seeley, wrote an article in the *American Kennel Gazette* in 1927. In it he advocated the stripping of Samoyeds in the summertime in addition to mere combing. This stripping comprises 12 to 30 hours of hard work on each dog and takes about two weeks. This caused quite a controversy among the owners, as most were violently against it. Today we comb out only the loose under-coat, which is the raw material for Samoyed yarn discussed later in the book.

Ch. Tarquin II.

The year 1927 also saw the importation of Maroosa, a daughter of Polar Light of Farningham bred to Nim of Farningham. She was imported by Mrs. Frank Romer, then transferred to the Reids of the Norka Kennels. Anka of Farningham came in bred to Polar Sea and went to Florida. In that litter, Capensis Alexis and Capensis Kara were registered by Mrs. Stanley Matthews.

The distinguished Yukon Mit and Barin lines were carried on through Tarquin, Ch. Tarquin II, Ch. Prince Igor, and Ch. Dobrynia in the kennels owned by Monsignor Keegan, who showed and bred Samoyeds from 1928 to 1948. Ch. Dobrynia, son of Ch. Norka's Lubiniey, was Best American-bred in the Working Group at the Westminster Kennel Club, 1936. Following the show, *The New York Times* reported, "Upon seeing the Samoyeds for the first time, there is no more beautiful dog in the world."

Msgr. Keegan was featured in the *American Kennel Gazette* in February 1937 in an article by Arthur Frederick Jones, which pictured his dogs, kennels, and home in the Adirondack Mountains. Msgr. Keegan was a believer in raising dogs in the natural state, and never kept them in heated buildings.

The number of California breeders increased when Mrs. J. C. McDowell of La Crescenta founded the Khiva Kennels and imported Ch. Snow Frost of the Arctic, who was to become the first Samoyed on the Pacific Coast to win a Working Group. (He achieved this in 1935 at the age of seven under judge Julius Dupon.) Mrs. McDowell publicized the breed by showing up and down the Coast as well as in the Midwest and East. She sold puppies to Admiral Byrd's niece, Miss Jacqueline Byrd, and the actress Miss Anna Sten, of Hollywood.

By the year 1929, the breed had arrived at some semblance of solidarity and the *American Kennel Gazette* stated, "The growth of the breed has been both conservative and constant, and augurs well for the future. The Samoyed is an established fixture in American dog circles, and becoming more popular in the right direction for the future of the breed."

Some consider the greatest import of 1929 to have been Eng. Ch. Tiger Boy, brought in by Mr. and Mrs. Reid of Norka Kennels, and renamed Tiger Boy of Norka. Tiger Boy was a son of the great Kara Sea. He had sired litters in England before coming to America, with such progeny as Surf of the Arctic and Riga of the Arctic (out of the bitch Susie). A later litter produced Kosca. His notable progeny in the U.S.A. included sons Ch. Norka's Moguiski and Ch. Duke of Norka, and daughters, Ch. Norka's Lubiniey and Ch. Norka's Pascova.

The first specialty of the parent Samoyed Club of America was held with the Tuxedo Kennel Club show in September 1929. An early summation of the progress of the breed was given by Louis Smirnow, first club president, prior to his judging of the Specialty:

> The progress of the breed depends largely on careful breeding. Those of us who have seen Samoyeds know we are apt to see some specimens shorter in body than others, and unless a short-bodied Samoyed is bred to a longer-bodied one, the results will be undesirable from the viewpoint of the standard of the breed.
>
> A careful breeder will try to eliminate the various faults of his dogs by breeding to a dog who is strong in the characteristics that this breeder is endeavoring to correct.
>
> Occasionally we see an excellent dog, big boned, excellent coat, proper size with a small head. Precautions should be taken to breed a dog of this type to one where the head condition will be improved.
>
> The real champions in England and the old champions in this country, such as Tobolsk, Olga of Farningham and Nico of Farningham, all had fine heads. Unless a champion has a real true head there cannot be the proper expression, which is a very strong point in the beauty of the Samoyed.
>
> The fact that a breeder may have 20 dogs among which are a half-dozen bitches and three or four studs is no reason why this

breeder should not endeavor to breed outside his kennel, if by so doing, the proper characteristics will be had.

It seems to me and to some of the old timers that too much stress is being laid on size. I need hardly emphasize the fact that the large dog lacking other features will not do as well in the ring as the smaller dog with good head. One of the largest dogs ever bred in the history of the breed is Snow Crest of English fame. I have seen many photographs and read many discussions of this dog, but he was too long in the muzzle for me; his head has the appearance of a collie. Yet the owner of this dog, by careful breeding, bred the finest champions of English fame. (The breeder referred to was Miss Thomson-Glover.)

This first specialty had an entry of 40 for Mr. Smirnow's judgment. With only 40 Samoyeds registered between 1906 and 1920, such a large entry less than a decade later was remarkable. Tiger Boy of Norka, owned by the Reids, only three weeks in America from England and reported by Miss Thompson-Glover as taller than most English dogs, made his debut and was Best of Breed. Reserve dog was Bruson, also owned by the Reids. Winners Bitch was Northern Light of Farningham, even though heavy in whelp. Reserve Bitch was Milka, Ch. Gorka's litter sister. Champions present were Ch. Mushinsh, Ch. Gorka, and Ch. Toby II of Yurak.

Another breed specialist judge of this early period was Miss Ruth Stillman. Although she was not a Samoyed breeder, she remained a great friend and supporter of the breed for many years, judging as late as 1952.

People as well as great dogs are needed to weld a breed together. Such a person was Mrs. Catharine S. Quereaux of Long Island and New York City. She joined the breed in 1926, and by 1929 was collecting pedigrees and information of the breed. As the parent club secretary and/or publicity director, Mrs. Quereaux disseminated this information to all, largely at her own expense, for the period 1929 through 1951. Her importation of dogs and bitches to aid the breed were generously placed with breeders throughout the country.

Mrs. Quereaux wrote a history of the Samoyed breed which was never published in its entirety. Parts of this, titled "Dog of the Ages," appeared in a few magazines and club bulletins, but the complete twenty chapters were still unprinted at her unexpected death. For many years, her columns in the *American Kennel*

Gazette aided owners. We offer two quick examples of their content. In an article in 1926, she stated,

"A purebred Samoyed must not be confused with the little under-sized hybrids that are sometimes offered by unscrupulous dealers under the false name of Samoyed and which, when matured, usually develop the snappy dispositions of mongrels. The dogs should be 20–22" tall and weigh 50–60 pounds."

Later, in the November 1929 issue, Catharine Quereaux wrote,

"The Samóyed of the future must be of true working dog size. He must have feet that will stand up under long grueling hauls, for each year the actual sport of working the dogs is increasing in popularity. He must have intelligence and alertness that have so long distinguished the breed. He must have the Samoyed expression, as their heads will receive the marked consideration from judges.

In the late twenties, Miss Elizabeth Hudson, an enthusiast since 1908, visited Russia. She reported, "There were no Samoyed dogs in Moscow or Leningrad, nor could I get any information about the breed. All apparently had disappeared in the Revolution. Undoubtedly, if the breed is preserved in Russia it was in the original habitat, with the Samoyed tribes." She brought back with her from England the influential Ch. Storm Cloud in 1929. Storm Cloud, pictured in this book, was by Ch. Sea Foam out of Ch. Vara. He too, was reported taller than most in England and weighed slightly over 60 pounds. In America, he became the sire of Ch. Tucha, owned by Mrs. Helen Harris. Later (1939), out of the great bitch Morina of Taimir, he sired Vida of Snowland, the foundation bitch for Mrs. Harris' Snowland Kennels. Ch. Storm Cloud won the second parent club specialty, held in 1930 at the Morris and Essex Show.

Early in the 1930s, Mrs. Helen Harris began her famous Snow-land Kennels at Merion, Pennsylvania, by importing Pedlar of the Arctic. She and her daughter were on a trip to Europe and in a park in London, became acquainted with a Samoyed dog. Her daughter, Faith, simply "had to have one" and so Pedlar was obtained. Unfortunately, this puppy contracted distemper and blindness resulted. This did not prevent Pedlar from enjoying a full and long life until 1942. The stories of the other dogs acting as his "seeing eye" are amazing; he seemed to rule the sighted dogs.

58

Two views of Ch. Storm Cloud (1927–1939). Bred in England by Miss J. V. Thomson-Glover, and imported to America by Miss Elizabeth Hudson.

Another trip to England followed, and Mrs. Harris purchased Sabarka of Farningham, and tried valiantly but unsuccessfully to obtain Kara Sea from Mrs. Edwards. In 1936, Mrs. Harris returned to England for a puppy of Ch. Kara Sea. This is the event which put so much of the bloodline of Ch. Kara Sea into America. Mrs. Harris requested a litter by Kara Sea and Pinky of Farningham. Due to the age of Kara Sea, 13 years at the time, it required some discussion. She agreed to take the entire litter home to America. The entire litter consisted of two, Siberian Nansen of Farningham of Snowland and his litter sister Martyska of Farningham. Both were brought to America, but the bitch died at an early age. Nansen proved to be a great stud dog. He sired many champions, even at the age of eleven years. Thus, we find Ch. Kara Sea on the paper of modern pedigrees spanning a period of twenty-four years. Included in his later progeny were Champion Pinsk of Snowland, owned by the Ralph Oateys, and Ch. Staryvna of Snowland, owned by the R. H. Wards. These dogs were showing as late as the 1950s. This is truly a remarkable span of time in dog bloodlines.

Mrs. Harris had earlier purchased Vida of Snowland (Ch. Storm Cloud out of Morina of Taimir), Toucha of Snowland, Ch. Sprint of the Arctic, and Ch. Moscow of Farningham of Snowland. When she bred Nansen, a son of Kara Sea, to Vida, a granddaughter of

59

Ch. Sea Foam, she had her first remarkable "N" litter—Champions Nim, Nadya, Norna, Nianya, and Nikita. There is scarcely a Group-winning or Best in Show dog of the breed that does not have one of these as an ancestor. These great examples of the breed were successfully shown by famous handler, J. Nate Levine.

The pride of Mrs. Harris' kennels, Ch. Nadya, in turn became the dam of Ch. Novik of Snowland, owned by the Ruicks. Ch. Nianya of Snowland, owned by the Masons, became the dam of Ch. Chum, Cleo, Soldier Frosty of Rimini and was behind many, many other famous Pacific Coast Champions.

The great contribution of the Snowland Kennels to the Samoyed breed in the United States was the fact that Mrs. Harris would sell her best bitches to other parts of the country. Never did she send second-rate bitches to other breeders. For example: Ch. Nianya of Snowland went to Mrs. A. E. Mason in California; Ch. Frola of Snowland to Mr. and Mrs. Joe Marshall in Chicago; Ch. Valya of Snowland to Mrs. Lucile Miller of New Mexico; Ch. Staryvna of Snowland to the Robert Wards in California; Ch. White Christmas of Snowland to Mrs. Pamela Rhanor in California; and the fine producing Sams, Ch. Noel of Snowland to Mrs. Grillo in New Jersey; Ch Zoveek of Snowland to Roy Brott in Ohio; Ch. Nikita of Snowland to the Ashleys of Oceanside; Nieko of Snowland and Ch. Vivotchka of Snowland to Mrs. Helene Bascom of New York; Lensen of Snowland to Vera Lawrence of California; and Voltorn of Snowland to Dr. William Ivens of Doylestown, Pennsylvania.

Mrs. Harris once wrote to us of meeting a French painter named Jacques Suzanne while at Lake Placid. He seemed to know the Samoyed breed well, and said he had painted the dogs and horses of the late Czar. He had traveled to Siberia and had something to say on the size of the Samoyed dog. He related that the majority of the native dogs were not as large or so beautiful as the good grooming and feeding provided by our society seems to make them. He believed that in their native habitat they were stunted by the infrequent feedings, for they varied in size, while the Samoyeds owned by the Czar were all beautiful big specimens. He presented Mrs. Harris with a picture of three puppies which came from the kennels of the Czar.

A fine article featuring the Snowland Kennels was published in the June 1936 *American Kennel Gazette*. Titled "Snowland Wants the Samoyed to Retain Its Primitive Charm," it was written by Arthur Frederick Jones.

60

Ch. Tucha of Snowland, at 18 months.

Ch. Nim of Snowland, Best of Breed at Westminster, 1939.

Ch. Staryvna of Snowland, a Ch. Kara Sea granddaughter, at left as a ten-weeks old puppy, and right, as an adult bitch. Acquired by the authors from Mrs. Harris.

61

A lineup of champions at Snowland: Ch. Siberian Nansen of Farningham of Snowland (a Kara Sea son) , Ch. Nim of Snowland, Ch. Nalda of Snowland, Ch. Nadya of Snowland and Ch. Norna of Snowland. Nim and his sisters, Nadya and Norna were of the famous "N" litter sired by Nansen out of Vida of Snowland.

The Snowland Team, owned by Mrs. Helen Harris. Trainer was Ernest Kanavel.

A long-time friend of Mrs. Helen Harris and a very long-time supporter of the breed is Mrs. Helene Bascom of Glens Falls in upstate New York. Mrs. Bascom has owned the breed since childhood, her first being acquired in 1913 from a kennel in Idaho. In 1930, she purchased a female, Nani of Laika, from the Pinkhams, and later bought Tasha of Laika. In the late 1940s, she obtained a puppy from Mrs. Harris destined to become Ch. Vivotchka of Snowland, sired by Voltorn. In 1951, she brought new lines to the United States by importing Ch. Snowland Marguerita from Mrs. Westcott of England.

Mrs. Bascom's fondest remembrances are of Msgr. Keegan's dogs all running together, as was the custom at the Pinkhams' and Msgr. Keegan's kennels. She purchased the puppy, Eclipse of Altai (by Tsiulikagta's Karafang out of Star's Katrina of Altai) in 1968. This record of 55 years of Samoyed ownership is a record to envy.

A sledding contemporary with Eddie Barbeau in the 1920s and 1930s was Harold Haas of St. Paul, Minnesota. His Kara Sea Kennels at first contained Sonia of Kara (by Nordak Kashka out of Ch. Roxanna Barin, (and thus back to Ch. Tobolsk and Ch. Donerna's Barin, as well as Ch. Snyeg, in two generations). Mr. Haas received the splendid Kolya of Farningham upon Mr. Seeley's death. Ch. Kolya of Farningham is a quite dominant sire behind the pedigrees of the central and Midwest United States.

Headlines in Boston on May 21, 1930, read "Famous Champion is Host to Byrd Dogs on Birthday." Ch. Donerna's Barin observed his 10th birthday surrounded by seven sons and four daughters and friends. Barin was pictured with Dinney and Torgnac, who served with Admiral Byrd's South Pole expedition. Persons who attended were expedition drivers Edward Goodale and Norman Vaughn, owners Mr. and Mrs. Pinkham, and visitor Mrs. E. P. Ricker, Jr. of Maine. Mrs. Ricker was the first woman to traverse the frozen reaches of the Kolyma River district in Eastern Siberia. Her famous racing teams of Siberian Huskies originated in that area. The dog Bonzo, International Derby Leader of the Ricker-Seppala Teams, was with her. Mrs. Ricker later married the son of the Dr. Fridtjof Nansen, who brought such notice to the Samoyed breed.

Importation resumed after the depression years of 1930 and 1931 with Bakou from France, registered in 1932. A grandson of Fingal, who was the finest Samoyed in France, he was a striking dog, on the small side. Bakou did not himself influence much, but left an only son, Bokar, who achieved much recognition. Five other imports

63

Eng. Ch. White Fang of Kobe, bred and owned by Mrs. Dorothy L. Perry, of the world-famous Kobe Kennels, Whyteleafe, Surrey, England. Fang, the all-time top winner of the breed in England until his record was surpassed by Mrs. Perry's Int. Ch. Gogalev Corbesky, was sire of Am. Ch. White Way of Kobe, whose importation by Mrs. Agnes Mason in 1939 proved so important to the success of her White Way Kennels.

Morina of Taimir (1933–1948), bred in England by Miss E. Creveld and chosen by Miss Thomson-Glover to be sent to America and Miss Elizabeth Hudson. Morina's mating with Storm Cloud produced Vida of Snowland and has had great impress on the breed.

A distinguished gathering: Am. Ch. Snow Frost of the Arctic, Silver Knight (at 6 mos.) and Lone of the Arctic.

were registered in 1932: Pedlar of the Arctic and his sire, Oleg; Kara Gem, who sired the sophisticated Sniejok of Norka, of the Dingledines' book *How to Train Your Owner;* from Canada, the English-born Canadian Champion Wizbang Laskeybelle, whose sire, Wizbang Laskey, was a litter brother to Ch. Tiger Boy of Norka; and Ivanski, who went to Martha Humphriss' Siberian kennels in Rhode Island.

Importation with greater influence came in 1934, when Mrs. Harris' personally selected Sabarka of Farningham. Ch. Ice Crystal of the Arctic followed. Sabarka sired some fine get, and Ice Crystal brought the sweet expression and coat to the breed which survives to the present day.

Other new bloodlines were brought to the Pacific Coast by White Countess of the Arctic and Ch. Snow Frost of the Arctic in 1931 and 1932. To the East came Barena of Farningham by Miss Humphriss. Mrs. Horace Mann brought in White Sprite who, mated to Ch. Gorka, produced Ch. Yorza. Note that Gorka was eleven years old at this mating. Scottish born Zahrina, eight years old and the mother of Ch. Kara Sea, came to the Norka Kennels. She was re-named Zahrina of Norka.

The first recorded activity of the breed in the far Northwest appeared in 1934 in Spokane, Washington, with the birth of Nanook VI (sired by Zarov of Snowland ex Kasha), bred and owned by Frank Beeson.

While a few dogs were being shown on the Pacific Coast in the early 1930s, and Mrs. McDowell was pushing hard with her Khiva Kennels from 1928 to 1938, it was Mrs. Agnes Mason with her skill in selecting bloodlines and organizing that gave the big push to Samoyed popularity there from the late 1930s through the 1950s.

Mrs. Mason, as a girl in Alaska, was very familiar with dogs, as her father had sled teams. Renewing her work with dogs, in 1935 she purchased a Samoyed for her daughter Aljean from M. D. Robison of Oakland, California. He became Ch. Czar Nicholas Levanov. His dam, ex Mitzi Aura, went back to Ch. Snow Frost of the Arctic and Patricia Obi. His sire, Nico of Creve, was by Nico of Farningham ex Semstra. Mrs. Mason gathered breeding stock from many States and England. Her English imports, Silver Spark of the Arctic (litter brother to Chs. Sport and Sprint of the Arctic) and Ch. White Way of Kobe were brought in in 1938. These added the bloodlines of Arctic and Kobe (through English Chs. Snow Chief of the Arctic and White Fang of Kobe) to West Coast pedigrees. Further, she combined her West Coast and English bloodlines with an infusion of the Snowland Kennels of Pennsylvania by obtaining Ch. Nianya of Snowland. With the addition of Dasha of Laika from the Pinkhams, she had the best in American bloodlines.

Mrs. Mason and her daughter, Aljean Mason Larson, owned and finished 14 champions and bred 22 champions. Many more would have finished, but for her preoccupation with other activities and strong interest in sled work and sled races. She wanted to prove that show dogs had stamina and endurance and that sled dogs are not vicious. She did.

Bill Tompson, her first sled trainer, once drove a team from San Francisco to Sacramento, with an assist from a river boat, to carry a message from Mayor Rossi of San Francisco to Mayor Monk of Sacramento. Lloyd Van Sickle was her second trainer, for a period of twenty years.

More of the American Snowland bloodline appeared upon the West Coast in 1935 when Miss Vera Lawrence purchased Lensen of Snowland, by Ch. Moscow of Farningham of Snowland out of Ch. Ice Crystal of the Arctic. Lensen was Best of Breed at the old Neptune Beach Show and at the Ventura Show with Helen Rosemont, Sr., judging.

Miss Lawrence began writing a breed column in 1933 for the *Western Kennel World Magazine* which soon became a permanent feature.

The get of Ch. Tiger Boy of Norka were proving themselves in the East, for at Westminster in 1937 Best of Breed was the Winners Dog, 4½-year-old Norka's Viking (by Tiger Boy ex Norka's Dutochka). This dog was of the same large type as Ch. Norka's Moguiski, who won the 1938 parent club specialty under the breeder-judge Msgr. R. F. Keegan, at the Morris and Essex show. Norka Kennels had six entries at Westminster, as did Msgr. Keegan, who won best novice with Krasan and Best Puppy with Prince Igor II.

Ch. Desstara of Farningham was brought over to Miss Humphriss and shown with success. She was bred to Ch. Icy King but very little of her progeny carried on.

In this same 1938, an interesting import from France was Inora Du Grand Nord. She was a great granddaughter of Fingal, but like the two prior imports from France did not leave much imprint upon the breed.

With the breed spreading and growing across the nation, a dog

66

Ch. Czar Nicholas Lebanov
(1936–1940), with young owner,
Miss Aljean Mason.

Time marches on. Mrs. Aljean Mason Larson, breeder-owner, handles Ch. White Way's Silver Streak to win of the Working Group at Glendale KC show under judge George Schroth.

from the Midwest significantly won the 1939 Parent Club Specialty. Ch. Prince Kofski, owned by Mr. and Mrs. Samuel Ruick, won at Morris and Essex over an entry of 43. He was a large dog, 24" tall and 85 lbs., but a stellar dog, in that he asked for and received Group placements. The Ruicks, Polly and Berta, emerged as leaders in the breed and aided in the expansion of the parent club into the Midwest Division. Mr. Ruick served as president of the parent club as well as of the Midwest club.

World-wide publicity was received by the breed when the Masons' sled team of champion Samoyeds performed at the World's Fair on Treasure Island at San Francisco, California. Their daily performances encouraged much picture taking and exposure to the public for attention and petting. Further publicity occurred when the picture of Ch. Sprint of the Arctic, Ch. Moscow of Farningham of Snowland, and Ch. Siberian Nansen appeared upon the cover of *Western Kennel World,* which began a tradition of the Samoyed as the "Christmas Dog" on the cover each December.

Ch. Ardcliff Snowstorm and Ch. Ardcliff White Cloud were the first Samoyeds to acquire many Group placings and add to the recognition of the breed in the Midwest. The owners, Mr. and Mrs.

"Looking for Juliet." An appealing shot of one of the Samoyeds of Miss Goodrich's Snowshoe Kennels.

Ch. Prince Kofski (1934–1946), owned by Mr. and Mrs. Samuel K. Ruick. Kofski's many wins included Best of Breed at Westminster in 1944, at almost ten years of age.

Clifford Chamberlain became life-long supporters of the breed. Later they moved to the East Coast, where, in addition to their own import, Ada of Snowland, they at times took care of imported dogs of Catharine Quereaux. Clifford, the parent club president and AKC approved breed judge, last judged at the parent club specialty at Westchester in 1962, which had been dedicated as a memorial to Ardath Chamberlain.

Contributions to the breed by Miss Juliet Goodrich were many and valuable. Not only did she import, breed, and show, but she was a pioneer in the field of eradication of hip dysplasia in the mid-1930s. Her Snow Shoe Hill Kennels was situated upon 5,000 acres of beautifully wooded land, complete with lakes, at Land O'Lakes.

CH. JACK FROST OF SACRAMENTO, a star of the late 1930s. Bred by M. D. Robison, Jr. and owned by Mr. and Mrs. E. L. McCleary.

Wisconsin. Here the dogs Jack Frost of Snow Shoe Hill, her first, and Keena (by Ch. Kandalaska Yena of Marne), had runs of several acres each if they so desired. Her winter home on Lakeshore Drive in Chicago was the scene of many educational meetings while she was Midwest Division President in 1940, 1961, 1962, and 1963.

Not only winning strains of beautiful dogs, but a great interest in Obedience, was given to the breed by Miss Margaret Schlichting of Katonah, New York. Her White Barks Kennels boasts many descendants outstanding in Obedience. Several of the Utility Dogs are pictured in this book. The champions Peter Pan, Barrie, and Wendy appear in many pedigrees. Miss Schlichting's interests included serving as parent club secretary, as well as the veterinary aids mentioned later.

When the great field of Obedience entered the dog shows in 1937, the first Champion and C.D. obedience title Samoyed, Ch. Alstasia's Rukavitza, C.D., was owned by the well-known breeder judge Mrs. Anastasia MacBain of Ohio. Mrs. MacBain was a pioneer member and founder of the Inter-State Samoyed Club. Rukavitza won the 1941 parent club specialty show at the Morris and Essex Kennel Club. He was shown 42 times and won 33 Bests of Breed with 13 Group placings. Other well-known dogs of Mrs. MacBain's were Ch. Alastasia's Glinka (by Ch. Kandalaska ex Alastasia's Tarranga) and the famous imported bitch Ch. Dawn of the Arctic.

The Inter-State Samoyed Club held the first separate specialty show for the breed in 1938 on the Friday before the Western Reserve Show. Ch. Jack Frost of Sacramento was Best of Breed.

The working ability and movement of the Samoyed was long supported by Roy Brott, a breeder for 30 years. He showed Ch. Zoveek of Snowland with great success. It was reported that he and Ch. Zoveek "moved as one." Mr. Brott owned many champions, such as Ch. Vodka's Snow Drift, but he reported that Snow Skipper (by Toby's Boris ex Sam's Sonja) had the finest gait and action that he had ever seen in a Samoyed. Snow Skipper appears behind many Pacific Coast and Midwest dogs.

Mrs. Marian Blake of Ona, West Virginia exhibited little but had fine bloodlines and great producers. Dobrynia's Girl (by Msgr. Keegan's Ch. Dobrynia ex Roy Brott's Icy King's Siberian Stara) and Whitecliff of Oceanside produced well. Whitecliff of Oceanside was a litter sister to Ch. Echo of Kobe of Breezewood and was thus by Nikita of Snowland out of the famous Ch. Nova Sonia of Kobe.

70

Wendy, C.D., wh. 1940. Bred by Msgr. Robert F. Keegan and owned by Miss Margaret Schlichting, she was the foundation in establishment of Miss Schlichting's White Barks Kennel. Dam of Chs. Peter Pan and Barrie.

Mrs. Blake imported Snowland Grettin (by Snowland Sarnac ex Snowland Glasha) from England.

Dogs with very close type to that of the American Snowland Kennels were developed by Mrs. Ruth Bates Young of Ohio. She bred her Olga Pogi of Obi to Natalie Rogers' import Sport of the Arctic, a brother to both Sprint and Spark of the Arctic. One of the puppies from this litter, Snow Chief, became the sire of the Poiriers' International Champion Kola Snow Cloud of Loralee.

Olga's second litter sired by Ch. Tangara (a grandson of Ch. Tiger Boy of Norka) produced Tarranga, the mother of the famous Ch. Alstasia's Glinka and Ch. Alstasia's Gusinaya C.D. Other well-

Ch. Barrie (1946–1952), placed in the Group the first time shown. Bred and owned by Miss Margaret Schlichting.

71

known dogs bred by Ruth Young included Ch. Frost Star C.D., who sired Ch. Dmitri of Snowdrift, and the award-winning brood bitch, Ch. Sparkle Plenty of Arbee (by Roy Brott's Ch. Zoveek of Snowland ex Nimreena of Snowland). Ten years later, in this over-30-year-career, the line carried down to Ch. Pratikas' Pilot of Bonnie Brae, Ch. Barney Boy of Arbee, Ch. Pratika of Top Acres, and the famous litter by Ch. Martingate Snowland Taz out of Ch. Sparkle Plenty of Arbee, with the five litter sisters named by the Shah of Iran. (More about this litter later.) Mrs. Young today is columnist for *Popular Dogs* magazine, and is a licensed handler and booster for the Samoyed breed.

Mr. and Mrs. Porter Proudfoot had brought two dogs from the Siberian Kennels of Miss Humphriss in 1937 and had taken Sammy of Petsamo through to his Championship, but the over-protective qualities of these dogs caused them to turn to Mrs. Pamela Rhanor of Hawthorne, California, for new stock. Mrs. Rhanor had been raising dogs with Mrs. McDowell's bloodlines of Ch. Snow Frost of the Arctic and Yancey's daughter, and had added Ch. Silver Star of White Way, Sooltan, Ch. Snohomish of Oceanside, Ch. Khatanga of Snowland from Dr. Ivens, and Ch. White Christmas of Snowland from Mrs. Helen Harris. Porter Proudfoot had supervised the laying of telephones with the use of dog-sleds in Alaska. He and Esther obtained the future Ch. Laska of White Way (by Sooltan ex Ch. Silver Star of White Way). Ch. Laska of White Way was the dominant sire of the line of the Balaiya Doroga dogs which have moved through southeast United States and have done well.

Mrs. Rhanor, using the titles of Sammy-Ed and of Petsamo in her names, had her bloodlines carried on extensively when she sent Snow King of Petsamo to Mrs. Betty Arneson in Seattle in 1944. That same year, Tynda of Petsamo went to Mrs. Margaret Tucker and was the start of the now famous Encino Kennels when she was bred to Ch. Starchak C.D. to produce Ch. Kun To of Encino.

Active in California in the late 1930s period were Lenore Thompson of Redwood City with Winter Dawn and Tekka Trebor Techol of White Tundra; Beverly Jones with Ch. Kara Kol, and the Jack Englerts with a son of Ch. Kara Kol. Tara Boy helped publicize the breed with a large 8' exercise wheel exhibition. Other breeders who aided in the formation of a breed club in this area were: Mrs. Bryce Dye with Empress Zita, the Clawsons of Berkeley, and the Bourgoins with the bitch Weyana. Ch. Prince Barlof (by Ch. Maelchek ex Empress Zita), was owned by the Perk Stangs of Mill Valley, who served as President and Publicity Director of the new group.

Prince Barlof was a good sized dog, 23½ inches tall, and weighing 75 pounds. To match the size of this dog was Ch. Ski Trooper of Tamaland, owned by Mr. and Mrs. Marcel Juilly and handled by their daughter Pat Healy. Knarf, as he was called, was one of the Snow White litter of 1941, nicknamed for the Seven Dwarfs. He was by Ch. White Way of Kobe out of Jooschka, who was by Prince Barlof out of Lady Mona.

The year 1940 was a banner one for Samoyeds, for they placed 17 times in the Working Group. Three won Companion Dog degrees: the MacBains' Ch. Rukavitza, the Kroepils' Ch. Icy King Duplicate, and the Burnettes' Polar Sea. The Cleveland Western Reserve Show had 56 Samoyeds with eight champions. Mr. Harold Danks, of Wisconsin, had his sled team on exhibition at the show and gave children rides in the Cleveland auditorium.

With 1941 came the war years, and breeding and showing was curtailed. But there was some activity.

The pioneers—the Romers, the Reids, the Pinkhams, the Seeleys, Mercy Argenteau, and the Van Heusens were gone, but the breed was reaching out to all parts of the country.

While the war travel restrictions imposed a 50-mile radius for exhibitors, Mrs. McDowell of California judged the classes at the Interstate Samoyed Club Specialty held with Western Reserve KC in Cleveland, Ohio, and awarded Jack Frost of Sacramento the top spot.

The Samoyed Club of the Pacific Coast held a Specialty in 1941 in conjunction with the Oakland Kennel Club. Best of Breed with an entry of 41 was Agnes and Aljean Mason's Ch. Petrof Lebanov.

Bloodlines were beginning to move back and forth across the land. Mrs. M. Perrin Wintz of Indiana purchased another bitch from Mrs. McDowell, a double granddaughter of Ch. Snow Frost of the Arctic. She believed that breeders should concentrate more on the size of bitches, and that they should be more of the size of the males. She owned the imported Ch. Kandalaska (by the English Champion White Fang of Kobe) who was 22½ inches tall and weighed 68 pounds with a four-inch coat.

The traveling during the war spread some other dogs around, a widening that greatly aided the breed. Captain and Mrs. Ashley's litter, sired by Nikita of Snowland out of Ch. Nova Sonia of Kobe, placed Ch. Echo of Kobe of Breezewood in Indiana. While stationed in Washington, they had bred their Nikita of Snowland to Niarvik of Inara, owned by Mrs. Edna McKinnon. This produced the males

Sooltan and American and Canadian Ch. Snohomish of Oceanside, who are behind Ch. Stormy Weather of Betty Blue and Ch. Chinde of Caspar.

Sooltan and Ch. Snohomish of Oceanside began siring new bloodlines in the Seattle area. Lewis and Claire Bajus in Milwaukee had the influential Ch. Yeinsei's Czar Nicholas II in their kennels. Their nephew, Joe Scott, brought Queen Senga of Lewclaire to the West Coast.

The Westminster show continued in the war years. At the 1942 show Harry Yencer, a breeder-judge, officiated. Mr. Yencer's Darya Kennels, located 10 miles north of Albany on the Hudson River in New York, had been in operation since 1933.

Another dominant sire appeared in 1943 from a breeding of Ch. Herdsman's Chattigan out of Ch. Silver Star of White Way, bred by the White Way Kennels in California. While Mr. Ward had owned a Samoyed pet from the Khiva Kennels of Mrs. McDowell in 1931, he and Mrs. Dolly Ward joined the showing and breeding end of the Samoyed breed with Ch. Starchak C.D. "Chatter," as he was affectionately called because of his talking, was the winner of the parent club Stud Dog Trophy in 1956. Starchak did much to further the breed. He sired over 120 puppies of which 16 were champions, and over 40 grandchildren became champions. Ch. Starchak's bloodlines, when combined with the bitch personally selected by Mrs. Helen Harris, Ch. Staryvna of Snowland, produced a strong line with great influence upon West Coast Samoyeds. The litter with Chs. Starchak's Witangemote, Starchak's Witan, and the bitch Ch. Starchak's Warnistura live in many pedigrees today through the White Way Kennels, the Startinda Kennels, the Oni-Agra Kennels, the Whitecliff Kennels, Tsusiligata Kennels, and Caribou and Vellee kennels, covering the states of California, New York, Oregon, Canada, Colorado, Idaho, Wisconsin, Florida and Texas.

Ch. Starchak's Witangemote went to Mr. and Mrs. Kenneth Bristol, and produced a dozen champions who were combined in a sled team. Ch. Starchak's Warnistura, called Sissy, went to Mrs. Agnes Mason and produced the great Champion White Way's Silver Streak, a many time Group winner. Ch. Starchak's Witan sired, among others, the elegant winner Ch. Starctic Storm. Among other Starchak puppies that influenced the breed was Ch. Rainier, bred by Miss Elizabeth Wyman and owned and trained by the authors.

Ch. Rainier was the second Samoyed to win a Working Group First on the Pacific Coast. He sired the International Champion

Ch. Starchak, C.D. (1953–1957), the
1956 Wimundstrev Stud Dog Winner.

Ch. Starchak's Witan, by Ch. Starchak,
C.D. ex Ch. Staryvna of Snowland.
Noted for tremendously powerful gait
and agility.

Ch. Starctic Storm (1950–1961) by Ch.
Starchak's Witan ex Mazzi's Duchess
(linebred to Starchak). At his first
show, Storm went BOB from the
classes, over SCA-supported entry at
Los Angeles KC, 1954, under judge
Major Godsol.

75

MacGregor of Glenstrae, who won four championships in Europe and the C.A.C.I.B. award. Another notable Rainier son was Suzanne's Racier Suraine (out of Ch. Suzanne of White Way). He is in many Midwest pedigrees through dogs of the Sneiders' Ell Tee Kennels.

Notable bitches were Ch. White Mesa, owned by the Warren Stephens; Ch. Princess Startinda, owned by the Bristols; and Ch. Victoria of Starctic, owned by the James Allens. Ch. Starchak's Witan had one daughter with great dominance, Capella C.D. owned by the Joe Dyers of Idaho, and one son, Ch. Starctic Storm, who became firmly implanted in hundreds of pedigrees through his son Ch. Kazan of Kentwood, and his grandsons, top-winning and producing Ch. Karshan and Ch. Sayan of Woodland.

In the years 1939 to 1943, an annual average of only about 195 all-breed and 150 Specialty Shows were held. In this connection, a point should be made that many fail to take into account when discussing great winners. Prior to 1950, a dog to win 20 or 30 Best of Breeds had to be a flyer, and shown extensively. For example, English Champion Kara Sea had 22 Challenge Certificates and was a hallmark of the breed. American Champion Donerna's Barin, a pillar in America, had only approximately nine Bests of Breed in the 1920s. Ch. Alstasia's Rukavitza U.D. earned 33 BOBs in the late 1930s and early 1940s. Ch. Starchak C.D. obtained 32 Bests of Breed in the late 1940s. One must learn to judge a record by the competition and the availability of shows. As we shall see, by 1970, there were approximately 540 all-breed shows and 480 Specialty shows held in America each year. This approximates a 300% increase. The opportunities for wins are proportionately stronger.

1945–1950

Dogs and owners had become so widespread that a new organization of clubs was necessary to keep the owners informed. The parent club expanded into divisions. The sectional clubs were formed into the Pacific Coast, Midwest and Eastern divisions of the Samoyed Club of America.

Thus, to begin the post-War era, Samoyed enthusiasts had a new parent club structure to aid in promoting the breed. The club had expanded from an Eastern group into a national club with three areas or divisions to promote more local activity and interest.

76

Ch. Kunto of Encino (Ch. Starchak, C.D. ex Rhanor's Tynda of Petsamo), first champion in the Encino Kennels of Charles and Margaret Tucker.

Ch. Kobe's Prince Riki of Encino, wh. 1964. A son of Best in Show winner Ch. Joli Knika. Owned by Mrs. Margaret Tucker.

The year 1946 was an explosive one for dog breeding and shows. Within each division of the new club formation, interest was high.

The show of the year was to be the renewal of the parent club specialty by the Midwest Division at the Chicago International Kennel Club. This would be the first time in the history of the breed that there truly would be dogs from all sections of the country for competition. Arrangements were handled by Col. Edward Wentworth, a long-time Samoyed owner and chief ring steward for the Chicago International Kennel Club. The Colonel did not exhibit, although he owned several, as he was a vice-president of Armour Company, and perpetual Chief Steward. He had owned the breed since his son had succumbed in a fraternity house fire, and his pet Samoyed stayed and perished with him.

Ten years before, the breed was not very widely distributed, but now there were entries from the West Coast: Ch. Nick of White Way, Ch. Starchak C.D., Ch. Chinde of Caspar C.D.X., Toby of White Way and Kara Sun of Sam Hill; from the Northwest: Ch. Dushka of Altai; from New York, Pinsk of Snowland; from Massachusetts, Miriam Clark's Matsar; from Pennsylvania, Voltorn of Snowland; from Michigan, Park-Cliffe Kisky Snow Frost; from Ohio, Roy Brott's Zoveek of Snowland and Alstasia's Glinka and Missie Kris of Obi; and from Canada the veteran Champion Nicholas.

Frolnik of Sammar was Best of Breed from the Open Dog class over a total entry of 77. Frolnik was by Ch. Yeinsei Czar Nicholas II out of Ch. Frola of Snowland, and he went on to win the Working Group handled by his owner, Clare Marshall. Best Brace in the Working Group was awarded to Toby of White Way and Ch. Nick of White Way.

New kennels continued to be formed and some of the older ones continued to produce. Mr. and Mrs. Charles Tucker bred their Rhanor's Tynda of Petsamo to Ch. Starchak C.D., and the resulting Ch. Kun To of Encino became a foundation sire. Two years later, Mrs. Tucker began importing with her first, Suretta of Kobe.

Dr. William Ivens, of Pennsylvania, who had been showing and breeding Samoyeds since 1937, registered a litter by Ch. Siberian Nansen out of Zorina of Snowland. He sent one puppy to Lenore Thomson in California, one to Princess Diane Eristavi of Massachusetts, and Svalbard of Snowland to Mrs. Helen Harris and Faith Harris. Dr. Ivens' earlier dogs included Ryn of Snowland, a Group-placement winner, killed at an early age within two points of his championship and Ch. Noel of Snowland, shown with success and found in pedigrees today. Dr. Ivens dropped out of the breed in 1950, but his import of Ch. Martingate Snowland Taz in 1946 made a permanent impression upon the breed in the Eastern section of the country.

Ch. Martingate Snowland Taz was selected personally for Dr. Ivens by Miss Thomson-Glover, through the efforts of Miss Ruth Stillman, who was visiting in England. Imported at the age of two years, Taz enjoyed a glorious show career through the years 1946 to

78

1950, garnering 50 Bests of Breed out of 54 times shown including four in succession (1946–49) at Westminster, 3 Group Firsts and 19 other Group placements.

Taz brought much substance and heavier heads to many of the kennels. He was quite in demand as a stud, and was the sire of 28 champions and 29 champion grandchildren. His mating with Mrs. Bernice E. Ashdown's Eng. and Am. Ch. Princess Silvertips of Kobe produced a litter of five champions that included two Best in Show winners—Ch. Silver Spray of Wychwood and Ch. Silvertips Scion of Wychwood. Others of Taz's progeny include: Ch. Jay Tee's Kharkovof Rothridge, owned by the Roths of Ohio; Ch. Sweet Missy of Sammar, the first Samoyed to win Best in Show, owned by Mr. and Mrs. J. J. Marshall, Jr.; Chs. Barrie and Peter Pan, owned by Miss Margaret Schlicting of New York; Ch. Tazson; Ch. Tazbell; Ch. Tazya; Ch. Tatiana of Sammar; Ch. Patty Duff of Sammar; Ch. Gay Boy of Sammar, owned by Mr. and Mrs. Ralph Longdens of Long Island; Ch. Pratika of Top Acres, owned by Ruth Bates Young, and Ch. Ekenglo's Jola, owned by Lucy Schneider.

In 1951, at age of seven, Taz was purchased from Dr. Ivens by Mrs. Elma Miller, and he was to add glory to her Elkenglo Kennels.

The Snowland Kennels of Mrs. Helen Harris had another outstanding litter in the 1940s by Ch. Siberian Nansen of Farningham of Snowland out of Dol of Snowland. A male, later Ch. Pinsk of Snowland, owned by the Ralph Oateys of New York, was Reserve to Martingate Snowland Taz at the 1946 Westminster show. Pinsk was Winners Dog at the 1947 Westminster, at which Ch. Martingate Snowland Taz was again Best of Breed. Pinsk's litter sister, Ch. Staryvna of Snowland, owned by the authors, finished in three five-point shows, meeting the West's finest bitches.

With this growth after World War II, the Samoyed began to be recognized in the show ring. Ch. Ardcliff White Cloud won the Group at Canton, Ohio in June 1946. A week later Ch. Chinde of Caspar, C.D.X., owned by Lois and Lillian Rayner of Eagle Rock, California topped a Group at Lansing, Michigan. Ch. Chinde is one of the most under-recognized dogs of the breed. By Sooltan out of Ch. Silver Star of White Way, Chinde was a half-brother to Champions Starchak, C.D., Laska of White Way, and Borealis of the Far Steppes. A grandson of Nikita of Snowland, he was three generations from Eng. Ch. White Fang of Kobe, and four generations from Ch. Kara Sea. His wins included 31 Bests of Breed and a Canadian Best in Show.

79

Ch. Martingate Snowland Taz, immortal winner and sire. Imported and originally owned by Dr. William Ivens, and later owned by Mrs. Elma Miller of Elkenglo Kennels. Taz was the first winner, in 1954 and 1955, of the Wimundstrev Stud Dog Trophy.

Am. and Can. Ch. Tazson (1946–1958). Bred and owned by Mr. and Mrs. Ashbjorn Ulfeng. Tazson's first show was at Madison Square Garden where he made a hit with exhibitors and sold "Taz" as a stud, the first of his great progeny in the ring. Tazson won two SCA Specialties and 55 Bests of Breed. His own offspring included Tazson's Snow Flicka and Ch. Nordly's Sammy (four-time Specialty winner).

Ch. Narguess of Top Acres, (1949–1963). By Ch. Martingate Snowland Taz ex Ch. Sparkle Plenty of Arbee. Bred by Ruth Bates Young, and owned by General and Mrs. Roderick Allen for all but the last three years of her life, when she was attended by Rev. and Mrs. Robert L. Seekins.

Am. and Can. Ch. Tazbell, 1950. By Ch. Martingate Snowland Taz ex Snowbelle. Bred by Borghild Ulfeng and owned by Antoinette Callahan, past honorary president of the Samoyed Club of America.

Ch. Pratika of Top Acres, by Ch. Martingate Snowland Taz ex Ch. Sparkle Plenty of Arbee. Bred by Ruth Bates Young and owned by Lucy Forbes. Best of Breed at Chicago International, 1957.

81

The Rayner sisters became traveling ambassadors for the breed. Travelling and showing over a period of four years, they went from California to Florida, to Nova Scotia, back through the Midwestern states to Vancouver, Canada, and south to California. While on their trip, the Rayners purchased the bitch Am. and Can. Ch. Dushka of Altai from the Willard Todnems of Seattle, Washington.

The Glendale Kennel Club show in 1947 had a special significance, for it was agreed to test the American Kennel Club rule which permits the entry of any dog over six months of age in Open class. Of this, Catharine Quereaux wrote:

This show was a test show where members were privileged to enter champions in the classes, contrary to our usual custom. The Wards' Champion Staryvna of Snowland was entered in the Open Bitch Class and was Winners Bitch in stiff competition with Snow Queen of White Way and Khatanga of Snowland among others. Though the Winners Bitch was beaten for Best of Winners by the yet untitled son of Ch. Starchak, Kun To, the win was a fact. True this one show proves nothing, but the day must come in this country that if champions are to be considered worthy of the title, they must be entered in the classes. My hat is off to those who have done it. It has always been done in England. This procedure is not unknown to America, for the Reids, when owners of the Norka Kennels, entered champions in the classes. Long before Tobolsk must have been entered many times in the classes after gaining his title. We are told Tobolsk won five championships. The more exhibitors that brave wrath by doing this the better for the breed, for better dogs will be found to defeat any one dog too long in a winning streak. Further, at big shows we often have five or six champions entered for Specials Only. One may be chosen Best of Breed, but there is no placement for the others. They may be infinitely better than the dogs entered in the classes, or may not be as good, but there is no rating given. In England they know their top ranking champions, their seconds, their thirds, and the day must come when we have the same knowledge of our own here. Mrs. Ward felt she could not, as President of the Pacific Coast Division, ask any one to make the test if she did not do it herself. Thus, taking it as a club matter rather than a personal one, she welcomed the win of the Winners Dog from her stud; this being the very thing which proves the desirability of such entries of champions. Perhaps after the June 8th, 1947 Specialty Show at Pasadena another test will be made, and the example should be followed by other divisions of the Samoyed Club of America.

82

The Samoyed winning increased. Mrs. Anastasia MacBain's Ch. Alstasia's Glinka was first in the Working Group at the Mercer County Kennel Club Show, September 13, 1947. Amer. and Can. Ch. Park-Cliff Kiska Snow Frost, owned by Mr. and Mrs. Leo Poirier of Highland Park, Michigan, won the Working Group at Bloomfield Hills Show over 553 dogs in the Group.

The Pacific Coast Division hosted the parent club specialty with the Pasadena Kennel Club in June 1947 and Ch. Staryvna of Snowland topped the entry of 47, the beginning of multiple Best of Breed awards for bitches. A Cinderella story was born at this show when a twelve-year-old girl invested a dollar on a raffle for a Samoyed puppy and won! Shirley Hill raised the puppy with great care, and won Best of Breed at the June Harbor Cities Kennel Club show in an entry of 36. In 1950, the dog, now Ch. Verla's Prince Comet, was Best of Breed in an entry of 110 Samoyeds at the parent club specialty show, and 4th in the Working Group at the same Harbor Cities show. He followed a year later with a Best in Show at the San Gabriel Kennel Club Show (under Judge Albert E. Van Court) over an all-breed entry of 750 present. He was a great winner, and resembled the picture of Ch. Storm Cloud, but unfortunately he did not reproduce himself.

The Startinda Kennels were begun in this era by Lloyd and Kenneth Bristol of Thousand Oaks, California, with Ch. Starchak's Witangemote, whose dam was Ch. Staryvna of Snowland, and Ch. Princess Startinda, a daughter of Ch. Starchak ex Princess Tina of Tonia. These two produced three Startinda Champions in one litter, Talnik, Sarana, and Chrinda. In 1956, Ch. Startinda's Talnik was second only to Ch. Yurok of Whitecliff as a winning Samoyed on the West Coast. While very active in shows, the Startinda Samoyeds are best known in sled dog racing in the West. For many years, the Bristols entered two full teams of five to seven dogs in many races from Donners' Pass, California to Williams, Ariz.

Not all dogs receive a Good Conduct Medal, but Soldier Frosty of Rimini (by Ch. Petrof Lebanov ex Ch. Nianya of Snowland), was awarded his with the Victory Medal. Frosty was presented the medal in a ceremony at Camp Stoneman, California. During World War II, he was number P–254 in the K–9 sled dog Corps. He served in Attu, Iceland and in Greenland as a lead dog to take supplies to marooned fliers. The ceremony and presentation was interesting in that it took place at a special luncheon in the Officers' Club. Frosty was given an

Ch. Chinde of Caspar, C.D.X. (1944–1958). The faithful traveling companion of his owners, Lois and Lillian Rayner.

"The Cinderella Dog," Ch. Verla's Prince Comet, won in a dollar raffle in 1947 by Shirley Ann Hill, and then shown by her to a fabulous career that included Best in Show in 1951. Pictured here in 1949 win under judge Joseph C. Quirk.

84

honorary commission as a Colonel in the Reserve Corps. When luncheon was served, his was roast beef and a pan of water, but his mistress, Miss Barabara Stewart, wouldn't let him eat at the table where he was seated. While age and time did not offer him a show career, his progeny gave him an added medal for his record. He left a mark as the sire of Ch. Omak, and thus the grandsire of the outstanding winner Ch. Yurok of Whitecliff.

Another son of Soldier Frosty that performed splendid public service was Ch. Samoyland's Vojak U.D., owned by Chloe and Tom Witcher of San Francisco. Vojak was the first and only Samoyed to make this dual championship on the West Coast, and was one leg away from his Tracking title when death came at the young age of six years. Ch. Vojak U.D. performed for television, service organizations, hospitals, for handicapped children and the March of Dimes, as well as for several years leading a team with Santa Claus into the Shriners' Hospital in San Francisco, where the children always enjoyed him and his teammates more than they did Santa.

A special trial of judging a Specialty by literally using the point scale then existing with the breed standard, was performed by Dr. William Ivens at the Los Angeles Kennel Club show in 1948. Individual scorecards were maintained and all entries ranked in each class. In his critique in the Fall 1948 SCA Bulletin, Dr. Ivens wrote:

> I have stated that I thought the calibre of the dogs above the average of those we show in the East. My scoring for males ranged from 92 to 60. Bitches were from 97 to 75. Specials were 94, 92 and 87.
>
> My Winners Dog, Laska of White Way, is, I think, one of the most spectacularly beautiful dogs I have seen. He has faults, to be sure, but the scoring system put him up in spite of several faults . . .
>
> In bitches I went overboard on the magnificent Gay of White Way, owned by Mrs. Mason. Since she has also bred her, she may be doubly proud. She is a great bitch, and as we all know, a great male is far more common. More than any entry, she was in full bloom, although her owner claims she is just coming into coat. She must be a great sight when Mrs. Mason feels she is in heavy coat. To look at her move from the rear was a joy. Had I anything to change on her, I would give her smaller ears, but even that is problematical. . . .
>
> I was very glad to see the famous Ch. Chinde of Caspar. He is an extremely handsome dog. Chinde was very short on undercoat due to the previous hot weather, but he is a dog to admire. Ch. Starchak was also not in full bloom of coat. He is a well-put-together dog,

beautifully moving, and fine-headed. In addition to his own beauty, he is proving himself, as in this entry, an excellent sire. My third Specials dog was another Starchak dog, Ch. Kun To of Encino, and unfortunately he did not seem as poised as the other two. I attribute this to the extreme heat and glare when I was judging this class.

Due to her high score, Gay went on to Best of Breed, and very justly so, I felt. Starchak was my Best Opposite. The exhibitors were very cooperative, as my scoring took endless time.

With the painstaking scoring, it took 5½ hours to judge the 31 dogs.

The silver anniversary of the Samoyed Club of America in 1948 found that among the parent club officers, were several charter members and two that joined the second year of existence: President Mrs. A. E. Mason; Vice-Presidents Louis Smirnow, Col. Edward Wentworth and Miss Lois Rayner. Other officers were Secretary Marie Grillo; Treasurer and American Kennel Club Delegate Miles Vernon; Publicity Director Catharine Quereaux. Two Governors were chosen for each Division: East, Miss Elizabeth Hudson, Ralph Oatey; Midwest, Robert Cahail, Mrs. Bolton; Pacific Coast, Perc Stang and Robert Ward. Governor-at-large was Mrs. Berta Ruick of Indiana.

An unusual show as held by the Interstate Samoyed Club in the underground Exhibition Hall of the Cleveland Auditorium in 1948. Three judges were engaged: Mrs. Enno Meyer, James Trullinger, and Mrs. F. H. Beddow. The judges drew their assignments at ringside prior to the judging. Assignments were for dogs only, bitches only, and Best of Breed Competition and non-regular classes. Show Chairman was A. L. MacBain. Other officers and committee members were H. W. Engleman, Rev. Wm. A. Fogarty, J. J. Marshall, Jr., J. T. Roth, and Mrs. Bion Wintz. Ch. Frolnick of Sammar was Best of Breed, with Ch. Alstasia's Glinka Best Opposite. Mrs. Ashdown's Rimsky of Norka U.D. was Winners Dog, with Roy Brott's Arbee's Sweetie Winners Bitch. This was the club's last specialty show.

The San Francisco area had two unusual shows in 1948. The one at the Golden Gate show in February was different because two 11-year-old girls with Samoyed exhibitor parents staged their own show in an adjacent lot. They bought ribbons out of their allowances and charged 25¢ per entry, giving all profits to the Guide Dogs for the Blind at San Rafael. There were three classes, Small, Medium, and

Large. Iva Stang and Madge Juilly, Samoyed exhibitors, were the judges and $35. was raised for Guide Dogs. Inside the show, 50 Samoyeds were judged by Julius Dupon. Ch. Ski Trooper of Tamaland was Best of Breed and Second in the Working Group, with Starchak's Witan Winners Dog, and Samoyland's Cinda Winners Bitch.

The Oakland Kennel Club in 1948 provided a Crystal Anniversary tribute to our Samoyed writer, Miss Vera Lawrence, who had not missed a column since 1933. Her pursuit of information of her beloved breed, and that of contributors, still appears in the *Western Kennel World* magazine. Ch. Chinde of Caspar was awarded Best of Breed, and the special trophy of a cover page on *Western Kennel World,* by the judge, Miss Vera Lawrence.

An entry of 50 or more was unusual at that period of time and yet in Chicago at the International, Mrs. Beatrice Godsol passed upon 51 Samoyeds and handed Best of Breed to the bitch Ch. Belita of Altai, a litter sister to Col. Edward Wentworth's King Eric of Altai.

Imports arrived in this period of expansion, but two great imported bitches passed from the scene in 1948. Both were truly foundation bitches for present American pedigrees. Morina of Taimir, born 1933, was imported by Miss Elizabeth Hudson of New York. Morina traveled here in luxury unknown to most dogs. On the *S. S. Aquitania,* she was under the care of the ship's butcher, and came over more than well-fed. She was daughter of Siberian Shaman out of Desreena, thus a granddaughter of Ch. Polar Light of Farningham, who won Best of Breed at Cruft's five years in a row. Morina, bred to Ch. Storm Cloud, produced Vida of Snowland, who produced Mrs. Helen Harris' famous "N" champions, Nim, Nadya, Nianya, Norna, and Nikita of Snowland. Further, she was the granddam of the Champions Nadine, Novik, Nalda, Chum, and Echo of Breezewood. Morina was only shown once and then at the age of 12 years. She was Best of Breed under the Samoyed breeder-judge Harry Yencer.

Nova Sonia was the other great loss. She came over in 1940 when the ships were running the U-Boat blockade. Nova Sonia was a daughter of the great English Champion White Fang of Kobe and Kosena of Kobe. Her full brothers (but not litter brothers) already in the United States were Ch. White Way of Kobe owned by Mrs. Mason, and the dog White Son of Kobe owned by the Allison Armours. Nova Sonia's litter brother Byfang of Kobe sired the

American Champion Kandalaska, owned by Mrs. Bion Wintz. Thus, this line is quite extensive in America pedigrees. Nova Sonia's bloodline is carried on in her famous daughters American and Canadian Champion Dushka of Altai and Ch. Belita of Altai. Through her daughter Echo of Breezewood, she was granddam to Ch. Zantok of Breezewood and Strog of Altai, both large Samoyeds who weighed over 85 pounds.

Adding to the growth of the breed in Southern California, Ch. Nicolette of Altai was returned to the States from the Canal Zone when Mr. and Mrs. Hal Wheelock moved to Los Angeles. Vicky Wheelock has worked diligently for the breed for the past 20 years, and was parent club Treasurer for many years. Their daughter, Anne, at the age of 10 years, trained and obtained a Companion Dog title for their latest Samoyed, Kobe's Nicole of Encino.

Other members in Southern California at this time that have carried on in bloodlines, sled dog work, and obedience titles for the breed were Mr. and Mrs. Charles Burr of Encino. Chastuska of Encino, from Mrs. Tucker, was trained and shown through the C.D.X. title. Later, in 1950, they obtained a grandson of Eng. Ch. Raff of Kobe out of Suretta of Kobe, the Ch. Tar-Ko's Kazan of Encino. Chastuska was later bred to the famous lead dog Rex of White Way, which produced their Winter Trails' litter. Included in the litter were Ch. Winter Trails' Blazer (used as an example of the breed in the American Kennel Club's *The Complete Book of Dogs,* 1961 and 1968), Winter Trails' Rogue and Winter Trails' Blitz. A picture of the three by Joan Ludwig that has won an international prize is included in this book. The Burrs worked their dogs in harness at their summer home at Big Bear Lake in the California mountains.

The Rocky Mountain area began activity in 1948 when Cleo, a daughter of Cheka out of Ch. Nianya of Snowland, was obtained by Mr. Rex Kanouse of Steam Boat Springs, Colorado. Cleo was a good-sized bitch, 22″ and 60 pounds, and had already produced, with the English import Silver Spark of the Arctic, the famous Champions Herdsman's Chattigan, Herdsman's Faith, and Herdsman's Victory Leader. Of Cleo and Samoyeds, Mr. Kanouse reported, "In the last 22 years I have raised ten different breeds of dogs and none of them were equal to the Samoyed when it comes to an all-round dog that can be trusted and taught to do anything." Cleo, with 10 points, two majors, started a fine strain in that area but was never finished to championship.

Ch. Ilma of Blakewood, of Ch. Dobrynia lines. Bred by Marian Blake and owned by Elma Miller. Ilma is the dam of Ch. Elkenglo's Zilma, owned by Madge and Esther Russell, and granddam of Sue Page's foundation bitch, Elkenglo's Esme.

Ch. Nicolette of Altai, owned by Mr. and Mrs. Hal Wheelock. Nicolette was by the English import Ch. Deyomas of Ibur (Deyomas is Samoyed spelled backward), and was imported by Catherine Quereaux.

Ch. Luchow's Pride of Top Acres, a grandson of Ch. Martingate Snowland Taz and Ch. Sparkle Plenty of Altai. Originally owned by Kurt Unkelback, but now with breeder Ruth Bates Young at Top Acres.

89

Christmas in Albuquerque, 1952. Mrs. Lucille Miller's Ada of Snowland, Ch. Snow Dawn, Ch. Snowland Stara, Ch. Peg O' My Heart and Koroleva of Altai.

Importations of 1948 included the bitch Snowland Vision from Mrs. Whiting of England, brought in by Miss Juliet Goodrich. The Irish Champion Snowland Stara was sent to Mrs. Catharine Quereaux and Lucile Miller. Snowland Stara, the first champion in the British Isles following World War II, was a half-brother to Martingate Snowland Taz through Ivanoff of Snowland. He was exported by Mrs. Kathleen Pyle of Ballygowan, Belfast, Ireland. Some of his progeny were Jingle of Sammar (out of Ch. Frola of Snowland), Ch. Tanga (out of Ch. Dushka of Altai), and the well-known Ch. Beliviosdi U.D., owned by Donald Heil of Chicago. Another son was Ch. Tam Tam, owned by Trudi De Carlo of New York.

Texas added to her Samoyeds with Starchak's Wainagium, owned by Bill and Freda Powell of Alpine, Texas. To their home at the college they added puppies sired by Snowland Stara which increased the popularity of the breed in the Southwest in 1949. After a visit to England in 1950, they returned to purchase Champion Raff of Kobe from his importer Ann Goekel.

The Morris and Essex show of 1949 with its entry of 81 Samoyeds under judge M. F. Rosenbaum topped all previous entries. The MacBain's newly imported bitch, Ch. Dawn of the Arctic, was Best of Breed, with Dr. Ivens' Ch. Martingate Snowland Taz the Best Opposite. Morris and Essex had a television show prior to the show and selected Ch. Noel of Snowland as the representative of the breed for the camera.

A son of Taz, Peter Pan, owned by Miss Margaret Schlicting, was Best in American-bred class at this Morris and Essex show. Ch. Peter Pan later had many Best of Breeds and Group placements. He was described by Miss Schlicting as "A real Sam, with the independence they are famous for. A ham and darling person, he was very sweet with children. Peter Pan was the boss of the dogs at White Barks Kennels. He died at the age of 15½. He was the best I ever hope to have and after 26 years of Samoyeds that's saying quite a bit."

A historic recognition was brought about in 1949 by the FIRST BEST IN SHOW AWARD TO A SAMOYED IN THE UNITED STATES. The award was made by judge Mrs. Marie Meyer at the Toledo Kennel Club Show, April 10, 1949. A beautiful puppy bitch, Sweet Missy of Sammar, owned by Mr. and Mrs. J. J. Marshall Jr., came up from the classes under the breeder judge Mrs. Anastasia MacBain, who also did the Group. Sweet Missy was also sired by Ch. Martingate Snowland Taz and was out of Ch. Frolene of Sammar.

91

In the wake of this first Best in Show in 1949, the Samoyed rose to great eminence in inter-breed competition in the 1950's. Spearheading this rise were the dogs of the Wychwood Kennel, owned by Mrs. Bernice B. Ashdown, and trained and shown by Charles L. Rollins. The kennel's slogan "The Samoyeds with the Winning Ways" was, if anything, an understatement.

Although Mrs. Ashdown owned Samoyeds as far back as 1930, it was not until about ten years later, when she acquired Rimsky of Norka, that she became seriously interested in breeding and showing. Obedience training was then still in its infancy, and Wychwood became one of the pioneers and missionaries for that phase of the sport. Rimsky became the third Samoyed to earn the title of Companion Dog, and went on to become the first to gain Companion Dog Excellent, and then the first to achieve Utility Dog Tracker. Concurrently, he finished his championship in quick time, and thus became the first champion with C.D.X. degree, and the first champion U.D.T.

Following right in his footsteps was Ch. Marina of Wychwood (a granddaughter of Mrs. A. L. McBain's Ch. Anastasia's Rukavitza, C.D., the first Samoyed to earn the Companion Dog title). Marina became the first bitch of the breed to win the C.D. (with three first place scores of 197, 198 and 199—a record that still stands), and the first to gain C.D.X. She also made her championship concurrently. The mating of Rimsky and Marina produced a sensational litter of four C.D. winners—Ch. Ballerina of Wychwood (Best Bitch at the 1950 Specialty), Bettina of Wychwood, Beau Brummel of Wychwood, and Barin of Wychwood.

With the importation of Eng. Ch. Princess Silvertips of Kobe in November, 1949, Wychwood winning went into high gear. Instrumental in securing Silvertips for import to this country was the eminent breeder-judge, Miss J. V. Thomson-Glover, who considered her "probably the finest Samoyed in Great Britain today." Princess Silvertips had been undefeated in England with nine Challenge Certificates to her credit. She was embarked on her American show career in 1950, at just a few months short of her sixth birthday. After completing her championship, she was temporarily retired to rear what was to be a historic litter by Ch. Martingate Snowland Taz, and then was returned to the ring in 1951 to begin her show career in earnest. Her American record included 48 Bests of Breed in 49 times

Charles L. Rollins watches Ch. Rimsky of Norka, first Samoyed U.D.T. winner, jump over littermates Bettina of Wychwood, C.D., Ch. Marina of Wychwood, C.D.X. and Ch. Ballerina of Wychwood.

Rimsky soaring the hurdles.

Eng. and Am. Ch. Princess Silvertips of Kobe.

Ch. Silvertips Scion of Wychwood.

Ch. Silver Spray of Wychwood.

Ch. Marina of Wychwood, C.D.X.

Ch. Silvertips Saba of Wychwood.

Eng. and Am. Ch. Snowpack
Loucka of Kobe.

shown (the one defeat being to her daughter, Ch. Silvertips Saba of Wychwood, of which more later), 33 Group placements including 14 Firsts and two Bests in Show. The first Best in Show, won at seven years of age, made her only the second in the breed to have gone BIS. Her second was won at nine years of age. Her winning is all the more remarkable when it is realized that her career was interrupted four times for the bearing of litters.

The phenomenal success of Silvertips and her progeny has been hailed as "the greatest family campaign in modern dog history."

Ch. Silver Spray of Wychwood, one of the five champions born of the mating of Silvertips with Taz, established an all-time record for the breed with win of five all-breed Bests in Show and a Best American-Bred in Show. Spray made his championship in just 34 days, finishing at but nine months of age. Undefeated in the breed after completing his title, he was Best Samoyed at Westminster four years in succession, matching the achievement of his great sire. He twice placed in the Group at Westminster, the only times that a Samoyed has placed at the Garden.

Ch. Silvertips Scion of Wychwood, a litter brother, won 82 Bests of Breed (including Morris and Essex 1955), had 58 Group placements including 13 Firsts, and scored three Bests in Show in 1953 to 1955.

Ch. Silvertips Saba of Wychwood, a litter sister, had a record of 7 Group Firsts, three in succession. She went from Open class to Best of Breed at Morris and Essex 1952 under judge William L. Kendrick, who explained his putting her up over her dam Silvertips with "They are alike in make, shape, type, soundness and symmetry. Youth prevailed to an edge in condition of coat and a slight superiority in front action due to her letter-perfect shoulder formation."

In 1953, Wychwood brought in Snow Challenger of Kobe (by Int. Ch. Gogoley Corbesky, half-brother to Princess Silvertips and the recordholder in England of 34 CC's out of famous Ch. Zeeta of Kobe) as a strong stud force.

In 1956 came the importation of Eng. Ch. Snowpack Loucka of Kobe (by Ch. Prince Bado of Kobe ex Ch. Joybelle of Kobe, who together hold the record for having produced the greatest number of English champions). Loucka won her American championship in six straight shows, and scored four Group Firsts and two Group Thirds before being retired for maternal duties.

97

Headstudy and full shot of Eng. and Am. Ch. Americ of Kobe.

In December of the same year, Wychwood brought over another of the all-time greats of the breed. This was the young English Ch. Americ of Kobe. At under two years of age, Americ had already gained the much coveted Junior Warrant, and had to his credit four CCs and a Reserve CC at Cruft's. He had the rare distinction of having won the breed CC at both the Samoyed Specialty Show and the British Specialist Show in 1956, and had won the Trophy for Best Dog in England for the year. Miss Thomson-Glover wrote that Americ had paid her a farewell visit before his departure to the United States, and "to see him was to covet him. All will praise his beauty and soundness." She added that she looked upon his departure with mixed feelings, as both he and Ch. Snowpack Loucka had an especial place in her heart, for they were both descended from the last litter bred by her at Oakburn, and were strongly inbred to their forebear, Ch. Storm Cloud.

Americ's introduction to the American show rings in 1957 was most sensational. At his first show, he went from Open class to Best in Show. This was followed by four other successive Working Group Firsts, totaling five in all, and establishing a Samoyed record that is not likely to be equalled for many moons to come—completing his championship undefeated by a Working dog of any breed. In all, Americ was shown in the United States 33 times, was undefeated in the breed, scored 29 Group placements including 19 Firsts, and won four Bests in Show.

On top of his outstanding show careers in both England and the United States, Americ was awarded the prized "Peter of Kobe" Challenge Cup for 1958 and 1959, an "open for all" award to the stud dog whose progeny win the most points at championship shows.

Wychwood continued its importations in 1958 bringing in Zamerina of Kobe, an Americ granddaughter; Gina of the Tundras, Reserve Bitch CC winner at the 1958 Samoyed Specialty under Miss Thomson-Glover; and Snowpack Silver Melody of Kobe, niece of Ch. Snowpack Loucka. Silver Melody quickly became a champion, was undefeated in the breed in 20 showings, won two Groups, and was Best of Breed at the 1965 Samoyed Club of America Specialty at Darien, Conn. under judge Alva Rosenberg.

The contribution of Wychwood in bringing the Samoyed to favorable all-breed attention has been tremendous. One of its Samoyeds was Best in Show in every year from 1951 through 1959 (except 1956), and in 1953 it was the only kennel of any breed in America to win Best in Show with three separate dogs. It is also interesting that much of this winning was done in a period of outstanding Working Group competition that included such all-time greats of their breeds as the Doberman Pinscher Ch. Rancho Dobe's Storm, and the Boxer Ch. Bang Away of Sirrah Crest. In fact, in 1952, when Spray placed third in the Group at Westminster, Storm was first (and on to Best in Show) and Bang Away was second.

The 1950's were to see the establishment of another of the all-time great show records of the breed. A strong strain had been started in 1948, when Mrs. Jean Blank of Fremont, California, began her career with Cheechako and Chumikan, completing their championships in 1949. She raised a few litters, and with Percy and Lena Matheron, co-owned Yurok of Whitecliff.

"Rocky," as Yurok was known, was by Ch. Omak out of Kara Babkrah of White Frost. Handled exclusively by Mrs. Blank, he was shown to a record that stands exalted in the history of the breed. Yurok was an outstanding dog and stayed in remarkable coat, which permitted continual campaigning. In the five-year period from 1956 through 1960, he acquired (by AKC records) a pace-setting total of 136 Bests of Breed, 98 Group placements including 26 Firsts, and 5 all-breed Best in Show awards. In the years 1958 and 1959 alone, he swept 85 Bests of Breed, 73 Group placements with 18 Firsts, and 4 Bests in Show, a pace that won him honor as the only Sam to place in the Top Ten of the Phillips System Ratings for all breeds—a system that awards its ratings in accordance with the number of dogs over which the wins were scored. Yurok's most monumental win was of Best in Show at Harbor Cities Kennel Club show in 1959, when judge Percy Roberts placed him tops in the entry of 2,500 dogs. It was Percy Roberts who—as a dog broker—had been instrumental in the important importation of Tobolsk back in 1920.

Ch. Yurok of Whitecliff was retired at five years of age to the wooded retreat of his co-owners, Lena and Percy Matheron, at Smartsville in Grass Valley, California. "Rocky" lived to be 15 years of age. At his death in 1970, he was eulogized by owners of his descendants. Some of the influential grandsons "carrying on" for him have been through Elliot Colburn's Ch. Barceia's Shondi of Drayalene, the Dan Morgans' Ch. Darius King of Snow Ridge and Doris McLaughlin's Ch. Nachalnik of Drayalene.

One other dog shares with Ch. Silver Spray of Wychwood and Ch. Yurok of Whitecliff the distinction of having won five Bests in Show—Ch. Sam O'Khan's Chingis Khan ("Jingo"). "Jingo," by Ch. Noatak of Silver Moon ex Ch. Sam O'Khan's Tsari Khan, was

100

Ch. Yurok of Whitecliff (1955-1970), handled by co-owner Mrs. Jean Blank, scoring win under author Robert H. Ward.

bred by Francis Fitzpatrick, and is owned by James and Joan Sheets of Alexandria, Virginia. Because their careers did not overlap, these three great BIS winners never met each other in the ring. Spray won from 1952 through 1954, "Rocky" from 1956 through 1959, and "Jingo" from 1966 through 1969.

Am. and Can. Ch. Lulhaven's Snowmist Ensign may well surpass all previous Samoyed winning records. As we close out pages on this book, he has already won 4 Bests in Show in the United States and 12 in Canada, to give him an overall total of 16. His more than 50 Group placements (won in both countries) include 28 Firsts. Ensign, owned by Ott Hyatt and Sonny White of Bellevue, Washington, is handled by Mrs. Pat Tripp.

102

The third of the three Samoyeds that have won five Bests in Show, Ch. Sam O'Khan's Chingis Khan. Bred by Francis C. Fitzpatrick in 1963, he is by Ch. Noatak of Silver Moon ex Ch. Sam O'Khan's Tsari Khan. Owned by James and Joan Sheets. The top winning Samoyed in the United States (Phillips' Ratings) for 1967 and 1969, he won the A. E. Mason Trophy (for top Samoyed winner) in the last three years it was presented—1966, 1967 and 1968, and the Juliet T. Goodrich Trust Fund award for top winning Samoyed in the first two years it was presented—1969 and 1970.

Ch. Stormy Weather of Betty Blue (1950–1962) and Ch. Misty Way of Betty Blue, owned by Martin and Georgia Gleason. Stormy Weather, a Group winner, was the Wimundstrev Stud Dog Trophy winner for 1958, and is behind many winning Sams of today.

Am. and Mex. Ch. Adrian of the Arctic (1958–1967). An English import from the famed Arctic Kennel of Miss Marion Keyte-Perry, Adrian was the pampered pet of the William Stanfields who raised him in Hamburg, Germany, before coming to America. A promising but undisciplined show dog, he was a challenge to Warren Stephens, who agreed to train and show him. Upon being transferred to another country, rather than subject him to another adjustment, the Stanfields sold him to Bob DiGiovanni, for whom he became the foundation dog of the White Tundra Kennels. He is pictured completing his championship, with Warren Stephens handling.

A change in show rules by the American Kennel Club had some effect upon our breed in January 1950. First, the Limit Class was dropped from the regular classes and replaced with the Bred-by-Exhibitor class from the non-regular classes. The other rule greatly changed the method of show preparation for many exhibitors. The use of chalk or other whitening agents had to be thoroughly removed from the dog's coat before entering the ring. Dogs were to be dismissed, and owners penalized, for artificial coloring or excessive chalk. Chalking had been a prevalent practice with white dogs. The rest of the rule pertaining to appearance altering by surgical means did not have an effect upon the Samoyed.

In 1950, other imports were still arriving. Elma Miller imported Rippleby Fanfare. Mrs. Ann Marie Goekel of New Rochelle imported Snowland Shelagh Janmayen from Mrs. Westcott's Kennels in England. Later the same year, she obtained Rikki Omydees sired by Snowland Rusky.

A combination of the new breeders and owners, the lifting of prior limitations from the war years, and the holding of only three parent club specialties since 1943, started a rebirth of Samoyed activity. Entries skyrocketed in Southern California, which hosted the largest benched specialty ever held for the Samoyed Club of America with an entry of 110 individual dogs at the Harbor Cities Kennel Club. After the showing, the judge, Christian Knudsen, jokingly hoped he would never see another white dog. The Best of Breed, Shirley Hill's Cinderella dog, Ch. Verla's Prince Comet, was placed fourth in the Working Group. Agnes and Aljean Mason's brace was second in the Working Brace at this 2,500 dog entry in the Long Beach Civic Auditorium.

This twelfth Samoyed Club of America Specialty was a resounding success in both numbers and geography, drawing dogs from many parts of the country, plus England and Canada. Samoyed owners enjoyed a nation-wide togetherness, seeing dogs and meeting owners from far away places, and talking with the 114 persons at the pre-show banquet. This number was greater than the total ownership of 20 years before.

Following the all-time record entry of the Specialty, interest stirred in the Pacific Northwest for the first time since World War II. Martin and Georgia Gleason obtained a Samoyed destined for distinction. Ch. Stormy Weather of Betty Blue was not only a good dog himself but proved to be a great sire, though bred only a relatively few times. Through his father, Maulcheck of Rhanor, he goes back to the famous "N" litter of the Snowland Kennels and through his mother, in two generations, also to Nikita of Snowland and Ch. Nova Sonia of Kobe. The Ken-Dor Kennels of Mr. and Mrs. Kenneth Kolb of Evergreen, Washington were begun in this same period, and have continued to this day to produce such fine specimens as Ch. Ken-Dor's Sky Komish, Ch. Ken-Dor's Princess Kim, Ken-Dor's Pat-Nak, and others.

This era was strengthened when Mr. and Mrs. John Butler rejoined the Samoyed fancy and began breeding outstanding dogs in the San Diego area. Their champions, Sergei, Chekuv, Samoa Saloma (litter sister to Ch. Yurok), and Mygei appear in today's pedigrees.

The increase in Best in Show awards came in 1951, and foretold the growth of the breed and the successful breeding, training, and exhibiting programs in existence. Judge Albert E. Van Court awarded Ch. Verla's Prince Comet Best in Show at San Gabriel Kennel Club in August 1951. Ch. Dawn of Samoyland, a homebred of Dr. and Mrs. C. S. Bezanson, was Best in Show in Nova Scotia, Canada. Ch. Spark of Altai, the sire of Dawn of Samoyland, followed in his son's footsteps by winning the coveted Best in Show award at Moncton Kennel Club in Canada under judge Mrs. Alva McColl. (Note that Spark is a grandson of one of Mrs. Helen Harris's Snowland Kennels' bitches, as was the first Best in Show winner, Sweet Missy of Sammar. Six other Best in Show Winners over the next twelve years traced to this same bloodline.)

While showing and breeding was somewhat curtailed again by more war years, some of the champions recorded in 1951 were: Ch. White Mesa, owned by Mr. and Mrs. Warren Stephens; Ch. Pratika of Top Acres, owned by Mrs. Ruth Bates Young; Champions Vrai of Lucky Dee and Bunky of Lucky Dee, owned by Mr. and Mrs. William Dawes; Ch. Verla's Tagenrod, owned by the Lickess'; Wm. Tien's Ch. Lady Kathriana; Ch. Snow Blizzard of Lewclaire; and Ch. Kun To's Palana, owned by the Johnsons.

Dramatic increase in the breeding and showing of Samoyeds in the Northwest, especially Washington and Oregon, led to formation of a group through which owners and breeders could share information and training tips. These people added a new phase to the activities of the Samoyed when they organized classes and trained their dogs for packing and hiking. The *point scale,* or number of dogs required for competition in a dog show to acquire championship points, rose above that of the East Coast. With activity such as this, the parent club added another division and the Northwest Division was born with the following people as officers: Mr. and Mrs. Kenneth Kolb, Mr. and Mrs. Martin Gleason, Mr. and Mrs. Clifford Collins, Miss Goldie Klein, and Marie Mueller.

An unusual exhibition marked the 13th Specialty Show of the parent club held at Bay Meadows Race Track in California. The Samoyed was the feature of the show. Following the judging, 25 Samoyeds were taken off the bench to give a demonstration of sled work and races. Five teams competed in a short race with drivers: Tom Witcher with Ch. Vojak U.D. at lead; Bob Ward with Ch. Starchak C.D.; Lloyd Van Sickle with Rex of White Way; Charles Burr with Ch. Nick of White Way; and Ken Bristol with Ch. Starchak's Witangemote. Each team consisted of five dogs. Later, an exhibition of a 25 dog hook-up was given with a Ford convertible as ballast. This demonstration is pictured in the text. A specially selected team of 15 was chosen for a demonstration for television and motion picture cameras. This team, led by Rex of White Way and including eight show champions, coursed the mile track, executing right and left turns and complete about turns.

Mrs. Catharine Self Quereaux's death in 1952 left a great void, but she left many monuments to the Samoyed. The breed has available 26 years of bulletins and extensive pedigree files that she kept in duplicate and for years offered generously to everyone. Her four imports mentioned in this text carried on with championship get to improve the breed, her lifelong aim.

Another import joined the American bloodlines of Colonel Frank Bowen and his wife Vickie when they brought in Van Guard of North Riding to join Frosty from the Encino Kennels and Van Allen and White Rose of North Riding at their home in Maryland.

Joining the list of proud owners of Samoyeds with stellar show careers were Major General Roderick Allen and his wife Maydelle. Their bitch, White Frosting, completed her championship at the 1953 Westminster Show, and their Ch. Narguess of Top Acres was Best Opposite Sex, ably handled by Len Brumby, Jr. The General also imported the English bitch Ch. Janet Jan Mayen. Ch. Narguess of Top Acres came from a most notable litter sired by Ch. Martingate Snowland Taz. Their dam was Ch. Sparkle Plenty of Arbee, with a strong American bloodline. (The name Arbee goes back to Roy Brott, a breeder of 30 years, with dogs direct from Snowland and Yurak Kennels.)

This famous litter consisted of five sisters, named by the Shah of Iran, who at that time was the house guest of Major General Allen who was then stationed at Ft. Knox, Kentucky. The Shah said they should be named for lovely white flowers: 1. Narguess or White Narcissus. 2. Pratika or White Rose. 3. Hadesse or White Myrtle. 4. Yasmin or Jasmin. 5. Sosanna or White Lilly.

Narguess, Pratika, and Hadesse became champions. Yasmin of Top Acres was taken to Japan. Ch. Narguess of Top Acres also went to Japan, and whelped one litter there. Yasmin of Top Acres was returned to the States, where she whelped one litter sired by Ch. Bunky of Lucky Dee. The Dawes kept one of the male pups, Ch. Bunky of Lucky Dee Jr. He later was Best of Breed at Chicago International, and at the 1956 Parent Club Specialty at Seattle (on to 2nd in the Working Group under judge A. E. VanCourt).

With the foregoing breeding, it was later possible for Dr. and Mrs. Wm. Herbst of Inglewood, California, to acquire from the Lucky Dee Kennels, a son of Int. Ch. MacGregor of Glenstrae out of Heather of Glenstrae who had a German champion father with a granddam that was a Japanese champion.

A highlight of 1953 was the legislation that the parent club annual meeting would be held in the area of the president's residence. For the first time in 30 years, the meeting was held outside of New York City. The 14th parent club Specialty was held with the Westchester Kennel Club in September. The long time friend and judge of the Samoyed breed Miss Ruth Stillman officiated. From the entry of 40 she selected Ch. Zor of Altai, owned by Alta and Roy Ruth. His grandparents were Ch. Zantok of Breezewood, Niavirik of Inara, and Irish and Am. Ch. Snowland Stara.

A new kennel owned by ardent sledding enthusiasts appeared in 1954—the Woodsam Kennels of Mr. and Mrs. Robert Wood in Chittenago, New York. The Woods worked their teams at Oneida Lake. Other advocates of working dogs, both as sled dogs and as packing dogs, sprang up in the far Northwest. The positive effect of these Northwest breeders was still felt in the 1960s.

Mr. and Mrs. Robert Bowles' Ch. Noatak of Silver Moon and Ch. Silver Moon have won the Stud Dog Trophy and the Brood Bitch Trophy three years in a row. They are behind the Best in Show winners Ch. Sam O'Khan's Chingis Khan, Ch. Sam O'Khan's Tian Shan, Ch. Karasea's Silver Nikki, Ch. Karasea's Silver Kim and the Alareds' Ch. Maur-Mik's Kim. John and Lila Weir planned a breeding program with their "Happy," Ch. Tod-Acres Fang, and Ch. Kobe's Nan-Nuk of Encino to produce the influential Best in Show Winner Ch. Joli Knika and his grandson Ch. Star Nika Altai of Silver Moon, a Best in Show winner in 1967.

108

Am. and Can. Ch. Sam O'Khans Tian Shan, wh. 1963, by Am. & Can. Ch. Noatak of Silver Moon ex Am. and Can. Ch. Sam O'Khan's Tsari of Khan. Best in Show winner in Canada, and a Group winner in the U.S. Bred and owned by Mr. and Mrs. George Fitzpatrick, of Washington state.

Ch. Timan's Williwaw, C.D., wh. 1957. This amazingly versatile dog scored a BOB at ten years of age over younger Specials. Wheel dog on sled team for 4½ years, at age of six he was conditioned for show and won 6 out of 7 to gain his championship. He is a fourth generation of C.D. titlists. Handled by Shirley Keepers Kennedy.

Ch. Buddy Boy of Williwaw, son of Ch. Timan's Williwaw C.D. Owned by Dennis and Gretchen Raymond.

109

Reflecting the successes of the breeders in the Northwest area in this period of time, we note the fact that when they began in the early 1950's, they combined bloodlines from all parts of the nation and disseminated them throughout the USA in the following years.

Constructive growth for the breed in the Pacific Coast area came when Miss Helene Spathold and her father Layard became enchanted with the Samoyed. Helene added much to the breed in her short life. She believed in, and worked with, the Bruce Lowe theory to establish a definite strain or type. Her strain was very strong and successful in winning top honors at three parent club specialties. Miss Spathold, as publicity director for the Pacific Coast, wrote excellent articles on grooming, showing and raising of puppies. Both she and her father were breed judges at the time of their deaths.

Parent Club Specialty number 15 found Judge Edward McQuown with 51 entries at the Chicago International. Best of Breed was Ch. King of Wal-lynn, owned by Ethel Smith. In Los Angeles, the supported show held at the Los Angeles Kennel Club found Major B. Godsol awarding Best of Breed to Starctic Storm in an entry of 57 including 9 Specials. This was the R. H. Wards' first entry for the 4-year-old double-grandson of Ch. Starchak C.D. Later Starctic Storm sired Ch. Kazan of Kentwood who in turn produced Ch. Sayan of Woodland who won the Parent Club Specialties #34 with an entry of 92 and #37 with an entry of 71, as well as the San Diego Club Specialty with an entry of 78.

In the 15-year period from 1940 to 1955, the Samoyed breed had grown from a concentration in the East, with a few dogs on the West Coast and a sprinkling in the Midwest, to a nationwide affair. No longer would the judges see the Samoyed only occasionally. For example, some representative 1955 Best of Breed wins were: Decatur and Bloomington, Ill., Kusang of Northern Frost (Beckman); Plainview, Texas, Polar Dawn of Wimundstrev: Cincinnati, Ohio, Nicholas of Geona (Leahy); Springfield, Ill., Frostar's Kauouli Karin (Beckman); Sewickley and Butler Pa., Ch. Tam Tam of Altai (DiCarlo); Huntington, N.Y., Snowcrests Norna (Grillo); Old Westbury, Park Cliffe Snowpack Anissa (Davis); Gresham, Oregon, Ch. Polaris Pan (Klein); Salt Lake City, Ch. Chin Chin Dan Mc-Grew (Tom Ralphs); Portland, Maine, Ch. Ranger (Brindle); Albany, N.Y., Ardcliff Lucky Star (Bascom); Troy, N.Y., Ch. Narguess of Top Acres (Allen); Kokomo, Ind., Ch. King of Wal-Lynn (Smith); Delaware, Ohio, Destiny of Top Acres (Young); Athens, Ga., Nanook (Herring); Atlanta, Ga., Balaiya Doroga Cela

110

(Ingram) ; Champaign, Ill., Lucky Day of Snow Shoe Hill (Goodrich) ; Pansacola, Fla., and Mobile, Ala., Balaiya Doroga Cela (Ingram) ; Syracuse, N.Y., Elkenglo's Glasha (Miller) ; Rockford, Ill. and Fort Wayne, Indiana, Ch. King of Wal-Lynn (Smith) ; Minneapolis, Minn., Royal Snodonn (Ronstron) ; Brooklyn, N.Y., Ch. Tazson's Snow Flicka (Ulfeng) ; Holtville, California, Ch. Smithson's Snow King (Smithson) ; Lansing, Mich., Sardarson of Bonnie Brae (Marquardt) ; Philadelphia, Pa., Ch. Silvertips Scion of Wychwood (Ashdown) ; San Francisco, Calif., Ch. White Ways Silver Streak (Mason) ; Cleveland, Ohio, Ch. Tazbell (Callahan) ; San Bernardino, Calif., Ch. Nicolette of Altai (Wheelock) ; Vancouver, Wash., Ch. Stormy Weather of Betty Blue and Group 1st (Gleason) ; San Diego, Calif., Ch. Startinda's Chimen-tagh (Soper).

As the Samoyeds increased about the country with the other breeds and the number of shows doubled, there was a request for more Specialty shows. In 1955, as in the previous year, the parent club had two shows. The first, at Westchester KC, had an entry of 16 for judge Clifford Chamberlain, who placed the bitch Ch. Tazson's Snow Flicka, owned by the Ashbjorn Ulfengs, Best of Breed. In December, at the Los Angeles KC, there were 83 Samoyeds including 20 Champions for Mr. A. Loveridge to pass upon. Ch. Polaris Pan, from Seattle, Washington, was Best of Breed. His owners, Marie Mueller and Goldie Klein, were strong advocates of training the dog to work as pack dogs on their hiking trips.

The Samoyed invaded the southwestern United States when bloodlines from the Encino Kennels went to Dr. and Mrs. Simpson in Tucson, Arizona. The Wm. Powells of Alpine, Texas, had the progeny of Ch. Starchak, Ch. Snowland Stara, Ch. Staryvna of Snowland, and Eng. Ch. Raff of Kobe. Mrs. Lucile Miller had her Altai Kennels with American Snowland lines, Ch. Zantok of Breezewood, Ch. Snowland Stara, and bloodlines of Ch. Deyomas of Ibur. Mrs. Elizabeth Morony with her Marylake Kennels of Alamo, Texas, became an ardent supporter and with another Texan, Mrs. Nell Roberts of Austin, Texas, publicized the breed with educational bulletins.

Hazel and Bill Dawes of Cupertino, California, created a lasting impression with a breeding program that produced Group winners and Best in Show dogs. Their first male champion, Ch. Lucky Labon Nahum, was by Sonolad of the Valley. So the male side went back to the early California dogs of the Perc Stangs. From Snow Mist Tanya,

111

his mother's side went back to Kharkov and Siberian Snow Sonia of Martha Humphriss' kennels of the early 1930s in Rhode Island. Their foundation brood bitch, Ch. Faustina Fauna, was by Ch. Frolnick of Sammar, thus back to the Midwest dogs of Ch. Czar Nicholas and Pennsylvania Snowland Kennels through Ch. Frola of Snowland. On the maternal side, Hope of White Way added all of Mason's lines including the Laika, Donerna, Kobe, and Arctic. With almost every old and new bloodline, their linebreeding program produced very stylish, elegant, and profusely-coated dogs. When they ceased breeding and showing Samoyeds, several of their dogs formed the foundation for Helene Spathold's kennel of the Drayalene dogs. Before the Dawes' Lucky Dee name ceased on current dogs, their Ch. Vrai of Lucky Dee had two Best in Shows, and the Group Winner Ch. Bunky of Lucky Dee had won a Parent Club Specialty.

Sammy owners and their dogs enjoyed the first of many annual sled races in February 1955 at Big Bear Lake, California. Arranged by an idependent group called the Southern California Samoyed Club, the Sunday affair featured seven dog teams composed, of course, of all Samoyeds. These became the annual races and snow games open to all breeds. At first, the teams were made up of dogs belonging to many different owners. The visit to the snow was the first time for many of the dogs. There were many novice drivers, team dogs, and lead dogs. Among the first participants were: Larry and Ruth Soper with Ch. Chimen-tagh; Alice and Ted Winecoff with White Ways' Tilka and Apex; Bob and Dolly Ward with Ch. Starchak, Ch. Witan, Ch. Victoria of Starctic, and Ch. Starctic Storm; Gene and Chas. Burr with Ch. Kazan, Ch. Blazer, Chatuska, Blitz, and Silver Trinket; Vicky and Hal Wheelock with Ch. Nicolette and George; Margaret Tucker with Ch. Kun To, and the Kenneth Bristols with Ch. Starchak's Witange-mote, Ch. Startinda, Chs. Startinda's Talnik, and Sarana. The club officers were the Norman Hills, with daughters Shirley and Jean, Joe Scott, and Vera Kroman. A hot chili social was served to all mushers by the club. It was the amateur fun beginning of the Annual Big Bear Valley Sled Dog Derby.

The second parent club Specialty of 1956, held at the Mason Dixon Kennel Club, brought to light a winning dog that dominated the Samoyed circles for the next four years. Judge M. B. Meyer awarded Best of Breed to Ch. Nordly's Sammy, owned by Mr. and Mrs. John Doyle of Doylestown, Pennsylvania. Butch, as he was known, was sired by Mrs. Ashborn Ulfeng's Am. and Can. Ch.

Ch. Silver Crest's Sikandi, owned by Helene Spathold.

Tazson out of Bluecrest Karenia, and was a grandson of Ch. Martingate Snowland Taz. Champion Nordly's Sammy won four parent club specialties, #19, #20, #21, and #22, in four sections of the nation from the East to the West Coast. In 1957 at Monmouth, New Jersey, he was Best of Breed under judge C. A. Swartz and 1st in the Working Group, as well as Best American-Bred Dog in Show under James Trullinger. The largest entry of Samoyeds he topped was 71 at the specialty at Santa Clara Kennel Club under judge Major Godsol, where he went on to 2nd in the Working Group. He has been the

Ch. Barceia's Shondi of Drayalene, wh. 1960, by Ch. Shoeshone of Whitecliff ex Ch. Silver Crest's Sikandi. Bred by Helene and Layard Spathold, and owned by Elliott Colburn.

113

only Samoyed to win four parent club Specialties in succession, meeting the representatives in four sections, South, East, Midwest, and Pacific Coast. Ch. Nordly's Sammy retired the Club's perpetual trophy (White Bark Kennels' Ch. Barrie Memorial Trophy) and was retired from competition.

The Best Opposite to Ch. Nordly's Sammy at the 21st Specialty Show held at the Chicago International Kennel Club was a rather close relative. Ch. Imp of Snow Shoe Hill, owned by Miss Juliet Goodrich of Wisconsin, was sired by Ch. Deyomas of Ibur, a half-brother to Martingate Snowland Taz. The imported Deyomas had sired six champions at that time, Ch. Tess of Altai, Ch. Nicolette of Altai, Ch. Balaiya Doroga Cela, Ch. Imp of Snow Shoe Hill, Ch. Dey's Kim of Breezewood, and Ch. Balaiya Doroga Boorya. Upon the death of Mrs. Quereaux, Deyomas lived his remaining days with Miss Ruth Kilbourn. Miss Kilbourn also inherited Ch. Imp of Snow Shoe Hill, who lived in the luxury provided by this kind and loving owner of Samoyeds for over 40 years.

Imports of the mid-fifties were Venture of Kobe (by English Ch. Gogalev of Corbesky ex Ch. Snow Queen of Raff of Kobe), from Mrs. K. L. Perry to Mr. and Dr. Chas. D. Hall, and Ch. Nimbus of Antarctica (by Somoffvar ex Eng. Ch. Snow Stara of Kobe) from Mr. and Mrs. K. B. Rawlings to Vera Compton.

Mrs. Jennette Gifford bred her Zenaide of Singing Trees to Venture of Kobe. Her Singing Trees Kennels included the littermates Ch. Glazier of Singing Trees and Ch. Jomay of Singing Trees.

The Midwest states were given a big boost in the 1957–58 period by the Ell-Tee Kennels of Tom and Lucy Schneider. They produced top winning bitches and dogs, and had 10 champions themselves in 5 years. They bred (and owned) the winner of the Tucker Brood Bitch Trophy, Ch. Luloto, in 1958. Progress of the breed's success was revealed in the Samoyed's rank of 33rd in registrations among all breds. The number recorded was 1299. It was a nice comfortable place to be, neither the most popular, nor unknown.

Ch. Stormy Weather of Betty Blue, the 1959 Wimundstrev Stud Dog Trophy winner, was living in Seattle, Washington, and had sired 7 Champions out of 6 different bitches. They included Ch. Ken-Dors Sky Komish out of Connee Pun of Nichi, owned by Mrs. Dorothy Kolb; Ch. Storm out of Ch. Glee-Sams Misty Weather, owned by Mr. and Mrs. Joe Alderson; Amer. and Can. Ch. Snow

Cloud of Cedar Wood out of Ch. Tod-Acres Tanga, owned by Bernice Cooper; Ch. Glee-Sams Ski Weather, a full but not litter brother of Sir Storm, owned by Cecil and Joyce Worsnop of Calgar, Canada; and Ch. Tod-Acres Fang out of Tod-Acres Starlet, owned by John and Lila Weir. Fang later won the Stud Dog award and sired the Best in Show winner Ch. Joli Knika. The sixth champion was Niptiluk Takoka of Nichi out of Piu-Lengi-Nichi, owned by Mr. and Mrs. Wm. Beattie. She won a Working Group 1st at the Whidbey Island Kennel Club Show. The seventh was Ch. Kapegah Okanok of Nichi out of the bitch Ch. Snauflicka Skylarkin, owned by Nell and Clifford Collins. The Collins worked diligently for the breed not only with their dogs, but as president of the Northwest Division and vice president of the parent club. They showed their typey bitch to her Canadian Championship in three days. Peggy, as she was known, went from Best of Breed to Best in Show at the Pacific Northwest Exposition Show in Vancouver, Canada. She also won several Group Firsts in the United States. Of interest to breeders is the fact that Peggy won at the age of 8 years old. She was Best of Breed at the Ventura Show in 1964, and repeated the next day at the Santa Barbara Show, handled by Porter Washington, in an entry of 62 under judge Major Godsol.

Ron Johnson, while at the University of Washington in Seattle, volunteered his Prince Kazan (sired by Ch. Stormy Weather) as mascot for their football team, the Huskies. The football team's first dog from Alaska did not look like a husky when he grew up so a real Northern type, the Samoyed, took over.

Ch. Luchow's Pride of Top Acres and his imported female companion inspired the Jan Mitchell Award trophy given each month for many years to a selected celebrity for exceptional devotion to dogs. This award was originated by Kurt Unkelbach, author of *Love on a Leash* and Jan Mitchell, then owner of Luchow's restaurant in New York City. When the Mitchells' interests turned to art, Ch. Luchow's Pride of Top Acres was returned to his breeder, Mrs. Ruth Bates Young in Ohio.

An educational method for evaluating dogs as a group was devised in California. A spot show for Samoyeds was held in Southern California which provided that the dogs would be judged strictly by the old point scale of the approved standard. Vera Kroman of the Southern California Samoyed Club hosted the event and Mrs. Mel Fishback drew large charts depicting the rights and wrongs of the various anatomical parts of the Samoyed to enable spectators to know what

115

values were being assessed to each segment being judged. (We are pleased to have her drawings in this book.) There were four judges, each in a different ring and the dogs moved from one ring to the next as they were individually evaluated. Handlers were other than owners. There was one score card for each dog by each judge. The four cards for each dog were averaged by scorekeepers and the dogs listed by ranking on the scale by their numbered entry, not by name. No one was embarrassed unless the owners did not have a poker face. It seemed to be a fair way to evaluate a dog when all of the amateur judges were breeders or approved Samoyed judges. Each winner from these matches finished his championship rapidly.

A bulletin called *Southern Samoyed Fanciers* appeared in the late 1950s. Published in Texas by the energetic breeder and exhibitor Nell Roberts, it carried educational information to the South and Southwest United States. Mrs. Roberts invited guest writers such as Helene Spathold, breeder-judge, and Mel Fishback, sled dog enthusiast and Western editor of *Team and Trail*.

New supporters and bloodline combinations appeared in Northern California to produce show-winning dogs under the direction of Mrs. Madeline Druse of Redding and Mrs. Leona Powell of San Leandro: Ch. Ruble, Ch. Juliet O' Snow Ridge, Ch. Prince Tyson and his son, Ch. Tyson's Rebel of Snow Ridge (who won a Group 1st at both the Blue Ribbon Del Monte Kennel Club and Silver Bay Kennel Club). Both owners were greatly interested in sledding and worked their dogs in the Mt. Lassen National Park in Northern California.

The parent club specialty show of 1962 was held at the Westchester KC in Purchase, New York and was a special memorial to Ardath Chamberlain. Ardath had given 30 years to the breed and served as publicity director of the parent club. Her husband, Clifford, was selected as the judge for the show.

Judge Clifford Chamberlain had 32 entries with 8 champions. He narrowed to an East and West battle between Ch. Elkenglo's Dash O'Silver and California's Ch. Kazan of Kentwood. Ch. Elkenglo's Dash O'Silver, owned by Mrs. E. L. Miller of Corning, New York, was the winner.

Dominating bloodlines were created in the state of Washington when the George Fitzpatricks of Richland, Washington, produced Sam O'Khan's Tsari of Khan. Sired by Amer. and Can. Ch. Zaysan of Krisland C.D. (1957–1967) out of Whitecliff's Polar Dawn, Tsari was destined to prove a Best in Show and Brood Bitch Trophy winner. They also owned Ch. Sam O'Khan's Tian Shan, and bred the current five-time Best in Show winner, Ch. Sam O'Khan's Chingis Khan. Littermates are Am. and Can. Ch. Sam O'Khan's Khyber Khan, owned by the Richard Woods of Wenatchee, Wash.; Ch. Sam O'Khan's Temushen O'Dudinka, owned by Bill and Ann Miller of Milford, Conn., and Pat Morehouse's Ch. Sam O'Khan's Kubla Khan in southern California.

As new Samoyeds arrived, some grand old ones left. Amer. and Can. Ch. Tazson's Snow Flicka died at the age of 14 years. She was one of the few bitches to ever win a parent club Specialty, and had many Group placings and a Group First. Flicka was a remarkable mother type bitch that assumed all puppies were her own. She was one of the few Samoyeds to enjoy a bath, and would jump into the tub when the bathing mats were brought out. Ch. Tazson, also owned by Mrs. Ulfeng, was a great winner with 55 Bests of Breed.

Donna Yocom and the Colorado group were inspired to prepare another outstanding Samoyed showing in the spring of 1963. The judge, Mrs. Dolly Ward, had a geographical representation of 37 including Best in Show Samoyeds. The quality was excellent and Best of Breed was Ch. Joli Knika (by Ch. Tod-Acres Fang out of Ch. Kobe's Nan-Nuk of Encino), bred by John and Lila Weir. Knika was owned and handled by a 17-year-old boy, Cliff Cabe, from Oregon. He climaxed his win by taking the Group under George Higgs, and going on to Best in Show under Louis Murr. The show was held on a floor over an ice rink. Prior to the first Group judging at this show, the automatic ice-making equipment "turned on". As the air and floor became colder and colder, judge Donia Cline was heard to comment, "It ought to be a good night for the Samoyed, for if it gets any colder he will be the only one that can take it."

In this same 1963, 44 Samoyeds made their Champion titles and one, Ch. Joli Knika won a Best in Show at Denver, Colorado, after none by a Samoyed in two years. There were seven Working Group Firsts won by three different Samoyeds; Ch. Joli Knika (2), Amer. and Can. Noatak of Silver Moon (4), and Ch. Frostars Princess Snowball (1).

Another English import arrived in 1964, brought in by Dr. Maurice Waller of Memphis, Tennessee. The puppy was sired by the Eng. Ch. Sleigh Monarch of Kobe. The Dr. and his daughter also own Marylakes' Princess of Shimar. The south was also represented

117

Ch. Prince Tyson of Snow Ridge, wh. 1959, by White Frost's Tybo ex Ch. White Way's Juliet O' Snow Ridge. Bred, owned and handled by Leona Powell.

Ch. Tyson's Rebel of Snow Ridge (1963–1968), by Ch. Prince Tyson of Snow Ridge ex Ch. Patrice of Snow Ridge. A Group winner. Owned and handled by Leona Powell.

Mex. and Am. Ch. Danlyn's Silver Coronet, wh. 1963. Winner of the Arctic Breed Olympiad at San Fernando KC, 1968 under Mrs. Milton Seeley. Owned by Louis Torres.

118

by Mrs. Kathryn Tagliaferri of Baton Rouge, Louisiana, who completed the championship of Ch. Chu San's Mei Ling O'Yeniseisk, and won the Ch. Suzanne award for the top winning bitch in the nation for 1964. Mei Ling's daughter, Ch. Ka-Tag's Memory in Silver, owned by Nelda Dendinger, won the same award in 1967.

Samoyed activity was indeed growing. The *Southern Samoyed Journal* noted that, "At the Montgomery, Alabama, show in May 1964, there were four Champions entered for the first time ever in the South."

Western dogs and bloodlines moved eastward as Sercheck's Long Trip completed his championship for owners, the Zollie Reids of Oklahoma City, and received an air-conditioned kennel at the same time. Ch. Sercheck's Long Trip came from Mrs. Anne Butler of San Diego, California. Sergi had 15 Best of Breeds and 3 Group placements at the age of two years. The Reids also owned Ch. Eve-ollie's Kgy-Gju and Ch. Tanya.

The long-time advocate of the Samoyed in the South, the Snowdrift Kennels of the W. R. Ingrams at Prattville, Alabama, imported the American and Australian Ch. Kobe Holm Storm. Mrs. Ingram introduced Mrs. Rita Bowling of Virginia Beach, Virginia, to Samoyeds, and Mrs. Bowling recently also acquired White Krystal's Luba and Startinda's Rabochi.

In 1964, the breed was still 32nd in number of registrations, but recognition at the shows was becoming apparent with 28 Samoyeds receiving 45 Group placings, and three winning Best in Show, Ch. Saroma's Polar Prince, Ch. Bazuhl of Caribou and Ch. Karasea's Silver Nikki. Twenty-four obedience titles were earned: 21 C.D.'s two C.D.X.'s, and one U.D. (Daniel Winn's Ch. White Bark's Chief Snow Cloud).

As determined by the Phillips System, Amer. and Can. Ch. Saroma's Polar Prince defeated the greatest number of dogs in 1964. Samoyeds with multiple Group placements were: Ch. Chu San's Mei Ling O'Yeniseisk, Ch. Wynterkloud of Silver Moon. Ch. Sercheck's Long Trip, Ch. Frostar's Princess Snowball, Ch. Darius King of Snow Ridge, Ch. Noatak of Silver Moon, and Ch. Joli Knika.

The Midwest Division hosted the 25th parent club specialty at the Chicago International Kennel Club, where judge Virgil D. Johnson selected Bernice Heagy's Best in Show entry, Ch. Winterland's Kim, as Best of Breed over an entry of 34.

A new era and the end of the old system by which the parent club had always held a Specialty show in conjunction with an all-breed show, took place in 1964. A fellow Samoyed owner, Richard Breckenridge, was selected to be show secretary, assisted by Lloyd Bristol. They operated without a professional show superintendent. Show chairman was Robert Ward. Parent Club President, Robert Bowles and the board selected the Southern Group of the Pacific Coast Division to host the show for the Samoyed Club of America.

The show was held on the beautifully landscaped grounds of the Mira Mar Hotel at Montecito, Santa Barbara, California. Mr. Albert E. VanCourt, who had placed the first Samoyed male to a Best in Show and who always exhibited fond interest in the breed, was invited to judge. He had 92 entries present, including 21 champions. He chose the beautiful open class bitch, Shondra of Drayalene, owned by Joe Dyer of Idaho, as Best of Breed. The magnificent Ch. Noatak of Silver Moon, owned by the Robert Bowles of Seattle, was Best Opposite. A son of Noatak, Karasea's Silver Kim, was Winners Dog. The authors were proud to assist in the engineering of this breakthrough for separate specialties for the Samoyed Club of America. Such an event had not taken place in the 41-year history of the Club.

The advantage of having the show separate from all-breed shows is that it allows special events spotlighting the breeding efforts within the breed, such as Best Puppy, Best-Bred-by-Exhibitor, or Best-American-Bred exhibit. A futurity match or a best puppy sweepstakes is best when held with an individual specialty show. Best of all, it is *always a Samoyed that is Best in Show*.

1965–1970

The Samoyed ranked 34th of all breeds in 1970 in registration totals. The fast pace of the increase in registrations is seen in this study of some yearly totals:

1907—1	1920—13	1955—1,066
1910—0	1925—119	1960—1,249
1911—3	1930—146	
1912—1	1935—125	1966—2,985
1913—2	1940—146	1967—3,671
1914—1	1945—199	1968—4,050
1915—4	1950—660	1969—4,622
		1970—6,129

120

The number of titlists each year has also grown apace. Listings in the AKC Gazettes from March 1969 through February 1970, reflecting championships completed in 1969, showed a total of 78 for the year. This brought the overall total of Samoyed champions in AKC history to 1,165.

Listings for the same period showed that 41 Samoyeds earned Companion Dog degrees in 1969, five made Companion Dog Excellent, and none Utility.

The number of dogs (and of owners with increasing interest) had risen so high that there were three parent club Specialties in 1965, two in 1966, and three in 1967, whereas there had been only ten in the first 25 years.

A new look began in 1965. The American Kennel Club suggested to the Samoyed Club of America that a new constitution and organizational set-up to allow more local activity was necessary. There was a need for breed matches and more Specialty Shows to aid new owners and puppies. In 42 years there had been only one independent breed club, the Interstate Samoyed Club, in Ohio, and it had been dissolved 20 years before.

First was the Samoyed Club of San Diego. In 1965 they held two Sanctioned A Matches, using American Kennel Club licensed judges, Mrs. Virginia Miller and Mrs. Dolly Ward. To illustrate the value of matches, the Best in Match, Tsarina of Lassen View (a daughter of Ch. Yurok of Whitecliff out of Jerasue of Draylene), so encouraged her owners, the Edwin Burns, that they took up showing, and quickly made her a champion.

Other local groups were formed, including the Hudson Valley Samoyed Club; Samoyed Club of Washington State; Potomac Samoyed Club; Silver Plume Samoyed Club and Continental Divide Club in Colorado; Greater Chicago Area Samoyed Club; Northern Calif. Fanciers; Samoyed Fanciers of Sacramento; Gem State Samoyed Club in Idaho; Wasatch Club in Utah; Southern Samoyed Fanciers; Samoyed Club of Los Angeles and the South Central Samoyed Club in Texas and bordering states. Many of these held their qualifying matches and the Los Angeles Club held their first Specialty in 1968 now an established annual event each September.

The nucleus of the Samoyed Club of Washington State, as the Northwest Division, hosted the second separate parent club specialty on August 21, 1965. It was a spectacular event, held at Bellevue, Washington. The judge, Mrs. Virginia Keckler of Ohio, had 83 Samoyeds with 110 entries (including 21 champions). With dogs from the Midwest, Oregon, Idaho, and California, Best of Breed was Ch. Shaloon of Draylene, owned by Lee and Sandra Wacenske of Washington, and Best Opposite, his litter sister Ch. Shondra of Draylene, owned by Mable and Joe Dyer of Idaho. If a breeder had been awarded the blue ribbon, it would have been to Elliot Colburn, who had bred the two top winners (both out of Ch. Barceia's Shondi of Draylene ex Silver Dede O' Snow Ridge).

In retrospect, we can see what happened to those young dogs and bitches that won their classes that day. Mrs. Keckler's opinions were upheld as the puppy dog winner, Lenora Sprock's White Krystal Balalika, completed his championship and carried on his mother's (Ch. Nadia of White Krystal) line, at their kennels in Steamboat, Nevada. Another class winner, Joli Rainie, owned by John and Lila Weir, carries on, as does Ch. Joli White Knight, the fourth in his litter to obtain a championship, the 8th champion by his sire (Ch. Tod-Acres Fang) and the 6th champion out of his dam (Ch. Kobe's Nan-Nuk of Encino). The Winners Dog, now Ch. Karasam of Misty Way owned by Peggy McCarthy of Oregon, won multiple Bests of Breed, Group placements, and Group Firsts for the Misty Way Kennels in Oregon. The Reserve Dog became Ch. Tyson's Rebel of Snow Ridge, who won Group Firsts at Del Monte and Silver Bay Kennel Clubs. More successful winners that also competed their championships were the Orville Merklein's Skookluk's Miss Chief, and the Reserve Bitch Leordan's Winter Wind of Ga-les owned by the Walter Simpsons of Renton, Washington. Their Ch. Winter Wind's Tamerlane won the breed at Westminster in 1965, and with 62 Bests of Breed and 25 Group placements was third Samoyed in United States ratings in 1965 and second top winning Sam in Canada.

A few of the many champions finished in this time period that will leave their mark in wins (and hopefully in progeny), are: The John Helinskis' bitch, Ch. Wynterkloud's Patyna Sno Mist (by Ch. Shadrack of Tindak out of Ch. Duchess Joh-ni of Silver Moon); Peggy McCarthy's Karasam of Misty Way (by Bel-Oras Valiant out of Ch. Tempest of Misty Way); the Lou Weltzins' (of Langley, B.C.), Ch. Kombo's Silver Prince (by Ch. Tod-Acres Fang out of Snow Ridge's Sonya). Leland Kusler's Kennels in Potlatch, Idaho, produced three champions by Joli Kaluna of Vellalee out of Ch. Saroma's Snow Beauty O' Vellalee: Ch. Vellee's Chayka, Ch. Vellee's Kloshe, and Ch. Vellee's Reddi, the latter owned by the John Vertunos of Illinois.

122

Ch. Tempest of Misty Way, owned by Mrs. Peggy McCarthy, Misty Way Kennels, Oregon.

Ch. Wynterkloud's Patyna Sno Mist, wh. 1963. Breeders-owners-handlers, John and Bernice Helinski, Colorado. Tyna's champion progeny includes Ch. Wynterkloud's Bil of Hilan Del (Scott) and Ch. Sherustar of Wynterkloud.

Ch. Vellee's Chayka, wh. 1963. First Samoyed bitch to win a Group in the Northwest in 13 years. Bred-owned-handled by Leland and Duvella Kusler, Idaho.

Many of the modern-day breeders are skillfully handling the strong and winning bloodlines of the past. Charles and Evelyn James (Frost River Samoyeds) obtained Frost River Lady in 1961 and bred to Silver's Rogue (by Silver Frost II ex Ch. Kobe's Nan-Nuk of Encino). A litter of three females resulted, all of whom made their championships: Ch. Anastasia of Frost River, owned by Gretchen Raymond; Ch. Mitzi, and Ch. Kara of Frost River (with daughter Ch. Kinta, handled to her championship in 1968 by Paul Barille). The James' have now produced five champions in five years.

Dennis and Gretchen Raymond have enjoyed considerable success. Their Ch. Buddy Boy of Williwaw and Ch. Anastasia have produced at least four champions. Ch. Mister Williwaw won the 1970 Samoyed Club of Los Angeles Specialty under Mrs. Kathryn Tagliaferri, and has earned Group placements. In 1971, Gretchen Raymond became the tenth current breeder judge of Samoyeds to be licensed by the AKC.

Mr. and Mrs. A. G. Bishop III have had great success with Ch. Karasea's Silver Kim, a son of Ch. Noatak of Silver Moon out of Kamchatka Princess Tamara, who is a full litter brother to Ch. Karasea's Silver Nikki. They are both pictured as Best in Show Samoyeds in this book.

The 1965 Specialty at San Fernando K.C. drew an entry of 60 for judge Forest Hall. He selected as Best of Breed, Ch. Danlyn's Silver Coronet, owned by Louis Torres. Silver Coronet's male line goes back to Ch. Timmy of the Highlands, Ru-Lares White Count and Ch. Startinda's Chimen-tagh. A new champion bitch appeared upon the scene with Trina of Taymylyr, owned by Mr. and Mrs. Thomas B. Tuttle, as Winners Bitch. Trina is by Ch. Barceia's Shondi of Drayalene ex Ellbur's Lady Ilsa.

In Colorado, familiar names and bloodlines are being preserved. The Harold McLaughlins' Ch. Nachalnik of Drayalene (by Ch. Rokandi of Drayalene ex Drayalene's Clarissa), is the fourth in his litter to complete a championship.

New dogs of credit to the breed appeared in Arkansas. The Max Moores' Ch. Samo-Silver Glo of Snowden placed second in the Working Group after winning 13 Bests of Breed in 1965.

Innovations were added to the separate parent club specialty in 1966 by the new young members and a few grayhairs of Southern California at the Hollywood Park Turf Club. The first Puppy Sweepstakes was held prior to the regular classes and judged by Jack

Ch. Anastasia of Frost River. Bred by Mr. and Mrs. Charles James. Owned by Mr. and Mrs. Dennis Raymond.

Ch. Darius King of Snow Ridge, wh. 1961, by Ch. Rokandi of Drayalene ex Ch. White Way's Juliet of Snow Ridge. Bred by Leona and Wade Powell, and owned by Mr. and Mrs. Daniel Morgan.

Dexter, a professional handler. The Puppy Sweepstakes winner, Karshan, later acquired his championship and through his dam, Ch. Dajja Mashad-E of Calaveras, perpetuated the bloodlines of sire Ch. Noatak of Silver Moon and grandsire Ch. Kazan of Kentwood. His sister, now Ch. Hoti-Ami of Starchak, was Winners Bitch. The Winners Dog, carrying on for his sire, Ch. Yurok of Whitecliff and dam, Apalita, was the now Ch. White Tundra's Little Yurok. The Best of Breed in this entry of 129, with 29 in the Puppy Sweepstakes, was Ch. Sayan of Woodland. Ch. Ts'arina of Lassen View was Best of Opposite Sex under judge Nicholas Kay.

In this period of decentralization, the group of southern California exhibitors who had been hosting the separate parent club specialties formed an independent club, The Samoyed Club of Los Angeles, as desired by the American Kennel Club. This club was to hold licensed events, show and Obedience Trials. The first board included Dianne Dalton, Thomas and Margi Tuttle, Tom and Mary Mayfield, Ed Adams, Bob and Evelyn Kite, the Robert Wards, and Vickie Wheelock. Obedience training was handled by Samoyed owner Laurel Alexander, who traveled a 300-mile round trip each week to conduct the classes.

The first independent group to conduct a Specialty was the San Diego Samoyed Club, in conjunction with the Silver Bay Kennel Club at San Diego in February 1967. President Maggi Simmons welcomed the owners of 73 entries for judge Robert Kerns. The winners were: Ch. Sayan of Woodland as Best of Breed, Ch. Ts'arina of Lassen View as Best Opposite, Winners Bitch Hoti-Ami of Starchak and Winners Dog, Williwaw Czar Nikkolas.

Old and new bloodlines across the country were typified by the news of Jean Brown of Colorado, completing the championship of Ch. Snoglo's Kistarr of Snomesa (granddaughter of the Australian Best in Show Ch. Starya of Kobe). Older bloodlines with new breeders produced Ch. Dudinka's Diva (by Ch. Barcea's Shondi of Drayalene ex Ch. Patrice of Snow Ridge) for Mary Nolan and Irene Eaton of Colorado. Diva won a Best in Match at five months of age and later became the winner of the Ch. Suzanne Award for the top-winning Samoyed bitch in the United States for 1966.

Lucile Miller of Albuquerque, New Mexico, returned to the breeding and showing of Samoyeds in 1965 after five years of absence. She had bred many great dogs in the 1930s and 1940s. The new start was a dog carefully chosen, Ch. Star Nika Altai of Silver Moon bred by the Robert Bowles' of Seattle. Nika came on strong,

Ch. Star's Boloff of Altai, wh. 1964. By BIS winner Ch. Star Nika Altai of Silver Moon ex Ch. Chu San's Princess Ghajar. Owned by Mr. and Mrs. Robert H. Ward.

Ch. Hoti-Ami of Starchak "Tiki," wh. March 1969, strong winning bitch, bred-owned-and-handled by Dolly Ward.

Boutique, exciting young offspring of Ch. Star's Boloff of Altai ex Ch. Hoti-Ami of Starchak. Spectacular winning includes BIM over 300 entries at San Luis Obispo KC "B" Match at 5 months, BIM at Samoyed Club of Los Angeles match at 6 months, and a Group First at Silver Bay KC of San Diego match at 7 months. Bred and owned by Mr. and Mrs. Robert H. Ward.

127

winning over 20 Best of Breeds in one year, including the supported entry show at Tulsa in 1967, followed by Best in Show at Heart of the Plains Kennel Club under judge Major Godsol.

The successful "mixing" of bloodlines from different areas, a growing trend in our breed, reached a new peak in Los Angeles in 1966 when the Parent Club Specialty Winners Bitch Hoti-Ami of Starchak, boasted a Washington State sire (Ch. Noatak of Silver Moon), and a dam (Ch. Mashad-E of Calaveras) bred from both northern and southern California lines. The Best Opposite Sex, Ch. Tei Juana of Viburnum, had a background of Far West, Midwest, and Eastern Samoyeds, having been bred in Illinois by Samuel Lawton and owned in San Diego by Leon Bill.

The 1967 Specialty, hosted by the Eastern members and held with the Trenton show, introduced a new import, Venturer of Kobe (by Silver Gleam of Kobe ex Koscena of Kobe), brought in by Mr. and Mrs. Donald Jordan of Sudbury, Massachusetts. Venturer was awarded Best of Breed by Mrs. Milton Seeley over 25 exhibits including 7 Champions. The Southern bloodlines were represented in the Best Opposite Ch. Quitos Sugar, owned by the A. Dougherty's from the Blairsdale Kennels. The Winners Bitch, Oni-Agras Silver Bunny, owned by D. and C. Richardson, typified the new look in today's breeding as compared to yesteryear, being the bloodlines of Ralph and Beverly Ward of New York and thus tracing to Eastern, California, and Midwestern dogs. Oni-Agras Silver Bunny traces back to Kobe's Oni Agra Chief of Encino and Silver Bunny of Encino, and from there to most of Agnes Mason's best sled dogs.

Carrying on the pattern of American breeders combining show type with working dogs, Mrs. Donna Yocom and her son Mike began with show dogs, used them as sled dogs, and then went back to show dogs. Among first dogs and bloodlines were Ch. Kenny's Blazer Boy of Caribou C.D.X., Ch. Chu San's Silver Folly, Ch. Chu San's Princess Ghajar, and Tsiulikagta's Kara Nor. Recent dogs which appear in later bloodlines are Ch. Tsiulikagta's Pepe San, Ch. Tsiulikagta's Yuki Fang owned by Richard Nelson, Ch. Tsiulikagta's Yuki Tai San owned by the Harry Coopers of Fort Worth, Texas, and Nancy Foster's Ch. Tsiulikagta's Lady Barchenok. She has added the bloodlines of Ch. Saroma's Polar Prince in recent litters and since moving her kennel from Denver, Colorado, to Albuquerque, New Mexico, has added combinations of the Altai Kennels.

The 1967 parent club separate specialty in the Midwest was a

Ch. Niarivik of Inara, wh. 1940. Through her daughter Snow White Lassie of Altai, grandmother of Ch. Kusang of Northern Frost, Niarivik is behind many Midwestern Samoyeds of today. Grandmother of eastern Ch. Zor of Altai, and through her sons Ch. Snohomish and Sooltan, behind many winning dogs of the Northwest. Bred by Mrs. Thomas E. Hearn, and owned by Mrs. Edna McKinnon.

Twenty-eight years later, at Casa de las Huertas in Albuquerque, Mrs. McKinnon is breeder of Niarivik's Sooltan of Inara, by Glacier Khan of Caribou ex Tsiulikagta's Nan-Nuk.

Ch. Kusang of Northern Frost, an important Midwest sire. and show star. By Northern Frost of Fairview (Ch. Frosty of Fairview-Snow White Lassie of Altai) ex T'Laska's Antonika.

tribute and memorial to Miss Juliet Goodrich, held at the Dane County Fair Grounds, Madison, Wisconsin. There were 47 Samoyeds including 16 Champions, and 11 puppies in the Best Puppy in Show competition. Best Opposite was Carol and Bruce Bradley's Ch. Bradley's Powder Puff (by Arctic Prince Borealis out of Sledgling of Baerstone). The Best Puppy was Baerstone's Kasija (by Ch. Stutz of Baerstone out of Ch. Tei Juana Cayenne of Virburnum), also bred by Mrs. Jean Baer. In a storybook finish for the weekend, the Winners Dog and Winners Bitch of the Specialty, Blizzard of Snoline (by Ch. Glen Echo Polar Sno C.D. ex Ch. Lady Sasha of Kazan C.D.) and Shestnustar of Wynterkloud (by Ch. Sam O' Chingis Khan ex Ch. Wynterkloud's Patyna Sno Mist), both completed their championships the next day at Paper City Kennel Club. The Reserve Dog and Bitch, Karshan and Kasija, owned by Dianne Miller and Jean Baer respectively, won the points at Madison Kennel Club the third day. Ch. Star Nika Altai of Silver Moon, handled by Virginia Hardin, was Best of Breed all three days under the three judges—Robert Ward, Henry Stoecker, and Phil Marsh.

This 1967 Juliet Goodrich Memorial Specialty had seen a Best of Breed of Northwest breeding, owned in New Mexico; a Best Opposite of Midwest breeding; a Winners Dog with an Oregon sire and a California dam; and a Winners Bitch from a combination of Washington and New Jersey bloodlines.

But one does not have to reach across the country to breed better ones every time. The 33rd parent specialty, held with the National Capitol K.C. the year before, was won by two champions bred from Mildred Sheridan Davis's Park-Cliffe Kennels, active in the same area for forty years. At one of the last judging assignments before her death, Mrs. W. L. Bonney selected Ch. Park Cliffe Snowpack Sanorka C.D. as Best of Breed from an entry of 50, including 17 Champions. He is owned by James and Janice McGoldrick of Long Island, New York. The Winners bitch, Best of Winners, and Best of Opposite Sex was Frosty Flakes Winter Mist, owned by Eileen Arena of Brentwood, New York, with bloodlines similar to the Best of Breed. She was sired by Ch. Park-Cliffe Frost Snow Flake ex Ch. Park-Cliffe Snowpak Kim.

The fifth separate parent club Specialty was also held at Hollywood Park. Mrs. Helen Wittrig, judging an entry of 71, and Mr. Warren Stephens passed upon the Puppy Sweepstakes entry of 19. Best of Breed was Ch. Sayan of Woodland. Best Puppy was Almost Christmas Chatter, owned by Mr. and Mrs. Joe Faria of Exeter, California.

Ch. Sno-Joke of Silver Moon, by Ch. Noatak of Silver Moon ex Ch. Silver Moon. Bred by Mr. and Mrs. Robert Bowles, and owned by Mr. and Mrs. Wilfred Stukey. Mr. Stukey was the delegate for the Samoyed Club of America to the American Kennel Club from 1963 to 1968.

The look alikes—mother and daughter. Left, Ch. Trina of Taymylyr (wh. 1964) by Ch. Barceia's Shondi of Drayalene ex Ellburs Lady Ilsa. Right, Holly of Taymylyd (wh. 1966) by Ch. Kazan of Kentwood ex Ch. Trina of Taymylyr. Best Brace at KC of Beverly Hills. Owners, Mr. and Mrs. Thomas Tuttle, California.

Ch. Tsarina of Lassen View, wh. 1964, a daughter of Ch. Yurok of Whitecliff ex Jerasue of Drayalene. A group placement winner. Bred by Dr. and Mrs. David E. Stanford, and owned by Mr. and Mrs. Edwin Burns, Californa.

131

The Delegate to the American Kennel Club of the Samoyed Club of America from 1961 to 1969, Wm. Stukey, and his wife, Ethel, owned the Winners Dog, Sno-joke of Silver Moon. Sno-joke, their fourth champion in 18 years, was from the country-wide known and winning lines of Ch. Noatak of Silver Moon, in-bred to his mother Ch. Silver Moon. One of their best was Ch. Tazsons' Snow King who was Best Opposite Sex at the 1955 Specialty in Rye, New York, to his litter sister Amer. and Can. Ch. Tazson's Snow Flicka. These two and their brother Ch. Nordlys Sammy were all get of the illustrious Ch. Martingate Snowland Taz.

Breed progress was aided by the Samoyed Club of Washington State when they held a Plan A Match on October 27, 1967 with an entry of 25 Samoyeds. Best in Match was T'Kope Toketie Kamook, owned by Beverly Anderson and Ruth Green. Best female was Starlite's Cascade Spring, owned by Robert Alma.

The last of the Division-hosted shows in the name of the Samoyed Club of America were held in 1968. At Far Hills, New Jersey, the Best of Breed was John Scovin's newly-acquired Ch. Siayes Schnegora Boickh (by Tara's Snow Boy, a grandson of Taz, and out of Ch. White Cliff's Polar Dawn, a granddaughter of Yurok, bred by Carmelita Avery of Tulsa, Oklahoma). Siayes beat 33 Samoyeds including 10 champions and went third in the Group. The BOS belonged also to the Scovins. She was Ch. Marylake's Nina Belle, bred by Mrs. Elizabeth Morony of Texas, by Can. and Amer. Ch. Samingo's Prince Charming out of Marylake's Nina. Winners Dog was the stunning Karandash Tym, C.D., by Elkenglo's CeeTee out of Torin, C.D. This was an Eastern bloodline going back to Ch. Rippleby Fanfare, imported by Elma Miller. Tym was bred and owned by Roberta Baird. Winfield and Marilyn Orr of Maryland finished their bitch, Bright Biscuit, owner-handled all the way. Her background includes the famous champions of the past: Janet Jan Mayen, Zor of Altai, Snow Flicka, and Nordly's Sammy, which include imported, eastern and western dogs.

Western exhibitors and members supported the last Pacific Coast Division show in 1968 at Santa Barbara Kennel Club (one of the few remaining benched all-breed shows), with a substantial entry of 71 for Mr. Anthony Hodges of Pennsylvania. He placed Ch. Karshan, Best of Breed; Ch. Williwaw's Frost River, BOS; Zeke, Czar of Entrophy, WD, completing his championship; and Belaya Anja Padrushka, WB a daughter of Ch. Karshan, WB. Bloodlines thus represented were Silver Moon, Starchak, Snow Ridge, Frost River and Yurok.

132

Ch. Velko of Chipaquipa, wh. 1966, by Ch. Beta Sigma's Mufti ex Sparkle's M'Liss of Top Acres. Bred by Ruth Bates Young and owned by Leslie and John Lueck, Michigan.

Shorewood's Nyeda, wh. 1967. By Ch. Vellee's Reddi ex Pinehill's Chantilly Lace. Owned by Lillian and Irvin D. Slusser, Illinois.

Ch. Dajja Mashad-E of Calaveras, wh. 1961, by Ch. Kazan of Kentwood ex Drifting Snow of Snow Ridge. Bred by Mr. and Mrs. James Allen, and owned by Mary F. Mollett and Dolly Ward.

The Samoyed Club at Los Angeles held its first independent and separate specialty show at the Hollywood Park Race Track, Inglewood, California, in September, 1968. Judge Mrs. Anastasia MacBain had an entry of 69, with 13 Champions. Mrs. Janet Kauzlarich judged 19 puppies in the Sweepstakes. Best of Breed Ch. Samovar of the Igloo, owned by Mr. and Mrs. Alan Stevenson, and Sweepstakes winner was Master Jack Frost of Coronet owned by Evelyn Jackson. A new award, that of Best Bred by Exhibitor chosen between the two class winners, was awarded to White Tundra's Eric, owned by Margaret and Bob Di Giovanni.

The Northern California Samoyed Fanciers supported the Richmond Dog Fanciers show in 1968. Familiar bloodlines were seen in Ch. Karshan (Ch. Noatak of Silver Moon ex Ch. Dajja Mashad-E of Calveras), who went Best of Breed. Ch. Yurok of Whitecliff was represented through his grandson Ch. Darius King of Snow Ridge, owned by Dan and Lavera Morgan, who won the Stud Dog Class with an impressive array of get. Officers and supporters of this Samoyed Club are Dan and La Vera Morgan, Walter and Jan Kauzlarich, the Burt Kimbels, the Tom Witchers, Mrs. Beckeye Austin, Wilma Coulter, Ed Altamirano, Virginia Arnett, and Margo Gervolstad.

The longevity of the Samoyed and his ability to preserve his youth were proven in 1968 when Kenny O'Brien's Ch. Timan's Williwaw C.D. was awarded Best of Breed over many younger champions and an entry of 30 of the breed. It is more proof positive that the Samoyed does not age early. Their prime is long past many breeds' show time span. Many a Samoyed does not reach his true maturity until five years of age. A few early finishers come back to win at five and six years, and defeat a whole new crop of youngsters. The pride of having a veteran continue to win is the epitome of Samoyed care and companionship.

A desire to promote better breeding and increase the number of good Samoyeds in the Central East Coast area led to the founding of the Potomac Valley Samoyed Club. Headed by Joan Turkus Sheets, M.D., Mr. and Mrs. Davis Richardson, Lillian Crist, Elsie DaCosta, Dale Herspring and Marilyn Orr, the new club adopted a superb "Breeders Code of Responsibilities." As with each new group, classes in care and grooming were held, and speakers were invited to special sessions. Representatively, Dr. Wayne Riser spoke to strengthen the work on hip dysplasia. An AKC-sanctioned "B" Match was held with 21 entries, and a Parade of Champions after the show. Local groups were in orbit, at last.

Winner of the first Samoyed Club of America Puppy Sweepstakes, held with the 1966 Specialty: Ch. Karshan, wh. 1965. By Ch. Noatak of Silver Moon ex Ch. Dajja Mashad-E of Calaveras. Bred by Mary F. Mollett and Dolly Ward, and owned by Murray and Dianne Miller.

Winner of the second Puppy Sweepstakes held with the SCA Specialty 1967: Almost Christmas Chatter, wh. December 26, 1966. By Ch. Kazan of Kentwood ex Ch. Trina of Taymlyr. Bred by Mr. and Mrs. Tuttle and owned by Mr. and Mrs. Joseph A. Faria.

Ch. Belaya Anja Padrushka, wh. 1967, by Ch. Karshan ex Ellbur's Bonnee. Bred by James Walker, Jr. and owned by John and Carol Chittum, California.

This exchanging and improvement on the local scenes was enhanced further by the Club's organizational evolution. The reformation which had gotten way in 1965 made the parent club a stronger force across the country.

The Midwest offered, through the Juliet Goodrich Trust Fund, projects to protect the breed and to further education on the Samoyed. A Special Awards Committee, with Mrs. Helen Bascom of New York as its head, was formed to initiate rules to govern awards to be made each year for the Top Winning Dog, the Top Winning Bitch, the Top Stud Dog, the Top Brood Bitch and the Top Obedience Winner. These awards, first made in 1969, were to replace the just-retired perpetual trophies: The Charles Tucker Brood Bitch Award, the Wimundstrev Stud Dog Award, and the A. E. Mason and the Suzanne of White Way Memorials. (A listing of Award Winners is included in the Appendix.)

Upon the retirement of Wilfred Stukey as the parent club delegate to the American Kennel Club (after seven years service), Ellis Snee of Washington, D.C., was elected to replace him in 1969. Ellis and Anne Snee were the importers of Ch. Silver Ray of Sword Dale, whose sire Silver Sable of Sword Dale was the "Stud Dog of the Year" in England for 1967 and 1968.

Pending the adoption of a new constitution, no national specialty was held in 1968. The breed club was reorganized into a national parent club, with independent local clubs, in 1969.

A spectacular national specialty was held in September 1969 at Conjego Park, Thousand Oaks, Calif. Show chairman was Tom Mayfield, and the show was acclaimed by many to be a model for all separately-held specialties. A splendid entry of 94 (including 14 champions) competed under breeder-judge Joyce Cain of Wisconsin. Best of Breed, scoring his fourth specialty win, was the Kites' Ch. Sayan of Woodland, handled by Jim Manley. Best Opposite was the authors' Ch. Hoti Ami of Starchak. Best puppy was Midnight Sun Kimba, owned by the Victor Monteleons.

A major highlight of the show was the publication by the parent club, for the first time, of a catalog which incorporated the breed history, the official standard, illustrations including the authors' "Fault Finder," pictures of great Samoyeds of past and present representing bloodlines from coast to coast, and a directory of all local clubs. Hailed as a reference work of the breed, this 38th Specialty catalog has become highly prized and copies continue to be purchased.

Ch. Cherski's Polar Koryak, by Ch. Saroma's Polar Prince ex Cascade's Cherski. Bred by Richard and Marilyn Hire, and owned by Mr. and Mrs. Richard Beal. Pictured in win of Group at Longview, Wash. 1968.

Ch. Silver Ray of Sword Dale, English import. By Silver Sabre of Sword Dale (Stud Dog of the Year 1967–1968 in England) ex Ch. Jewel of Sword Dale. Imported by Anne and Ellis Snee of Washington, D.C.

Ch. Samantha of Snow Basin, by Ch. Sayan of Woodland ex Gary's Snowball. Bred by Ellen and Douglas Lovegrove and owned by Thomas and Mary Mayfield.

137

Ch. Baerstone's Kasija watches one of her puppies, sired by Ch. Star's Boloff of Altai, take his first steps to her. "Kasi," by Ch. Stutz of Baerstone ex Ch. Tei Juana Cayenne of Virburnum, was herself Best Puppy at the 1967 parent Specialty. Bred and owned by Mrs. Jean Baer, Wisconsin.

Ch. Pepe Le Pieu, by Ch. Glen Echo Polar Sno ex Ch. Queen Ann of Joli White Knight. Pepe finished at the 1970 Samoyed Club of Los Angeles Specialty. Bred by Laurel Alexander and Barbara Doss, and owned by Mr. and Mrs. Virgil Pelligrino.

The 1970 parent specialty, hosted by the Samoyed Club of Washington State and held in August on the eve of the Olympic KC show at Renton, Wash., established a new high for entries with 150 (122 actual dogs). Show chairman was Dick Beal. Judge Joseph Faigel selected Ch. Darius Karlak Cheetal (owner-handled by LaVera Morgan) as Best of Breed. Best Opposite and winner of the Helen Harris Memorial Trophy for Best Bitch was Ch. Tsonoqua of Snow Ridge, owned by Margo Gervostad, and handled by Paul Booher. The fine souvenir booklet of the show was a sellout.

Indicative of the nationwide character of the Samoyed impact is the list of the top five winning Samoyeds for each year as compiled by the Phillips System, a feature of *Popular Dogs* magazine. (The Phillips System computes inter-breed winning by awarding points for Group placement or Best in Show wins, in accordance with the number of dogs over which the win was scored.) It can be seen that quality in the breed is well-distributed across the nation.

1967:

1. Ch. Sam O'Khan's Chingis Khan
   Owners, James and Joan Sheets, Alexandria, Va.
2. Ch. Star Nika Altai of Silver Moon
   Owner, L. L. Miller, Albuquerque, N.M.
3. Ch. Silver Cloud of Mapleshade
   Owner, Mrs. P. Morgan, W. Richfield, Ohio
4. Ch. Sayan of Woodland
   Owners, J. and E. Kite, Woodland Hills, Calif.
5. Ch. Karasea's Silver Kim
   Owners, A. G. and L. E. Bishop, III, New York City

1968:

1. Ch. Maur Miks Kim
   Owner, J. and L. Aldred, Detroit, Mich.
2. Ch. Sam O'Khan's Chingis Khan
3. Ch. Karasam of Misty Way
   Owner, P. McCarthy, Eugene, Ore.
4. Ch. Honey Babe of Gro Wil
   Owner, Grover Walls, Burlington, Iowa
5. Ch. Sayan of Woodland

139

1969:

1. Ch. Sam O'Khan's Chingis Khan
2. Ch. Maur Miks Kim
3. Ch. Sayan of Woodland
4. Ch. Snow Stars Polaris Rex
   Owner, C. Willoughby, Sun Valley, Calif.
5. Ch. Lulhavens Nunatat
   C. Lutham, Auburn, Wash.

1970

1. Ch. Maur Miks Kim
2. Ch. Lulhavens Snow Mist Ensign
   O. Hyatt and S. White, Bellevue, Wash.
3. Ch. Mister Williwaw
   Dennis and Gretchen Raymond, Anaheim, Calif.
4. Ch. Honey Babe Stone of Gro Wil
5. Ch. Frosty of Blue Mountain
   N. Bartz, Orchard Park, N.Y.

Some Best in Show Samoyeds don't take it seriously. Ch. Spark of Altai relaxing after taking top honors at Nova Scotia show in June 1952. Owned by Dr. and Mrs. C. S. Bezanson.

140

Am. and Can. Ch. Maur Mik's Kim, top Phillips System winner in 1968 and 1970, pictured scoring Best in Show at Grand Rapids KC 1970. At mid-'71, Kim was already sire of 18 champions. Owned and handled by Jack and Linda Aldred, Jac-Lin's Samoyeds, Michigan.

One may question our emphasis on show-winning Samoyeds. We appreciate that along with these Samoyeds whose above average quality has been confirmed by a variety of judges, there may be excellent Sams who never see a ring. But people in the dog world do not hear of them. It avails little for a spectator to say, "My Sam at home is better than the one who won today." The proof is in the competition. And while a Samoyed need not be shown to be appreciated by his owner, it remains that those that are shown and win deserve their applause for maintaining the quality of the breed at a high level.

Japanese Ch. Cire of White Luck, bred by Eileen S. Whitlock of Tulsa, Okla. and owned by Yayoi Maki and Midori Imatake of Tokyo.

American-bred Samoyed winner in Europe, Int. Ch. Macgregor of Glenstrae. By Ch. Rainier ex Dusha's White Feather, bred by Evelyn Morrisey, Mac was the choice of litter by the authors. Owned by Captain and Mrs. Robert M. Hunter of California, and handled by Herr Robert Helfrich of Heidelberg, Germany.

142

The Samoyed in Other Lands

Australia

The Samoyed Club of Victoria was founded in 1948 as the Samoyed Club of Australia, and is the oldest club in the country. The Samoyed Club of South Wales was founded in 1958. At present, there are four clubs in Australia, each in its own state. Each club is licensed and affiliated with its own State Kennel Club and under the National Kennel Control Council in Australia. This has now given a standardized method of awarding championships which did not exist prior to 1961.

Since January 1962 champions are known as Australian Champions. Prior to this they were state champions. To become a champion, a dog needs to earn 100 points. Points are acquired as follows: 10 points for each Challenge Certificate, plus 5 points extra for a Best in Group, and another 5 for a Best in Show. At every championship show in Australia, unless it is a Specialist show, every breed competes for Challenge Certificates, even if there is only one entry in the breed. When the judge believes the dog worthy of a Challenge Certificate, it is awarded. It is remotely possible to obtain a championship with no competition, but this rarely happens.

Dogs are bred and judged by the English standard, and this standard cannot be changed nor altered except by permission or instruction of the English Kennel Club.

Roy Anderson, a member of the Samoyed Club of America, has been for many years our only S.C.A. representative member from the land down under.

Australia and New Zealand had the first opportunity to develop the Samoyed breed, for the explorers Amundsen, Borchgrevink, and

143

Shackleton all left dogs there in greater number than the few that were brought to England. But the greatest activity has come in the last thirty years. At the Sidney Royal Show, an entry of 150 to 200 Samoyeds is not uncommon.

Australia has now taken great interest in sled dogs and at the station in Little America is developing a special breed of sled dogs for permanent use in the area.

Europe

We have found little past history of the breed in European countries, except for England. In 1952 the authors sold a dog to Captain Robert M. Hunter, who took it to Germany. Captain Hunter was a member of the Allied Military Police Forces in Berlin. He tried most diligently to uncover histories of the Samoyed for us. All sources through the Russians led to nothing. His dog was exhibited in Germany, France, Holland, and Belgium and won four Championships. Ch. Macgregor of Glenstrae won his *Sieger* title (German Championship) at Mannheim, Germany, and followed this with the C.A.C.I.B. title at the International Exposition, Brussels, Belgium in 1954. "Mac" was awarded the Dog World Award of Canine Distinction for being the first American-bred Samoyed to hold the title.

Another American Samoyed was in Germany in 1961, Mrs. Lorelei Jordan's German Champion Leordan's Snow Fury of Pan-San. Fury was bred by Goldie Klein and Marie Mueller in Seattle, Washington. He was sired by Ch. Polaris Pan out of Kendor's White Sandra. Fury won his C.A.C.I.B. title in 1961.

Mrs. Jordan wrote that the Samoyed is shown in the Spitz class or group in Germany. A spitz-hund is any prick-eared dog. The Samoyed is called a *Samojedenspitz*. The manner of showing varies from country to country, and in Germany baiting of dogs and double handling is permitted. Gaiting is done at a slow pace and you may not stack your dogs. Natural stances are required. Dogs are judged and evaluated upon their own merits. There is no first, as we know it. If you decide to show or breed dogs in Germany, note that a bitch may be bred only once a year for registerable puppies. A limit of six puppies in a litter may be registered. There is no central agency of Kennel clubs such as the American Kennel Club.

144

Instead, each club has its own set of rules. Luckily, they are almost identical.

There are records of the Russian Prince Paul Troubetskoi raising Samoyeds in France in the period of 1900 to 1910, and we do know of the importation of Baklu in 1926.

In 1954, we received a letter from J. Fornier de Savignac of Ariege, France, telling of the Samoyed activities at that time.

> In France there are only two or three good breeders, which does not make for a big production of puppies. This is too bad, for the Samoyed is such a likeable dog that many people would like one. It is sad that with such a shortage they cannot have the satisfaction of owning one. Before the war, I was very busy with dogs I had brought into France from England and they turned out very well. During the war, all kennels were destroyed. After the war in 1945, I no longer wanted to begin my kennel again, but I have helped and advised some fanciers, and little by little they have begun to breed litters. In 1951, with a very small membership, we formed the Samoyed Club, and it now has some 200 members in France.
>
> There are in France some judges who know Nordic, Samoyed and Eskimo dogs well. I was the one who most specialized in them. I have often judged abroad in England, Switzerland, Italy, and Germany, but now can no longer travel around.

While there are Samoyeds in the Scandinavian countries and certainly more than a few in each show, the only one with an effect on pedigrees would be a dog imported by Mrs. Frank Romer from Norway in 1916. Samoyeds from California went back to Norway through their puppies and a few of the half-Norwegian puppies stayed here by a breeding in 1947 of Northern Chieftain, bred by Mrs. Agnes Mason and owned by the Collicots, to a nice Norwegian Samoyed bitch named Kari, owned by Captain I. Halbert of Norway. Capt. Halbert sailed his ship, the S. S. *Lutz,* into San Francisco Bay in 1947 and arranged the breeding. Five lovely puppies were born on July 1947 while the ship was at sea. One of the females was owned eventually by the Norwegian Consulate at Philadelphia.

The Orient

While unregistered Samoyeds from China were shown in California and Texas in the 1920's, none were ever registered, and none appear in present bloodlines. Good examples of the breed did find

Mrs. Ivy Kilburn-Morris with Samoyed "Polar Bear" swimming in the waters of Hong Kong in 1940.

their way to the Orient in 1934. Miss Hazel I. Shadell, a stenographer missionary, purchased a puppy from Mrs. Ivy Kilburn-Morris, then in Shanghai. Mrs. Kilburn-Morris had lived in Japan in 1932 with her two dogs, Farningham Polar Bru and Farningham Tosca, and five litters were placed in that country also. Miss Shadell's puppy, Snow Wrangle, travelled far and came to Mrs. John H. Thomas of Mt. Vernon, Ohio, and Mt. Rainier, Maryland. Here this Samoyed bloodline completed its trip around the world. A litter by Ch. Siberian Nansen of Farningham of Snowland out of Snow Wrangle was pictured in the Washington *Post*. Many people came to see these dogs, described as rare in 1940. Most startling was the fact that a puppy, Snegurochka, went to the Russian Ambassador, Mr. Constantine A. Oumansky, who had sent his undersecretaries to purchase the puppy for his daughter.

South America

Little is known of the Samoyed activities in South America, but the breed is there. Mrs. Margaret Tucker exported a bred bitch from her Kobe Kennels in Encino, California, to Mr. Humberto Orias of Lima, Peru, in 1965.

146

Ch. Queen Ann of Joli White Knight (by Ch. Joli White Knight ex Ch. Lady Sasha of Kazan, C.D.), bred at the Snolines Samoyed Kennels of Nancy and Laurel Alexander, has been sold bred (to Mardee Faria's Almost Christmas Chatter, a son of Ch. Kazan of Kentwood ex Ch. Trina of Taymlyr) to Laura Regini of Argentina. Queen Ann, and her litter due in October 1971, will travel by air with her owner to Buenos Aires to become foundation stock. Due to the fact that only three of a litter may be registered in Argentina, the rest of any litters will be utilized as sled dogs in the Mar de Plata area, 200 miles southeast of Buenos Aires.

Alaska and Puerto Rico

While Alaska and Puerto Rico are not "other lands," they are mentioned here as being outside the Continental limits of the United States. Presently, the Wayne Denzlers, who have obtained their Samoyeds from Margaret Tucker's Encino Kennels for the past fifteen years, have set up their own kennels in Puerto Rico.

147

Father Hubbard, "The Glacier Priest."

In Alaska, the Glacier Kennels in Juneau, owned by the Findlays, are a tourist attraction. They keep a guest book and average 100 to 200 visitors per week during the tourist season. Their guest book shows visitors from as far as Japan and Newfoundland, and all the areas in between. Their puppies have gone to Norfolk, Va.; Silver Spring, Md.; Washington D.C.; Great Falls, Montana; Grand Junction, Colo.; Carmel, Calif.; Whitehorse, N.Y.; and Key West, Florida.

Other Alaskan breeders include J. Idesta Green and R. B. Williams of Juneau and F. O. Montgomery. Mr. Montgomery freighted with dogs near and over the Mendenhall Glacier. Father Hubbard, known as "The Glacier Priest," was so taken with the Samoyed and their affectionate nature that he obtained one from the Encino Kennels in California with the idea of having a team. His subsequent heart attack and retirement to Santa Clara College prevented that. However, he did breed some Samoyeds at the college.

148

PART II
Standards and Judging

The constancy of the Samoyed is graphically shown in these photos, almost four decades apart. At top is Eng. Ch. Riga of the Arctic, pictured as a 10-months-old in 1928. Riga was by Ch. Tiger Boy ex Susie and was a litter sister to Ch. Surf. She was owned by Miss Keyte Perry of the Arctic Kennels, England. At bottom is Ch. Sam O'Khan's Sali Sarai, whelped in 1953. Sarai, by Am. and Can. Ch. Noatak of Silver Moon ex Can. and Am. Ch. Sam O'Khan's Tsari of Khan, is a litter sister of BIS winner Am. and Can. Ch. Sam O'Khan's Chingis Khan and Am. and Can. Ch. Sam O'Khan's Tian Shan. She was bred by Frances C. Fitzpatrick, and owned by Mr. and Mrs. James A. Sheets of Virginia.

Background of the
Samoyed Standard

AN explanation of the whys and wherefores of the breed standards is due the reader who is new to the purebred dog sport.

For each of the 116 breeds recognized by the American Kennel
Club, there is an officially approved standard in accordance with
which the breed is judged at the shows. The American Kennel Club
does not write these standards. They have been propounded and
formulated by the parent clubs of the breeds, or adopted by these
parent clubs from standards of other countries.

Obviously, much research and discussion has been required in
each case to construct a description of the breed upon which a large
majority of the parent club, breeders and owners can agree. In
other countries, each breed club does its own policing, and changes
in the standards can be effected easier. In the United States, however, after winning the approval of a majority of the parent club
(which must be a member club of the American Kennel Club),
proposals for change are then submitted to the Board of Directors of
the AKC. If the proposal is tentatively approved, it is published in
the official *AKC Gazette* to bring it to the attention of any owners
or breeders who were not aware of the intended revision. After an
ample period of time, the proposal is again presented to the AKC
Board of Directors for approval.

There are few breed standards which can claim the completeness
of the one used to measure and evaluate the Samoyed. As we shall
see, only a few changes have been made, and the dog described in
the American standard of today could well be the expedition dog
that modeled the first standards.

There have certainly been no changes in structure, coat, or disposition. As in his native habitat, the Samoyed remains a friend of man, a hunter, a protector, a herder, a beast of burden, and a draft animal.

The question of the use of the Samoyed has long been a matter of controversy. Is it a herd dog? Is it a sledge dog? Is it a guard dog?

It may be said generally that all work dogs were originally hunting dogs. Certainly this is true of the remaining breeds which are still in their native form, and not reshaped by man. Our research shows that the true Samoyed dog was a hunter for his master. It was not possible for nature to create him as strictly a herd dog. The animals to be herded in his native land were the reindeer, but they did not live in the deep snow country because of the lack of forage and moss. And certainly the Samoyed was not designed as a sled dog by Mother Nature. While his natural attributes lend themselves to draft work, the Samoyed was put to this use by man, and not by birth. When exploration was the "in" thing, the northern dog, used to the climate and lack of food, met a need for the explorers, who lacked other means to conquer the frozen lands.

Early Samoyed breeders met with great resistance to breed popularity when people admiring the "white teddy bear" puppies discovered that they were dogs that had been used for sled work in the arctic lands, and falsely publicized them as "fierce and savage beasts descended from wolves." To counter this reputation, many original breeders openly stated that the herd dog aspect was the one to foster, as whoever identified a Collie tending his flock, and nuzzling a lamb, as a "fierce beast"?

There have been many other breeders who have just as loudly proclaimed their Samoyeds' abilities as draft dogs. In the early days in England, even the Kilburn-Scotts trained their dogs as sled dogs until the English laws prohibited it. The sled dog activities were carried on in America and Canada by the majority of early breeders and large kennels. The Reids (Norka Kennels), the Romers (Yurak Kennels), the Seeleys and the Pinkhams all worked their dogs in harness in the early twenties and thirties, and thus bred for sledding abilities. The kennels of Ernie Barbeau, Harold Haas, and Agnes Mason continued to breed for sled work in the thirties and forties. In the forties and fifties, breeders such as the Weirs and Gleasons in the Northwest, the Ralph Wards and the Seekins in New York, Juliet Goodrich and Harold Danks in the Midwest, and the Wards, Witchers, Van Sickles, Burrs, Keepers, Allens, Bristols,

King, Goldwater, Tom Witt, and Breckenridge in the West, all trained Samoyed sled teams.

Appreciating this background, a standard was written to include all of the above-mentioned qualities except that of hunting. Mr. Kilburn-Scott cited the Samoyed's ability as a herder and sled dog in his first standard description in 1910, and this description of points has been little changed since. Size is the usual point of difference among breeders and countries, but isn't size a question in many breeds?

The Samoyed standard serves the purpose of maintaining a natural, original type of animal. It is not a created breed. Its characteristics have been developed over centuries of living with simple nomadic peoples who had no outside contact with other tribes, and thus no interbreeding of their dogs with others from other areas. The Samoyed was one of the family; he provided an extension of the master's hands and feet. His disposition had to fit into their communal society. His character is as splendid and pure as his snowy white coat.

The Early Standard

Ernest Kilburn-Scott, responsible for so much of the beginnings of the Samoyed in the Western world, formulated a first standard for the breed in the early 1900s. This standard was quite closely followed when the official English standard was adopted in 1909 and 1911 with the formation of the first Samoyed associations in England.

The standard as formulated by Mr. Scott read:

Colour—Pure White; with slight lemon markings; brown and white; black and white. The pure white dogs come from the farthest north, and are most typical of the breed.
Expression—Thoughful and remarkably pretty in face; fighting instincts strongly pronounced when aroused.
Intelligence—Unusual intelligence, as shown by the many purposes for which dogs are used by the Samoyede people and the ease with which they can be taught tricks.
Size and Weight—Dogs 19 to 21½ inches at the shoulders; bitches 18 to 19½ inches at the shoulders; weight about 40 lbs.
Head—Powerful-looking head, wedge-shaped, but not foxy. Wide and flat between ears, gradually tapering to eyes; stop not too pronounced; absolutely clean

muzzle, not too long, with no lippiness; strong jaws and level teeth. The nose may be either black or flesh-coloured.

Eyes—Very expressive and human-like, sparkling when excited; set obliquely and well apart. Eyes should be dark for preference, but other colours are admissible.

Ears—Pricked, set wide apart, and freely movable; set slightly back in contradistinction to the ears of the Eskimo and Chow-Chow, which are forward; shape triangular, and not too large; tip slightly rounded.

Body—Body shapely, but not cobby, with straight back; muscular, with deep ribs; chest wide and deep, showing great lung power; straight front and strong neck.

Legs—Good bone, muscular and not too long; thighs well feathered; forelegs straight; hindlegs sinewy, and set for speed.

Feet—Long, and slightly spread out to get good grip; toes arched and well together; soles hairy and well padded to give grip and protection from ice and snow.

Brush—Long, with profuse spreading hair; carried over back or side when on the alert or showing pleasure; when at rest, dropped down, with slight upward curve at end.

Coat—Long and thick standing well out all over body, especially along back; free from curl; undercoat very soft and wooly; large, bristling ruff; hair on head and ears short and very smooth.

The standard was little changed through the years. There were occasional efforts to expand or change it, such as in 1948 when an attempt was made to require that the coloration of the nose and pigmentation be black, thereby eliminating all throwbacks to the original dogs, which had had light and liver points in many cases.

Bianca of Kobe, at two years. Owned by Mrs. Trudie McElnae-Westwood, Surrey, England.

154

In 1900, Major F. G. Jackson had proposed that "the typical Samoyede should be pure white and have a flesh-coloured nose." In formulating the standard, Kilburn-Scott had not gone as far as that, for they had many good dogs with a little lemon color about the ears, and with black noses. Actually, the black nose and dark eyes add greatly to the expression, making some of the faces of the dogs almost human-like.

It is interesting to see how closely the current English standard, which follows, has evolved from the original Kilburn-Scott standard.

Current English Standard for the Samoyed:

Characteristics: The Samoyed is intelligent, alert, full of action, but above all displaying affection towards all mankind.

General Appearance: The Samoyed being essentially a working dog should be strong and active and graceful, and as his work lies in cold climates, his coat should be heavy and weather-resisting. He should not be too long in back, as a weak back would make him practically useless for his legitimate work, but at the same time a cobby body such as the Chow's would also place him at a great disadvantage as a draught dog. Breeders should aim for the happy medium, viz. a body not long, but muscular, allowing liberty, with a deep chest and well sprung ribs, strong neck proudly arched, straight front and exceptionally strong loins. Both dogs and bitches should give the appearance of being capable of great endurance, but should be free from coarseness. A full grown dog should stand about 21 inches at the shoulder. On account of the depth of chest required, the legs should be moderately long, a very short-legged dog is to be deprecated. Hindquarters should be particularly well-developed, stifles well angulated, and any suggestion of unsound stifles or cowhocks severely penalized.

Head and Skull: Head powerful and wedge-shaped with a broad, flat skull, muzzle of medium length, a tapering foreface not too sharply defined. Lips black. Hair short and smooth before the ears. Nose black for preference, but may be brown or flesh-coloured. Strong jaws.

Eyes: Almond shaped, medium to dark brown in colour, set well apart with alert and intelligent expression. Eyerims should be black and unbroken.

Ears: Thick, not too long and slightly rounded at the tips, set well apart and well covered inside with hair. The ears should be fully erect in the grown dog.

Mouth: Upper teeth just overlap the underteeth in a scissor bite.

Neck: Proudly arched.

Forequarters: Legs straight and muscular with good bone.

Body: Back medium in length, broad and very muscular. Chest broad and deep ribs well sprung, giving plenty of heart and lung room.

Hindquarters: Very muscular, stfles well angulated; cow hocks or straight stifles very objectionable.

155

Feet: Long, flattish and slightly spread out. Soles well cushioned with hair.
Gait: Should move freely with a strong agile drive, showing power and elegance.
Tail: Long and profuse, carried over the back when alert, sometimes drooped when at rest.
Coat: The body should be well-covered with a thick, close, soft and short undercoat; with harsh hair growing through it, forming the outer coat, which should stand straight away from the body and be free from curl.
Colour: Pure white, white and biscuit; cream.
Weight and Size: Dogs, 20–22 inches at the shoulder.
                      Bitches: 18–20 inches at the shoulder.
                      Weight in proportion to size.
Faults: Big ears with little feathering.
        Drop ears.
        Narrow width between ears.
        Long foreface.
        Blue or very light eyes.
        A bull neck.
        A long body.
        A soft coat.
        A wavy coat.
        Absence of undercoat.
        Slack tail carriage. Should be carried well over the back, though it may drop when the dog is at rest.
        Absence of feathering.
        Round cat-like feet.
        Black or black spots.
        Severe unprovoked aggressiveness.
        Any sign of unsound movement.

The Americans, Canadians and Australians all originally adopted the English standard, with minor variations. As of today, however, only the Australians maintain the exact same standard as the English.

The Canadian Standard, while maintaining the English suggested height ranges for dogs and bitches, added several variations. Their "general appearance" section is much more descriptive and comprehensive. A section is devoted to a description of the gait desired in the dog. More description is added to the type of head desired and more exacting details on the flews or lips of the dog. The weight limits for both dogs and bitches were dropped.

Under disqualifications, the Canadian Standard goes further than the American or English. Specifically, they add as disqualifications: Blue eyes, dewclaws on the hindlegs, and any color other than pure

Am. and Can. Ch. Kapegah Okanok of Nichi (1957–1968). Winner of Best in Show at Vancouver, Canada, and of numerous Group placements. Owned by Mr. and Mrs. Clifford Collins of Seattle, Wash.

white, cream, biscuit, or white and biscuit. The American Standard has some of these, but the English none.

Both the Canadians and Americans heavily penalized bad disposition toward mankind and unprovoked aggressiveness toward other dogs.

The official Canadian standard for the Samoyed (July 1957)

General Appearance: The Samoyed, being essentially a working dog, should present a picture of beauty, alertness, and strength, with agility, dignity, and grace. As his work lies in the cold climate, his coat should be heavy and weather resistant, and of good quality rather than quantity. The male carries more of a "ruff" than the female. He should not be long in the back as a weak back would make him practically useless for his legitimate work, but at the same time a close coupled body would also place him at a great disadvantage as a draft dog. Breeders should aim for the happy medium, a body not too long but muscular, allowing liberty, with a deep chest and well sprung ribs, strong arched neck, straight front and especially strong loins. Males should be masculine in appearance and deportment without unwarranted aggressiveness; bitches feminine without weakness of structure or apparent softness of temperament. Bitches may be slightly longer in back than males. They should both give the appearance of being capable of great endurance but be free from coarseness. Because of the depth of chest required, the legs should be moderately long. A very short legged dog is to be depreciated. Hindquarters should be particularly well developed, stifles well bent and any suggestion of unsound stifles or cowhocks severely penalized. General Appearance should include movement and general conformation indicating balance and good substance.

Gait: A Samoyed should gait with a good, well-balanced movement. He should move with an easy agile stride that is well timed. The gait should be free with a good reach in the quarters and a sound, driving power in the hindquarters. A choppy or stilted gait should be penalized.

157

Coat: The body should be well covered with a thick, close, soft and short undercoat, with harsh hair growing through it forming the outer coat, which should stand straight away from the body and be quite free from curl. The legs should have good feathering.

Head: Powerful and wedge shaped with a broad, flat skull, muzzle of medium length, a tapering foreface, not too sharply defined. The stop should be not too abrupt, nevertheless well defined. Ears should not be too long but rounded at the tips, set well apart and well covered inside with hair. Eyes dark, set well apart and deep with alert, intelligent expression. Lips black, flews should not drop predominantly at the corners of the mouth. Hair short and smooth before the ears. Nose and eye rims black for preference, but may be brown. Strong jaws and level teeth.

Back: Medium in length, broad, and very muscular. Bitches may be slightly longer in back than males.

Chest & Ribs: Chest broad and deep. Ribs well sprung giving plenty of heart and lung room.

Hindquarters: Very muscular, stifles well let down, cowhocks or straight stifles should be severely penalized.

Forelegs: Straight and muscular. Good bone. In or out at the elbow to be severely penalized.

Feet: Long, flattish and slightly spread out. Soles well padded with hair.

Tail: Long and profuse carried over the back when alert, sometimes dropped when at rest. A judge should see the tail over the back once when judging. A double hook should be penalized.

Size and Weight: *Dogs:* 20–22 inches at the shoulder; *Bitches:* 18–20 inches; Weight in proportion to size.

Color: Pure white, cream, biscuit, or white and biscuit.

Disposition: Alert and intelligent and should show animation. Friendly but conservative. Unprovoked aggressiveness to be severely penalized.

Scale of Points:

Gait	15
General Appearance	10
Coat	10
Head	10
Back	10
Chest and Ribs	10
Hindquarters	10
Feet	10
Tail	5
TOTAL	100

Disqualifications: Blue eyes. Dew claws on the hindlegs. Any colour other than pure white, cream, biscuit or white and biscuit.

Penalties: Over or under allowed height. Cowhocks or straight stifles. In or out at the elbow. Choppy or stilted gait. Double hook in the tail. Unprovoked aggressiveness.

Revision of the American Standard

In 1945, there had been constant complaining about poor judging of Samoyeds throughout the United States. It was felt that the standard was inadequate. Many judges had expressed their thoughts that the standard was in parts unwieldy, and in other parts too flexible for uniform judging.

As the breed was increasing in numbers, and being exhibited in areas never before known, the parent club president, S. K. Ruick, appointed Mrs. Agnes Mason to be chairman of a Standard Committee, with purpose of revising the standard. Wisely and carefully, Mrs. Mason formed a committee representative of all areas of the club. The members were Helen Harris, Berta Ruick, Lucile Miller, Martha Humphriss and Louis Smirnow. Country-wide participation in local discussion groups aided the committee. The committee worked to form an illustrated standard, but the American Kennel Club advised that illustrations should be used as an aid rather than as part of the actual standard.

Comments, examples, measurements and photographs were exchanged across the country. In 1946, the size specifications were altered, with suggested heights for bitches raised from 18"–20" to 19"–21", and the dogs from 20"–22" to 21"–23½". This was done when over 50 champions were measured, and it was found that there were only four within the previously suggested heights.

In 1952, Mrs. Mason added the breeder-judges Robert Ward, Vera Lawrence, Joe E. Scott, C. H. Chamberlain, and Miles Vernon, and the breeders Gertrude Adams and B. P. Dawes to the Committee. The Divisional Presidents added Mrs. Robert Seekins, Warren Shelley, Georgia Gleason and Charles Burr. Mrs. Mason, now president of the parent club, appointed Mrs. Adams to be Committee Chairman.

A re-opening of the issue of the height of bitches as suggested by the breed standard occurred in 1953. The problem was that the membership had voted by mail (133 yes to 25 no) to raise the height of bitches to 22" because there was a desire to have it theoretically possible to have some bitches and dogs of the same height. There is no overlapping in either the American or the English Standard. Many breeders and judges believed that in natural growth, some are always the same size regardless of sex, quite like other breeds and animals. However, the American Kennel Club did not approve the change of the standard.

159

Work toward the new standard continued. The committee prescribed percentages to be used in the new standard in an attempt to avoid indefinite phrases such as *moderately long,* or *medium,* or *shorter than.* Precise angles and degrees for measurement came from hundreds of measurements taken of actual dogs, and of many photographs of past celebrated dogs. The actual number of degrees used to set the lay-back of shoulders and angle of the stifle, for example, were based upon the average of many measurements.

A great deal of opposition was encountered by the committee in setting a description of the head. Many believed that if percentages were used, or if the muzzle were defined as big, medium or short, we might be "keying" to one particular strain or individual. The description of the muzzle in ratio to the skull was finally adopted, as it allows for variance in size as well as slight variances to fit the balance of the dog being judged. A description of the style and expression of the head creates perhaps the greatest divergence of opinion among breeders in all breeds. Each is much attached to his or her own "line-breeding," which stamps the slight variance in heads. No matter what, however, the head must conform to the characteristics of the breed, and with the overall balance of the dog.

The committee, after reading comments from all sections of the country, decided to drop the weight suggestions of the old standard. Weight is a variable, based upon condition and health, and since the standard explores soundness and movement in such detail, it was felt that correct substance should be recognizable to the breeder or judge.

Disqualifications were held to a minimum by desire of both the Standard Committee of the Samoyed Club, and of the American Kennel Club. It was felt that a fault that would properly disqualify an animal should be quite objective, quite disabling, quite permanent, and quite foreign to the breed. Great variance in size is not foreign to any breed, although objectionable to many breeders. It was decided to state in the standard that penalties should be assessed to the extent to which the dog appears to be over or undersize, according to suggested heights.

The greatest dissent came over disposition. This has always been the greatest asset of the breed. Even the earliest accounts of the explorers mentioned how they could detect the Bjelkiers from the other dogs in the dark because they would be poking and nuzzling for attention and affection. They would be the dogs first upon the sleeping bags, seeking human companionship. The dogs were able to run in groups. These qualities endeared the breed to the early breeders, and there are many who still prize this trait above all others in the breed. However, to disqualify permanently for misbehavior in the ring has a note of finality about it that is hard to accept, based as it is on a brief moment's determination. Really, it is up to the breeder to eliminate this fault in training, and in choosing the sire and dam of a litter. A severe penalty is assessed in the ring for such behavior, and should prevent such animals from winning and thus being desired as breeding stock.

The new standard was approved by the American Kennel Club in February, 1957. It had thus required eleven years of work and research and writing to reach an agreement within the parent club for this revision.

One further change was made in 1963. The point scale to assess a value for each area of the standard met with great resistance by both the club members and the American Kennel Club. Originally, it had been used to call attention to the various points, and to assign relative importance to the different parts of the dog. It was felt by some members that this created a system whereby some would ignore the whole dog because it was found to be lacking in one area. In other words, the point scale promotes "fault judging" rather than assessing the whole value of the dog upon his good qualities and nearness to the standard. After much discussion, upon the recommendation of the Standard Committee, confirmed by a vote of the membership of the Samoyed Club of America, and with the approval of the Board of Directors of the American Kennel Club, the entire point scale was dropped in 1963.

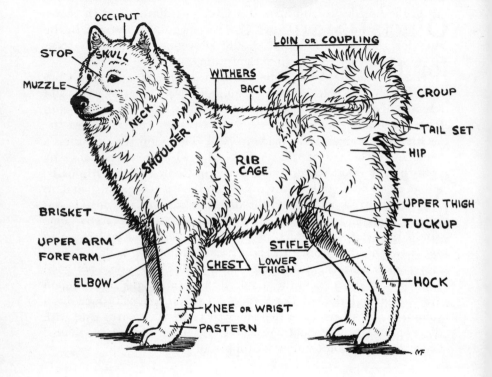

-PARTS OF THE DOG-
ALL COAT DRAWINGS MINIMIZED TO EMPHASIZE STRUCTURE

Official Standard
for the Samoyed

As submitted by the Samoyed Club of America, and approved by the American Kennel Club, April 9, 1963.

GENERAL CONFORMATION

(a) **General appearance.** The Samoyed, being essentially a working dog, should present a picture of beauty, alertness and strength, with agility, dignity and grace. As his work lies in cold climates, his coat should be heavy and weather resistant, well-groomed, and of good quality rather than quantity. The males carries more of a "ruff" than the female. He should not be long in back as a weak back would make him practically useless for his legitimate work, but at the same time, a close-coupled body would also place him at a great disadvantage as a draft dog. Breeders should aim for the happy medium, a body not long but muscular, allowing liberty, with a deep chest and well-sprung ribs, strong neck, straight front and especially strong loins. Males should be masculine in appearance and deportment without unwarranted aggressiveness; bitches feminine without weakness of structure or apparent softness of temperament. Bitches may be slightly longer in back than males. They should both give the appearance of being capable of great endurance but be free from coarseness. Because of the depth of chest required, the legs should be moderately long. A very short-legged dog is to be deprecated. Hindquarters should be particularly well-developed, stifles well-bent and any suggestion of unsound stifles or cowhocks severely penalized.

General appearance should include movement and general conformation, indicating balance and good substance.

163

(b) Substance. Substance is that sufficiency of bone and muscle which rounds out a balance with the frame. The bone is heavier than would be expected in a dog of this size but not so massive as to prevent the speed and agility most desirable in a Samoyed. In all builds, bone should be in proportion to body size. The Samoyed should never be so heavy as to appear clumsy nor so light as to appear racy. The weight should be in proportion to the height.

(c) Height. Males, 21 to 23½ inches; Females, 19–21 inches at the withers. An oversized or undersized Samoyed is to be penalized according to the extent of the deviation.

(d) Coat. (Texture and Condition). The Samoyed is a double-coated dog. The body should be well-covered with an undercoat of soft, short, thick close wool with longer and harsh hair growing through it to form the outer coat, which stands straight out from the body and should be free from curl. The coat should form a ruff around the neck and shoulders, framing the head (more on males than on females). Quality of coat should be weather resistant and considered more than quantity. A droopy coat is undesirable. The coat should glisten with a silver sheen. The female does not usually carry as long a coat as most males and it is softer in texture.

(e) Color. Samoyeds should be pure white, white and biscuit, cream, or all biscuit. Any other colors disqualify.

MOVEMENT

(a) Gait. The Samoyed should trot, not pace. He should move with a quick agile stride that is well-timed. The gait should be free, balanced and vigorous, with good reach in the forequarters and good driving power in the hindquarters. When trotting, there should be a strong rear action drive. Moving at a slow walk or trot, they will not single track, but as speed increases, the legs gradually angle inward until the pads are finally falling on a line directly under the longitudinal center of the body. As the pad marks converge the forelegs and hind legs are carried straight forward in traveling, the stifles not turned in nor out. The back should remain strong, firm and level. A choppy or stilted gait should be penalized.

(b) Rear End. Upper thighs should be well-developed. Stifles well-bent—approximately 45 degrees to the ground. Hocks should be well-developed, sharply defined and set at approximately 30 percent of hip height. The hind legs should be parallel when viewed

164

from the rear in a natural stance, strong, well-developed, turning neither in nor out. Straight stifles are objectionable. Double-jointedness or cowhocks are a fault. Cowhocks should only be determined if the dog has had an opportunity to move properly.

(c) **Front End.** Legs should be parallel and straight to the pasterns. The pasterns should be strong, sturdy and straight, but flexible with some spring for proper let-down of feet. Because of depth of chest, legs should be moderately long. Length of leg from the ground to the elbow should be approximately 55 percent of the total height at the withers—a very short-legged dog is to be deprecated.

Shoulders should be long and sloping, with a layback of 45 degrees and be firmly set. Out at the shoulders or out at the elbow should be penalized. The withers separation should be approximately 1–1½ inches.

(d) **Feet.** Large, long, flattish—a hare foot, slightly spread but not splayed; toes arched; pads thick and tough, with protective growth of hair between the toes. Feet should turn neither in nor out in a natural stance but may turn in slightly in the act of pulling. Turning out, pigeon-toed, round or cat-footed or splayed are faults. Feathers on feet are not too essential but are more profuse on females than on males.

HEAD

(a) **Conformation.** Skull is wedge-shaped, broad, slightly crowned, not round or apple-headed, and should form an equilateral triangle on lines between the inner base of the ears and the center point of the stop.

> *Muzzle*—Muzzle of medium length and medium width, neither coarse nor snipy; should taper toward the nose and be in proportion to the size of the dog and the width of the skull. The muzzle must have depth.
> *Stop*—Not too abrupt, nevertheless well defined.
> *Lips*—Should be black for preference and slightly curved up at the corners of the mouth, giving the "Samoyed Smile." Lip lines should not have the appearance of being coarse nor should the flews drop predominately at corners of the mouth.

Ears—Strong and thick, erect, triangular and slightly rounded at the tips; should not be large or pointed, nor should they be small and "bear-eared." Ears should conform to head size and the size of the dog; they should be set well apart but be within the border of the outer edge of the head; they should be mobile and well covered inside with air; hair full and stand-off before the ears. Length of ear should be the same measurement as the distance from inner base of ear to outer corner of eye.

Eyes—Should be dark for preference; should be placed well apart and deep-set; almond shaped with lower lid slanting toward an imaginary point approximating the base of ears. Dark eye rims for preference. Round or protruding eyes penalized. Blue eyes disqualifying.

Nose—Black for preference but brown, liver, or Dudley nose not penalized. Color of nose sometimes changes with age and weather.

Jaws and teeth—Strong, well-set teeth, snugly overlapping with scissors bite. Undershot or overshot should be penalized.

(b) Expression. The expression, referred to as "Samoyed expression," is very important and is indicated by sparkle of the eyes, animation and lighting up of the face when alert or intent on anything. Expression is made up of a combination of eyes, ears and mouth. The ears should be erect when alert; the mouth should be slightly curved up at the corners to form the "Samoyed smile."

TORSO

(a) Neck. Strong, well-muscled, carried proudly erect, set on sloping shoulders to carry head with dignity when at attention. Neck should blend into shoulders with a graceful arch.

(b) Chest. Should be deep, with ribs well-sprung out from the spine and flattened at the sides to allow proper movement of the shoulders and freedom for the front legs. Should not be barrel-chested. Perfect depth of chest approximates the point of elbows, and the deepest part of the chest should be back of the forelegs—near the ninth rib. Heart and lung room are secured more by body depth than width.

(c) Loin and Back. The withers forms the highest part of the back. Loins strong and slightly arched. The back should be straight to the loin, medium in length, very muscular, and neither long nor short-coupled. The dog should be "just off square"—the length being approximately 5 percent more than the height. Females allowed to be slightly longer than males. The belly should be well-shaped and tightly muscled and with the rear of the thorax, should swing up in a pleasing curve (tuck-up). Croup must be full, slightly sloping, and must continue imperceptibly to the tail root.

TAIL

The tail should be moderately long with the tail bone terminating approximately at the hock when down. It should be profusely covered with long hair and carried forward over the back or side when alert, but sometimes dropped when at rest. It should not be high or low set and should be mobile and loose—not tight over the back. A double hook is a fault. A judge should see the tail over the back once when judging.

DISPOSITION

Intelligent, gentle, loyal, adaptable, alert, full of action, eager to serve, friendly but conservative, not distrustful or shy, not overly aggressive. Unprovoked aggressiveness to be severely penalized.

DISQUALIFICATIONS:

Any color other than pure white, cream, biscuit, or white and biscuit.
Blue eyes.

Commentary on the
Current AKC Standard

"**General appearance**" is an attempt to picture the dog as he evolved in his native habitat and the natural attributes which made him survive in that severe, barren, and cold climate. The coat possesses density and quality to withstand not only weather and cold, but the formation of ice which would prevent movement and survival. The spikey stand-off guard hair keeps the snow and ice away from the undercoat. The white coloration, which is most natural to Northern Arctic animals, is for the conservation of warmth. Studies have shown that the make-up and color of the fur from Arctic animals prevents the conduction of heat from the body. Inexperienced people feel that such a thick coat must entail a lot of suffering in hot weather. Wrong! Mother nature automatically substitutes a lighter overcoat every spring; a body covering like this is just as good an insulator to keep heat out in summer as to ward off cold in winter. It has been proved beyond a shadow of a doubt that the Samoyed, Arctic Dog though he is, can withstand hot weather. You may see him in Africa, Puerto Rico, Southern United States, South America, and Japan.

The head described is the **typical wedge** of the wolf, the bear, the fox, the ermine, and the seal, which gives the powerful jaws and the ability of the teeth to rip and tear which a hunter must have. The eyes, through centuries of squinting in the bright Arctic sunlight, have the slightly slanting Mongolian look so necessary to survival. Note that the ponies taken on the Polar expeditions all suffered from snow blindness and became quite helpless.

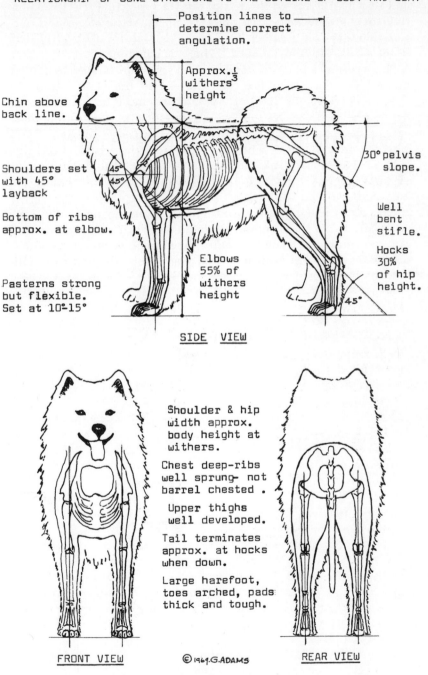

Position lines to determine correct angulation.

Approx. $\frac{1}{3}$ withers height

Chin above back line.

Shoulders set with 45° layback

Bottom of ribs approx. at elbow.

Pasterns strong but flexible. Set at 10°-15°

45°
45°

Elbows 55% of withers height

30° pelvis slope.

Well bent stifle.

Hocks 30% of hip height.

45°

SIDE VIEW

Shoulder & hip width approx. body height at withers.

Chest deep-ribs well sprung- not barrel chested .

Upper thighs well developed.

Tail terminates approx. at hocks when down.

Large harefoot, toes arched, pads thick and tough.

FRONT VIEW

© 1969.G.ADAMS

REAR VIEW

The ears are extremely functional and movable to avoid freezing, and very heavily haired inside and out for protection. Do you know that there are no long-eared animals in the Arctic Regions? Long-eared dogs in cold weather have a tendency to form blood blisters in their ears, with subsequent freezing and gangrene.

"Expression" is the sum total of the expression created by the set of the eyes, the tilt of the ears, the size of the mouth, and the upward curve of the lip line. A Samoyed must have tight, close flews. The right expression has an intelligent, penetrating look, with a devilish and quizzical attitude which says to you, "Well what do we do now?" The Samoyed faces the world cheerfully, confidently, with a frank candor that is unmistakable. He returns your gaze squarely, honestly, and without trace of calculation. He has nothing to conceal.

The centuries-long association with humans, living in the huts and 'chooms,' of the Samoyed people has created a disposition and expression unmatched by any other breed. The primitive harshness one might expect in both man and dog is subordinated to kindliness and friendship.

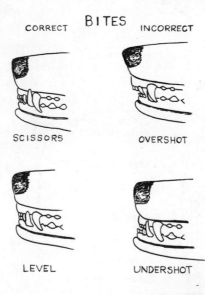

170

HEADS

DARK
ALMOND SHAPE
EYE

THICK, ROUNDED
MEDIUM SIZED
EARS, WELL
FURRED.

BROAD, FLAT
FOREHEAD

STOP
WELL-DEFINED

STRONG
LEVEL
JAW

LIPS
BLACK &
CLOSE
FITTING.
"SAMOYED
SMILE"

Acceptable head.

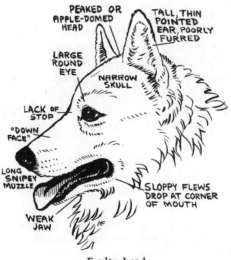

PEAKED OR
APPLE-DOMED
HEAD

TALL, THIN
POINTED
EAR, POORLY
FURRED

LARGE
ROUND
EYE

NARROW
SKULL

LACK OF
STOP

"DOWN
FACE"

LONG
SNIPEY
MUZZLE

SLOPPY FLEWS
DROP AT CORNER
OF MOUTH

WEAK
JAW

Faulty head.

COAT

Acceptable coat type, quality and distribution.

The dense undercoat is a vital part of the Samoyed make-up; but it is quite wrong to blame the lack of an undercoat for the lack of a stand-off outercoat. True, the perfect coat is both the under and outer coats, but when the outer coat is of a proper texture, it stands up without any aid from the undercoat even during the period of heavy shedding. It is a matter of texture, not length. The outercoat must be harsh to enable it to stand up. When you pat or dab the open palm of your hand flat on the guard hair, it should bend under pressure and spring back to the upright position immediately upon release. The hair should appear to protect the animal, like the spears of the porcupine, from the weather, dirt and snow, and wetness. The profuse coat dòes not lay down unless it is the improper texture. A flat lying coat is just about as poor a coat as a Samoyed can have. This type of coat is useless for the life which the Samoyed is born to lead and for the work it is supposed to do.

The proper coat on the Samoyed is the type which shakes free of water upon coming out of the lake, which does not permit snow and ice to pack into it and freeze, and which shakes free of dirt and mud when the dog dries and rolls in straw or grass. Quality of texture and type of coat are more important than quantity.

All details of body and leg structure listed in general appearance are for that all-purpose animal, the hunter, the herder, the hauler. These details give us a nimble yet sturdy dog that will not give up in the snow or long chases of game.

172

SOFT LONG HAIR PARTS ON BACK

TAIL HAIR HANGS LIMP, PARTS

RUFF HAIR DROOPS LIKE COLLIE'S

WAVY DROOPY FEATHER

FAULTY

NO TAIL PLUME

GOOD TEXTURE, BUT TOO SHORT

NO FEATHER

FAULTY

LACK OF RUFF

THIN, SCANTY COAT POORLY DISTRIBUTED

(LENGTH OF RUFF HAIR SHOULD EXCEED ALL BUT TAIL)

NO UNDERCOAT ON LEGS.

THIN FEATHER

FAULTY

173

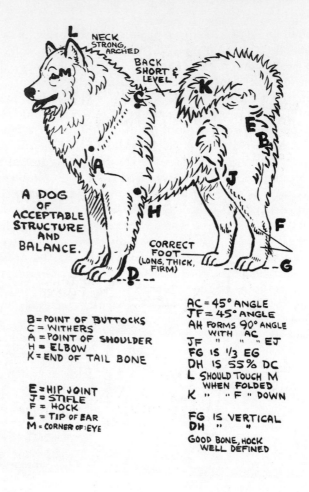

NECK STRONG, ARCHED

BACK SHORT & LEVEL

A DOG OF ACCEPTABLE STRUCTURE AND BALANCE.

CORRECT FOOT (LONG, THICK, FIRM)

B = POINT OF BUTTOCKS
C = WITHERS
A = POINT OF SHOULDER
H = ELBOW
K = END OF TAIL BONE

E = HIP JOINT
J = STIFLE
F = HOCK
L = TIP OF EAR
M = CORNER OF EYE

AC = 45° ANGLE
JF = 45° ANGLE
AH FORMS 90° ANGLE WITH AC
JF " " " EJ
FG IS 1/3 EG
DH IS 55% DC
L SHOULD TOUCH M WHEN FOLDED
K " " F " DOWN

FG IS VERTICAL
DH " "
GOOD BONE, HOCK WELL DEFINED

The concept of **substance** is misunderstood in Samoyeds when individual dogs are praised for possessing massive bone. Substance goes with soundness and, in its broadest sense, indicates that the dog shall be so constructed as to be capable of doing his native job well. The Samoyed is only a fast sled dog when he is first a fast herder. Too many articles lead one to believe that the Samoyed is a massively boned dog. This great emphasis upon "good" and "heavy" bone emerged because of the fine-boned and weedy-type specimens exhibited in the early 1900s. Many of those owners obtained the idea that the bone on the Samoyed would be like that of an Eskimo

174

or a Chow. Once Mrs. Kilburn-Scott said, "If a dog possesses unusual bone, he is right-off type." In working dogs, if you have a dog with too heavy bone, I can show you a dog that lacks speed, agility and grace to do his work as a herder, hunter, or sled dog.

Picture the Samoyed people hunting wild reindeer in Siberia. They build a corral with large wings of fences to guide the herds into the corral traps. Men and dogs spread out in huge fan-like net and drive the reindeer into the trap. The reindeer are quite fast and nimble. The men and dogs are chasing them most of the day, and sometimes for several days. Think of the nimbleness and endurance that is required to run in the ice and snow. This certainly is no occupation for a Newfoundland or a Chow Chow.

Personally, from working dogs in teams, we know that the exceptionally heavy-boned dogs have actually passed out after several hours of intense work; likewise smaller dogs have given up and have been brought home on the sled. One would know better if one follows the accounts of the explorers and the dogs which survived their journeys best. Not the largest and not the smallest, but his 59 to 69 pound dogs were the last to be in harness. Strangely enough, in the sport of Greyhound racing at the tracks, rarely do you find a dog over 70 pounds or under 55 pounds. It is not because larger and smaller do not exist, but because there is an optimum size for strength and speed.

PASTERNS: ① UPRIGHT ② NORMAL ③ DOWN (WEAK)
FAULTY — NORMAL — FAULTY

— FRONT FAULTS —

Ⓐ. TIGHT SHOULDER, "NARROW FRONT," TOEING OUT.

Ⓑ. NORMAL.

Ⓒ. LOOSE SHOULDER, OUT AT ELBOW, TOEING IN. "WIDE FRONT."

① ② ③

REAR MOTION:

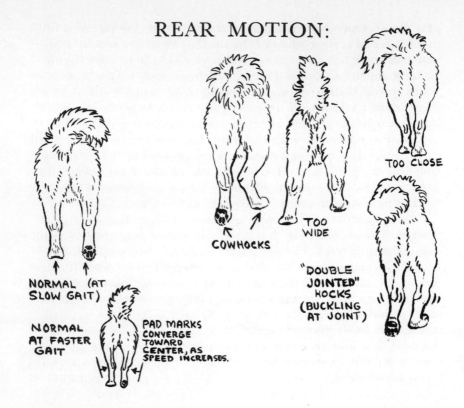

NORMAL (AT SLOW GAIT)

NORMAL AT FASTER GAIT

PAD MARKS CONVERGE TOWARD CENTER, AS SPEED INCREASES.

COWHOCKS

TOO WIDE

TOO CLOSE

"DOUBLE JOINTED" HOCKS (BUCKLING AT JOINT)

If our ideal Samoyed is to be graceful as well as beautiful, it must have sufficient body length to permit graceful movement. A compact body does not lend itself to good action, and using either males or females of this kind for breeding is to accentuate a fault of cobbiness.

"Torso" includes the neck, chest, loin, and back. We should begin with the neck and agree that, as we are describing neither a racer nor a draft animal, the neck should be moderately long. An animal, when he runs, uses the length of the neck to balance himself while at the gallop; therefore, a racing animal has an extremely long neck, while the draft animal has a short neck to consolidate strength at slower speeds. The Samoyed shall therefore have a proudly arched, moderately long neck, set for speed but not racy.

The definition of **chest** has caused much difficulty among owners, because the phrase "broad chest" has often appeared. Even in the new standard some misinterpretation occurs. One should not call

176

the front of the dog his chest; this is his front or brisket. The chest rightly is at the lowest point between the front legs. The breadth is measured more by the arch in the rib cage. The barrel-chested effect is to be avoided to eliminate the comparison to purely draft animals. The approved standard is quite explicit and clear upon this point.

The **loin** and **back** are well described in the standard, but the important part they play in producing a proper topline could be expanded. The topline of the Samoyed is level except for the slight rise at the withers and slight slope at the croup. The full view of the topline may give the impression of quite a slope to the topline, but you will find that this is caused by the arch of the neck and the rounding out by the proper coat, which grows with a maned effect over the shoulders.

Description of the **tail** is excellent, but mention should be made of the disastrous effect upon the dogs in the Arctic which do not have the proper loose tail to protect themselves while sleeping. The explorers who docked their dogs found out that within three weeks their dogs had died of pneumonia. Tails too loose or too tightly curled are incorrect.

Special features in the standard which must be observed while judging are: tail up and over the back at least once, moveable ears for protection, a topline which is neither too steep from front to rear nor too high in the rear. The gait in action, never clumsy, must be a graceful, natural trot and an eagerness to move. In other words, does he *want* to move?

The description of **disposition** is fairly thorough in the standard. The unadvertised ability of the Samoyed to get along in groups in kennels and at shows benched without dividers was a standardized fact for over fifty years. No one thought much about this quality, it just happened. But unfortunately, in some instances it does not happen now. The Canadian standard is most severe about poor disposition. We in America do not emphasize this strongly enough these days. It seems that which we most take for granted is the last to be missed.

The greatest fact to learn from the standard is to evaluate your dog against the standard. Never evaluate your dog against another dog. The approved standard has been developed by many breeders of long experience, and approved by AKC. They based their observations upon the standards originally set down by men who knew the dogs under working conditions and the observations set down by explorers.

FAULT FINDERS:

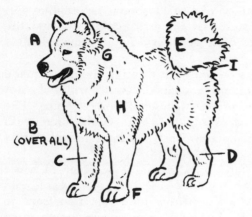

A: COARSE, BULKY HEAD
B: ENTIRELY TOO SHORT & COBBY
C: EXCESSIVE BONE
D: HOCKS TOO LOW SET (ALSO PASTERN 'KNEE')
E: TIGHT CURLED, DOUBLE CURLED OR HOOKED TAIL
F: FEET TOO LARGE AND ROUND
G: BULL NECK (SHORT, FLESHY)
H: LOADED SHOULDER
I: TAIL SET TOO HIGH

A = SHALLOW CHEST
B = SLAB (FLAT & NARROW) SIDES
C = ROACH BACK
D = GAY (FLAG) TAIL
E = COWHOCKS
F = WEAK LOIN "WASP WAIST"
G = OVERANGULATED
H = "SICKLE HOCKS" (CANNOT STRAIGHTEN LEG)
I = TOO RANGY
J = TAIL SET TOO LOW
K = HOCK SET TOO HIGH ("LONG HOCK") MORE THAN 1/3 HIP HEIGHT

178

A = UPRIGHT (STRAIGHT) SHOULDER
B = INADEQUATE LETDOWN OF ELBOW
C = HIGH REAR, LEVEL CROUP
D = STRAIGHT STIFLE
E = "SNAP" OR "SQUIRREL" TAIL
F = HOLLOW FRONT (LACK OF FILL IN BRISKET)
G = SWAYBACK

A: EWE NECK
B: FLAT, THIN SPLAYED FOOT
C: LONG WEAK BACK
D: STEEP CROUP
E: RING TAIL
F: LIGHT BONE
E: TAIL TOO SHORT

FAULTY

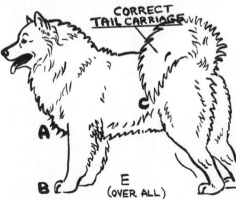

CORRECT TAIL CARRIAGE

A: "PIGEON BREAST" (PROTRUDING & FLESHY)
B: SMALL HIGH "CAT FOOT"
C: SLACK LOIN
D: DOUBLE-JOINTED HOCK; LOOSE HOCK
E: TOO SHORT LEGGED

E (OVER ALL)

179

Are the dogs larger or smaller now than they were in the past? Neither, for Fridjof Nansen listed his males as averaging 59 lbs. in working condition and his bitches at 50 lbs. Records show that Antarctic Buck was the tallest dog of the breed in 1909, and most of the descendants spring from him. He was reported by some at 21½ inches, and some at 22″ measured at the shoulder, not at the withers. (In America, we measure at the withers—the highest point of the shoulder.) In 1925, the English Ch. Snow Crest was reported at 23 inches and 70 lbs. In 1930, English Champion Kara Sea was measured at 22.6 inches and 65 lbs. The English import Ch. Tobolsk measured at 23 inches and over 65 lbs. in 1922. At the same time, the English import Ch. Donerna's Barin was reported to be 22½ inches and 65 lbs. In 1948, Irish import Ch. Snowland Stara, the first champion in the British Isles after World War II, was 23½ inches and 68 lbs. As recently as 1954, the imported Ch. Raff of Kobe was 23 inches tall and weighed over 90 lbs. before he was placed on a strict diet by the Powells of Alpine, Texas.

There have been a few males at 21 inches and a fewer number at 24 and 25 inches. Catharine Quereaux, in America, stated:

It is up to us as members and individuals who wish to keep the Samoyed a medium sized working dog type to know our standard and to impress it on our judges, and to impress upon them that a dog should win only in the degree in which it conforms to the standard. That variance in size is as much a defect as variance in other respects. Smallness is a greater sin than largeness. For in the smaller dog, defects are more easily concealed than in the larger dog. Anyone can measure from the floor to their own knee and knowing that measurement can thereby gauge size. Size must be considered in judging the breed or all that has been fought for in the breed will be lost.

Further, we must impress upon our judges that the requirement of good bone does not mean massive bone. "Piano legs" as they are familiarly called have no place in our breed; the natural work of the Samoyed as sledgedog and reindeer shepherd must be considered. The Samoyed today is largely a pet, but must be judged as a workdog and its fitness for the massive boned dog would do little in sled work, and the massive bone would be a great detriment in reindeer herding where fleetness is a requisite.

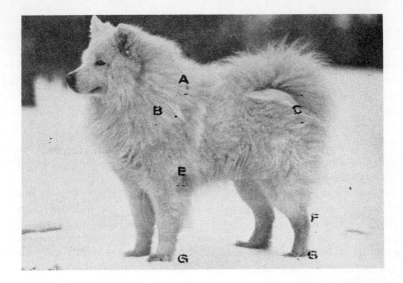

Withers A–G (highest point of shoulder)	19"	20"	21"	22"	23"	24"
Length B–C (shoulder point to hip point)	20.25	21.50	22.50	23.00	24.25	25.00
Height at rear	19.25	19.75	20.75	22.00	22.50	23.50
Barrel or circumference	24.50	26.00	26.75	28.00	28.50	29.00
Pastern or ankle	3.50	3.75	4.00	4.25	4.62	5.25
Depth of chest	8.50	9.00	9.25	9.50	10.25	10.75
Length of ear	3.10	3.25	3.375	3.50	3.87	4.00
Distance between eyes	1.87	2.00	2.00	2.12	2.25	2.25
Length of head (Occiput to tip of nose)	8.00	8.12	8.37	8.50	9.00	9.50
Length of Muzzle	3.25	3.37	3.50	3.87	3.90	4.125
Hock to ground F–G	5.75	6.00	6.25	6.50	6.75	7.00
Elbow to ground E–G	10.45	11.00	11.55	12.10	12.65	13.20

These measurements are the averages taken from the detailed measurements of more than 50 champions of the breed. Even the few details of the great champion of 40 years ago, Ch. Kara Sea are included in the averages. To show the similarity to the dogs today, Kara Sea was 22.6" at the withers, 5.5" at the pastern, 12.2" elbow to ground and 29.6" in circumference.

Miss Thomson-Glover wrote in 1930,

With regard to breeding, owners are far from blameless; some have foolishly made a fetish of white coats and black points and let the more important points go hang. Others have inter-bred with no adequate reason beyond that it is more convenient, or cheaper. Now at long last, the novices of some years ago, are themselves bemoaning the shortage of fine bitches.

Size is an unimportant factor compared with type and soundness. If an exhibit has balance, powerful easy movement, deep chest, well-sprung ribs, good front and hindquarters, coupled with a beautiful head, off-standing and weather resistant coat, and good feet, an inch more or less hardly counts. The owner of a small dog with type but perhaps a narrow chest, too light bone, indifferent shoulders and pasterns and softish coat, is apt to complain of great clumsy creatures above the standard and quite wrongly utterly ignoring their being far nearer the standard in essentials than their own exhibits. Owners of big dogs are prone to view the wins of small fry with surprised contempt, even if their own are leggy, plain, and shelly in body. Whatever comes nearest the standard at all points, whether big or small or medium, is the one who should win.

These opinions, no matter how varied, return us to the matter at hand. How do our present-day Samoyeds measure up to the Standard? All breeders have experienced what happens when we lose sight of the original purpose of the breed and over-emphasize something else. When size goes beyond nature's standard or the animal is bred smaller, many difficulties arise. Proportion of boning, soundness, disposition, and the like are affected. As a result, the dog can no longer do the job intended by nature.

A summation well appreciated by breeders and exhibitors in America was made by Miss Gloria L. Gittoes of Australia following a trip to America and England. She commented: "In a comparison of the three standards, the English, Canadian and American, it is interesting to note that under each heading the American Standard is lengthier. I do trust the more words, the more specific or the more descriptive. Certainly there is more on Gait in the American Standard."

Judging the Samoyed

(Author's Note: In supplement to our own observations, made in the commentary on the Standard (p. 168) and throughout the text, we here present observations on judging by some of the most respected authorities.)

by Mrs. Robert L. Seekins, Jr.:

As a Specialty judge, i.e., a breeder licensed to judge his own breed, I feel I can elaborate on some of the finer points in judging a Samoyed. Every all-round judge is highly qualified for all the breeds he or she may judge. But in any breed, naturally, a specialty judge will have the awareness of many of the finer points as well as, in a breed such as Samoyeds, the time and care that must go into presenting a Samoyed at its best. Only a person who has washed, carefully groomed, and tried to keep a pristine-clean Samoyed ready for a judging, can really know and appreciate the effort that has been made. Therefore, any specialty judge will probably take more time in going over the entry.

First I shall take the Samoyed itself. Since there are no absolutely perfect dogs (although there have been one or two almost perfect ones) one has to first look at the overall picture that the dog presents. It should be one in absolute proportions, viewed from the side. In other words, a good Samoyed has no exaggerated parts. The head, body, and tail are all a composite, and the judge can really see what the dog looks like if he has been trained to stand still. Sometimes, a really good specimen will be overlooked in this phase because of not standing so one can see the whole dog. I feel that a good medium-sized dog and slightly smaller bitch is the ideal. I personally would never penalize an entry if it were large, as long as it were within standard of course, providing it was a good specimen, but I do feel that the true Samoyed is a medium-sized dog. I am partial to feminine bitches, and do not like to see the so-called doggy bitch type.

Next we move the dogs, and I look for a flowing gait—no pacing. In explanation to the novice, *pacing* is the moving of both legs at one time on the same side—in other words, right front and right hind leg moving together. This is not only a tiring gait, but one absolutely wrong for a Samoyed. It is an attractive, showy gait, and has been used to advantage in some other breeds, but it is absolutely incorrect in a Samoyed. Even many dogs who can gait beautifully will fall into a pace when being shown, so watch for it, and do not go on with the gaiting until the dog changes gait. I want the dog shown on a loose lead, as I do feel that this is a natural gait and I can see the movement of the dog much, much better. I want the tail up during this gaiting, but there again, there are circumstances which may cause a Samoyed to drop tail. However, I feel that the tail should be over the back naturally—that is, not held there—at some time during the judging. I go over every entry for any weakness in the hindquarters, which can be ascertained by watching or touching.

The close examination of the Samoyed comes next. Starting with the head: a good even bite, with correctly placed (clean) teeth; eyes medium sized; dark, black eye rim preferred, black lip line preferred, black nose (allowance made for snow nose). The eyes make a great deal of difference in a Samoyed. They should have no tendency to either bulge or be sunken in and be set well apart. I also like to see a sparkle in them and not the sort of lackluster, dull look that we see occasionally. The muzzle should be full, not snipey, with no tendency to fall in under the eyes, and in proportion to the skull, on which should be set medium sized ears, well-furred and set well within the circumference of the head; ears at angles, pointed, large, or cubby bear tiny are all unfavorable. I feel the head is very important to the beauty of the Samoyed; and without that sweet, appealing smile, and an attractive head, the dog loses much in appearance.

The body, as stated before, should be in proportion: not cobby, but of medium length; legs set well with no tendency to stand out at the shoulders. Forelegs should be boned well, with feathering to be desired. Barrel chests are undesirable. There should be good depth in chest, but no bulging. I like to see a good length of neck, a

184

The authors as judges:

Ch. Joli Knika (1959–1965) by Ch. Tod-Acres Fang ex Ch. Kobe's Nan-Nuk of Encino. Pictured winning breed under Dolly Ward, en route to Best in Show all-breeds under judge Louis Murr at Colorado, 1963. Bred by John and Lila Weir, and owned by Helen and Cliff Cabe of Oregon.

Ch. Blizzard of Snoline, by Ch. Glen Echo Polar Sno, C.D. ex Ch. Lady Sasha of Kazan, C.D., owned by Lori Ann and Nancy Alexander, pictured in win under author Bob Ward. Handled by Mrs. Laurel Alexander. Blizzard was BOB at the 1970 Specialty of the Samoyed Club of Los Angeles under judge Kathryn Tagliaferri.

185

firm, well-muscled body, muscular hindquarters, and no tendency to cow-hocks (evidence by weakness in lower hock). Feet should be well-furred, not splayed, but I do not like "cat" feet.

The coat makes the difference in evaluating two otherwise equal specimens.

by Miss Helene L. Spathold:

Upon the dogs' entrance to the ring I request dogs be circled around in a counter-clock-wise circle, giving me an idea of the dogs' general appearance, type and over-all balance. I call a halt with the dog I believe most outstanding in that particular class and request dogs be stood or posed sideview, at which time I begin complete examination of each. Upon approaching the first dog I request the exhibitor to open the dog's mouth to check teeth, bite, jaw formation, and lip lines or points. I continue my examination with muzzle, face, eyes, skull, ears, neck, soundness of shoulders, reach of forelegs, spring of rib, depth of brisket, breadth of chest, forelegs. I check again for straightness, bone, soundness of pasterns, shape of feet and pads. Then I go on to levelness of and soundness of back, substance, shape of body, length of loin, and tuck-up. Overall general appearance again is considered, then on to hindlegs for bend of stifles, angulation of hindlegs, soundness of hocks, and a check to see if elbows and stifle joints meet at same approximation for balance of each for these parts of structure. I check testicles or sex of dog, examine tail carriage, and inspect coat for texture and quality. The same procedure is followed for each dog in the class, comparing each with and to the first dog examined. Now I request dogs be moved, separately at a fast speed and then again at slow speed, to the end of the ring, to determine, while dog is in movement to or from me, whether there are any faults of forelegs, shoulders, hindlegs, hocks, elbows, back, feet, pads, and pasterns.

The handlers are asked to again stand the dogs front view for final visual comparison. Then I select the winners according to their merits of qualities, overall balance, and weaknesses against those same merits or demerits of the competition present.

The faults I know and have seen the Samoyed to possess are unsound hocks, straight stifles, cowhocks, weak or broken down pasterns, short legs, long backs, long bodies, high rears, cobby or Chow-like bodies, double curled tails, barreled rib-springs, toe-in, toe-out, out at elbows or shoulders, lack of pigmentation, shy dispositions, aggressive dispositions, narrow fronts, and long, slab-sided bodies. There are many more serious deviations in structure from our accepted standard, as well as the American Kennel Club disqualifications—orchidism, blindness, blue eyes, any color other than the four standard accepted colors of our breed.

by Mrs. Agnes Mason:

Mrs. Mason was, until her death in 1970, an honorary life member of the Samoyed Club of America, Past President and Past Honorary President of the parent club, and honorary member of the Samoyed Club of Los Angeles. Her impact upon the popularity of the breed is exceeded only by her influence upon the quality of the breed. After nine years of Samoyed breeding, she forecast as clearly as if it were 29 years. In 1944 she wrote as follows:

First and foremost, it is my opinion that in order to determine the standard we should decide if it is the desire of the majority of Samoyed owners to keep our breed in the Working Dog class. If they continue to place in the Working Dog class as they have in recent years they will soon find their place at the top as Best Dog in Show. This will publicize the breed more than anything else could, and a breed judge should always place Best of Breed the dog that has the best chance in the Group. Judge Julius DuPon of California told us at one of our meetings that this was his consideration. If every judge regardless of his knowledge of the breed kept this in mind, I believe we would have more sincere and better judging.

A working dog is one of the most interesting of breeds and this last war has made the public more work-dog conscious. A 35- or 45-pound Samoyed hasn't the chance in the Working Group that a larger one has, regardless of type. I believe to arrive at a larger standard, we should be influenced to some extent by Nansen's experience on his expedition when he advises that the medium-sized Samoyed endured the longest. As near as I can figure this would be about 60 pounds. Personally, I like the 60- or 65-pound male standard and advocate our enlarging the standard to 45 to 60 pounds for females, and 50 to 65 or 70 pounds for males. We find that in our dog teams the females work as well as, if not better than,

Eng. Ch. Kosca of Kobe, owned by Mrs. Dorothy L. Perry, England. Agnes Mason commented on this photo as follows: "Good front legs, good stifles, feet, tail. Well-balanced dog. Head well set."

males. This gives plenty of leeway for a judge to consider type. Any Samoyed over this weight could be penalized accordingly, yet if he were outstanding he could still win.

Naturally, frame should conform to weight. I think an over-weight Samoyed is as much out of condition as one too thin. We have both in our kennel. However, the largest percentage are in condition as we like them for sled work. A Samoyed so large that his heavy bone makes him clumsy rather than agile and graceful is not a good sled dog, nor good at herding. Neither should they be bred cobby merely for show purposes.

A Samoyed with long hair should not be given the advantage over a shorter coat merely because of length of coat. Different judges have told me they did not care for the long Pomeranian coat. We naturally breed for good coat, but I think a sound Samoyed with shorter coat of good quality should be considered over a less sound one with a longer coat that might help his percentage on general appearance. We have had judges who judged on general appearance only, never going over the dogs for soundness, or gaiting them for leg action. I remember when we purchased Dascha from Mr. Pinkham he said, "A Sammy should never lose his waistline." At the time I did not understand just what he referred to. Of course, a deep-chested Samoyed in condition for work would have a waistline. Too long a coat on the back covers the beauty of the contour of our breed.

188

I do not think the short-legged Sammy is as attractive as the medium-size, or rather the larger present standard of today. Our present standard states they should not be short-legged, but a height of 19 inches could not be anything else if the chest is deep. Body and legs in my estimation should be given preference over head and tail carriage, and coat over black points. One judge said, "I like a black nose but a Samoyed does not work with his nose; gait is more important."

In a kennel with several as we have, it is easy to study comparisons and my likes or dislikes may apply to standard as far as show points are concerned. I have never seen a Samoyed that I did not admire for some special trait or beauty all its own. I have so much to learn about Samoyeds that I hesitate to pass along my observations for publication, but I hope that some of my conclusions agree with others who really know the breed better than I do.

by Louis Smirnow:

Mr. Smirnow, the first Parent Club President and a breeder-judge, wrote the following in 1948, after 30 years' experience with the breed:

Whenever I have had an occasion to write something for publication during the past 30 years of my interest in Samoyed matters, I have emphasized as a matter of greatest importance that of breeding properly. If breeders will keep before them the standard of the breed and try to breed in an effort to obtain the closest possible to the standard, our breed will improve. We must do away with the Collie-faced, narrow chested, long bodied Samoyed. And I must again caution breeders to breed properly. This means checking your own dog for faults carefully and trying to eradicate those faults in their offspring.

I do not believe that we have enough good females, at least I have not seen them at the big shows. This should receive the consideration of breeders and exhibitors.

I have witnessed judging at some shows and have particularly noticed that the judges give no consideration to the undercoat of a Samoyed, which is an important consideration for a work dog. I should like to see more attention paid to proper expression in the Samoyed. Without it, much of the wistfulness and charm of the Samoyed is lacking.

by Clifford Chamberlain:

Mr. Chamberlain bred and judged Samoyeds in the period from 1940 until his death in 1962.

I want a Samoyed who stands solidly, squarely, with all four legs meeting the ground at right angles. I don't like that slope that indicates weak pasterns. I want to see only two legs, front and back, when the dog is going away or coming toward me, or I don't want to see back toes peeking out around his front feet as he runs towards me or vice versa. We should see majesty, dignity, a real aristocrat in all good examples of our breed.

Often good bitches have the grace and power, and solid substance I like to see, to greater degree than the males, and I have noted with interest that this trait is passed on to at least one or two in a litter, no matter how rangy the stud. Bitches should be judged as Samoyeds first, and then as the female of the species. A bitch should have the same qualities in feminine proportion. Without good bitches, embodying what we want in a Sam, there will be breed deterioration. Snipeyness in a bitch's head is unpleasing to the eye but not as serious as structural faults. These crop up unto the 3rd and 4th generations. A good-headed stud, however, will help to eliminate some of the bitch's faults.

by Miss J. V. Thomson-Glover:

In the consideration of Samoyed judging, two excerpts from a 1930 critique by the highly respected Miss Thomson-Glover are rather interesting:

A born showman looks about him, proudly interested in everything within range. I do not care to see Samoyeds standing about, or tailing around like a flock of sheep. People think a dog shows well if it stands motionless, with its eyes glued to whatever the handler has in his hands. . . .

An eye entirely foreign is creeping into the breed, and perhaps novices do not realize how much beauty and Samoyed character is thus lost.

PART III
Breeding, Care, and Training

In the pages that follow, we bring you advice on the selection, breeding, care, training and enjoyment of your Samoyed —puppy to adulthood—from authorities whose interests, training and experience particularly qualify them to the assignment.

Suretta of Kobe, the first of six imports from the famous English Kobe Kennels of Mrs. D. L. Perry, is pictured with her puppies sired by Ch. Raff of Kobe, completing the foundation of the Encino Kennels of Charles and Margaret Tucker in California.—*Photo by Ludwig.*

Breeding the Samoyed

IN writing this book, we have come to a conclusion about breeding Samoyeds. While we do not disparage the reading of books on genetics, or acquiring and using the knowledge on the use of line breeding and inbreeding, we would recommend outcrossing as a frequent program for the novice to follow, especially outcrossing based upon the physical attributes of the parents and grandparents. Many of the top winners in this book were so bred.

This advice is based on the Samoyed's beginnings as a breed. Man has not cross-bred the original; therefore, they breed true in spite of man's learnings and theories.

It is sometimes felt that line breeding to "stamp" a particular feature is to glory in the comment "Oh that's a So and So line or kennel. You can tell by looking at it." Some breeders interpret the standard according to their human likes. By creating a dominance for a particular look, they may also double the "bad genes" as well as those they have selected as "good." This would be particularly true in the case of hip dysplasia, straight stifles, or double hocks.

We have been warned through the years by Louis Smirnow, Helen Harris, and Agnes Mason, among others, that we should *breed to the standard of the breed*. That means *Type* (it must look like a Samoyed ought to look); *Soundness* (it must be free of anatomical weaknesses of hips, legs, or angles, and gait properly); *Temperament or Disposition* (it must be *absolutely* dependable, *stable* and *happy*); and *Style* (that intangible something which sets a good Samoyed apart from the outstanding specimen who exudes an elegance in ring presence and *quality* with or without a good handler).

Handsome Lord Snowden, pictured as 11-weeks old puppy. By Am. and Can. Ch. Shaloon of Drayalene ex Ch. Tanna of Snowden, bred and owned by Mrs. Dorothy Moore, Pinehill Kennels of Arkansas.

Canadian Ch. Ker-Lu Sunniray of Kobe, English import pictured at 10 months. By Eng. Ch. Lealsam Snowigleem ex Eng. Ch. Sunray of Kobe. Owners, Shirley and Roy Curran, Ker-Lu Kennels, Reg'd., Canada.

Starlight's Noatak (at 5 months). Noatak's sire, Snowdrift Starlight's Kayak is out of Ch. Kobe Holm Storm, Australian import. His bloodline relates to Ch. Starya of Kobe and Ch. Icemist Beauty of Kobe in Australia. Owners, Mr. and Mrs. Mike Loughran of Phoenix, Arizona.

Therefore, in breeding, a knowledge is needed of the strengths and weaknesses of the grandparents as well as the parents to know how to evaluate the choice of a mate. For instance, to improve a too-broad or too-narrow front one does not select a mate with the opposite fault thinking to come out with an "instant mixture." Consider the dominance of the stud and brood bitch by *studying the get.* Heads are the most diversified, but Sams should have a Samoyed expression.

Before you breed, we would suggest these requirements:

1. You have a bitch that is above average stock, sound in body and temperament.
2. The plan for her breeding has been studied and carefully made on paper after thorough study of compatible bloodlines. That the bitch and the prospective sire will offset each other's possible weaknesses.
3. That both are X-Rayed normal.
4. That your aim is to produce puppies better than either the father or the mother.
5. That your bitch has been wormed about one month before her season.
6. That her booster shots are up to date, as the puppies receive immunity from their dam's milk *only* if their dam has immunity.
7. That she has had a complete health check by your Veterinarian.
8. That she is between one and two years of age before being bred for the first time.

Munronav's Kobe of Hillhead, wh. 1968, by Eng. and Am. Ch. Demitrio of Kobe ex Eng. Ch. Sunnistar of Kobe. "Poppy," pictured at 10 months, is a great granddaughter of Eng. and Am. Ch. Americ of Kobe. Bred by A. J. Whiteway, Quebec, Canada, and owned by C. W. and M. W. Van Ornum of Cincinnati, Ohio.

Diet for a Brood Bitch in Whelp
by Jan Kauzlarich & Elva Libby

During pregnancy and nursing, a dog's nutritional needs are very special. Most malformed puppies (and malformation in human babies too) are caused by malnutrition during the pregnancy.

A bitch in whelp needs more protein, which means lots of eggs, meat, and fish. The most crucial times are from the sixth week of pregnancy to birth, during which time nutritional needs are doubled, and from birth to about the fourth week of nursing, when the nutritional needs are almost tripled. Feed her smaller meals, but more frequent meals.

> **Morning:** Hard boiled eggs; cottage cheese; beef.
>
> **Evening:** Meal or kibble; ground beef; cottage cheese. Canned fish, chicken or cooked liver should be fed instead of beef in the evening meal two or three times a week.
>
> **Supplements:** One tablespoon poly-unsaturated vegetable oil; two Natabac capsules (a human pre-natal vitamin) a day from sixth week of pregnancy to weaning of puppies; Forty to sixty units of Vitamin E in wheat germ oil or tocopherol.

Diet for a Brood Bitch While Nursing

> **Morning:** Hard boiled eggs; beef; meat or kibble. In a separate dish, two cups of milk and one egg yolk.
>
> **Noon:** Cottage cheese; beef or fish. Two cups of milk and egg yolk.
>
> **Evening:** Same as morning. Feed supplements with this meal. In a separate dish, milk and egg yolk.
>
> **Bedtime:** Beef or fish; cottage cheese.
>
> ALWAYS have fresh water available for her.

While most Samoyeds whelp normally, and do not require that a veterinarian be in attendance it is a wise and comforting precaution to have one ready "on call." It is recommended that arrangements with him will have been made for that extraordinary emergency.

196

Whelping and Puppy Care
by Joyce Cain

Development of traits and characteristics begins in newborn puppies the moment they are born. Keeping the puppy clean the first months of life forms a pattern of cleanliness. This does not imply frequent bathing, but does suggest a sparkling white puppy without the necessity of a bath.

The dam should be as clean as a top show competitor when the puppies first arrive. Although her last bath should be at least three weeks prior to whelping, special care may be taken by bathing her feet and allowing her to sleep or rest on clean rugs. If necessary, she should be exercised on a leash.

When the time for whelping approaches (any time from the 58th day to 63rd day or so), line the whelping box with clean rough material for better footing for both dam and puppies. Newspapers are not recommended for Samoyeds as the ink rubs off on the white coats.

Begin your paper work. Record her temperature daily from the 57th day on. Normal is between 100 and 101 degrees. About three days before actual whelping, her temperature will drop to 99 degrees and "hold." Now watch temperature twice a day. When it drops to 97 degrees, and the water breaks, you may expect her first pup within hours.

During the whelping and the time when the dam has a heavy discharge, an absorbent disposable pad with a plastic lining may be placed under her. After each puppy is born in its membraneous sack filled with fluid and as soon as the dam has severed the cord from the whelp's abdomen, the pad can be rolled up with the placenta and discarded. The dam will be busy cleaning her whelp and will hardly notice. She may be allowed to eat one or two afterbirths, which is normal, but disposal of the others is recommended. Most important is to count them and account for every one.

Some breeders prefer to remove the newly born puppies to another warm box during each successive whelping, thus keeping them clean and dry and out of danger of being smothered by the dam. Between whelpings they should be returned to her if possible. Always keep the puppy box in a place where she can see her babies.

The fewer people around the better. Please, no strangers.

The whelping may take any time from two hours to twelve hours with pups arriving at any interval of time from five minutes to two hours.

Do not delay if any of the following danger signals develop:

Call your veterinarian:

1. If the bitch is straining, squatting, has a pup only partially expelled or has hard labor for more than an hour without any delivery.
2. After whelping is finished, if bitch begins heavy panting, or trembling, is restless and has a worried expression, or if mucous membranes are pale. Though conscious, she may become paralyzed and unable to stand. Immediate care is needed and your veterinarian will give an injection of calcium gluconate. This eclampsia is a condition occasionally encountered by the bitch at whelping. It usually occurs twenty-four to thirty hours or even four or five days after whelping.

When the puppies have been whelped and fed, the dam will need to be let out for elimination. Before she returns to her pups, bathe her skirts and dry them thoroughly. It will encourage her to keep herself clean. This is also an excellent time to change the bedding in the whelping box.

Puppies will start nursing usually when whelping is completed. Give the bitch warm milk and broth to aid her milk flow. The first two days are critical in newborn puppies. They must be kept warm and they must nurse. A puppy should have a round full stomach and be contented. The dam must clean and lick her pups, especially in the abdominal region. This action stimulates peristalsis, setting proper elimination. If the bitch fails to do this, you must gently rub the abdomen from the head to the tail with thumb or fingers, rhythmically, so the puppy will urinate and pass its fecal matter.

A post-whelping checkup should be made at the veterinarian's as soon as possible.

Your paper work consists of recording time or arrival of each pup and its sex and weight, and accounting for the afterbirths. Record the bitch's temperature twice daily for two weeks so you may see the doctor if her temperature increases above 102 degrees.

At three days, cut the dew claws, if any, on both front and hind legs. Take litter to the veterinarian for this or do it yourself as follows:

Use sterilized curved sharp scissors to cut the gristle—nub and paint with ferrous sub-sulfate, i.e.—Monsell's powder. Have some-one take the dam for a walk during this minor surgery, so she will not be upset. It is not difficult but be sure to get the whole piece as deep as necessary so they won't grow back.

Puppies are bathed by the dam during the first weeks of their lives; therefore, the breeder's only concern is keeping the dam and the whelping box clean.

Supplement feeding of Pablum and ball of hamburger (thumb size) may start during the third or fourth week. Added to this chore will be the beginning of house-breaking. Some dams will refuse to remove the excreta from the bed, others will continue after the supplemental feeding has started, and a rare few keep the whelping box clean through the eighth week. Once again, newspaper is not recommended. Training the puppy on paper condones elimination indoors and helps them to acquire a habit which must be broken later.

Take each puppy outdoors before feeding when they have awakened from a nap and again after a meal. The reasoning to all this added work of carrying one at a time is teaching the puppy discipline. You get his complete attention and training is simplified. The younger the puppy the more frequently he will have to relieve himself. Mistakes will happen, and if they do, clean them up at once. Clean bedding when needed will discourage mistakes and by the fifth week each puppy will beg to be first.

Wait until the pups have had their first serum shot before show-ing them off to friends and neighborhood children.

The puppies' eyes will start to open at seven to fourteen days from birth. The lids part first at the inner corner and extend to the outside.

Cut sharp puppy toe nails every five to seven days while they are nursing.

When feeding them, hold the pan so that they do not step into it. Try an orange juice squeezer dish to discourage stepping in dish. Allow the dam to remain close by and allow her to clean up any puppy that has gotten dirty while eating. When they have finished, remove the pan immediately. If the dam starts washing their faces to clean them, they soon will learn to wash one another.

Offer the puppies water frequently but do not leave it where they will walk in it or spill it. If they do get wet, towel them dry. The puppy who loads himself with water will not eat his ration of feed and will make more puddles than you can wipe. He must have water but he need not fill up on it.

Television star Betty White and author Dolly Ward at taping of "Pet Set" show, with 6-weeks-old litter of Samoyeds by Almost Christmas Chatter ex Boutique, bred by Mardee Faria. Actor Jim Nabors, a guest on the show, now has a puppy of the litter, named "Chatique."

Selecting a Puppy

THE selection of the puppy is of paramount interest to both the breeder and the buyer.

The prospective buyer should:

1. Read about the Samoyed.
2. Write to reputable breeders asking for explicit information on their stock and evaluated potential. Show superintendents and judges are sources for leads to reputable breeders.
3. Visit all possible breeders. A breeder does not necessarily own a large kennel.
4. Attend Sanctioned Matches, shows, and specialty shows.
5. Look at as many Samoyeds of all ages as possible.
6. Talk to their owners.

If you are in a well-populated area, you may be able to pick out your own puppy from the litter. This may be fortunate or not, depending on how well you have studied the breed.

If you are in an area in which there are no Samoyeds being bred or shown, you will have to depend on a sort of mail order business between you and the breeder. This may be fortunate or not, depending on how "good" the breeder is. BEWARE. There are many breeders who wish only to make a sale and may not know much more than you about how to evaluate puppies.

If you want a pet Samoyed, you should study the breed first. Selection of your pet is as important as selection of a show dog. You may end up with both, though you "do not plan to show." We think the ideal purchase is a pet who may be shown, or the show dog who may be your pet. They are always in this dual role anyway.

Most people would not deliberately buy a Samoyed with an eye to "campaigning" this breed at shows all over the country unless it were their pet.

The initial investment in a puppy or half grown (6 months-2 years) Samoyed is the smallest fee, compared with the care, time, and monetary and emotional costs you spend on your pet-show dog. It "costs" no more to raise your show dog than to raise your pet. The costs involved in entering the show game may be written off as "entertainment," as there is no better family sport than the dog game. It may intrigue both the child and the gray haired grandparents in the family. That is togetherness.

The puppy is most frequently chosen at the age of eight weeks; but don't disregard the advantages of selecting a half-grown Samoyed. Starting with the head, notice the placement (not too close) and shape (almond) of the eye as well as the degree of darkness. Check the circumference of the muzzle, especially for depth and breadth on either side of the nose button. You do not wish a snipey muzzle when he grows up. Ears may not be up yet, but check the thickness and strength of cartilage to determine whether the ears will "come up," as well as their placement on the head. Ears should not be too low set or too large, as this will detract from the expression.

Grasp the knobby knees to judge the bone. If the knobs are missing, the puppy may lack bone and size. Knobs are more observable about three to four months.

Hold the puppy securely around his chest and observe the legs hanging down. Do they hang straight in both the front and rear? If they toe out while gaiting, the puppy may walk or stand improperly. Watch him move about. Does he walk and trot with some spring and rhythm of gait? Do his feet point straight ahead? Does the rear match the front, or is one too strong for the other?

Tail set is quite obvious, so see that it is not too low or too high. Measure the spring of the rib cavity with your hands. If you feel a barrel shape, don't choose that darling one. If you feel a heart shape, it's probably A-okay. All coats look fluffy—you'd better check the sire and dam—and better yet the grandparents—to predict the type and amount of coat.

Study the pictures again—imagine the dog without any coat. Proportion of length of neck and squareness of the whole puppy standing is a matter of how the parts combine to make the whole picture. Legs should not be short. We have included pictures that show puppies at different ages and what they grew to look like as adults. *Notice disposition. Never* choose the shy one, the wetter, or the withdrawn pup.

Even the best "picker" can be disappointed, but evaluation of the ancestors and the puppy "on the spot" is the best you can do. In addition to the puppy's inherited potential, tender loving care, nutrition, exercise, and some *luck* combine to give you the "pick of the litter."

Some items to expect from the breeder to take home with you besides your new puppy:

1. His registration paper. A common error in terminology is the interchange of the words "papers" and "pedigree." The registration *papers* are issued by the AKC from the litter number previously recorded by the breeder with the AKC. With a bill of sale, it is evidence of ownership.
2. The pedigree is provided as a courtesy by the breeder to give you a document which lists the sire and dam, the grand-parents, great grandparents—as far as a six generation pedigree usually. This is his family tree!
   If an older dog or a puppy that is already named by the breeder changes ownership, you will need to send his papers to the AKC with a fee for transfer to the name of the new owner.
3. A reputable breeder will give you a record of the puppy's shots and dates of worming.
4. Also, he will provide a menu list of his current diet and even a supply of kibble to carry him over in his new surroundings, thus avoiding changes of diet as well as environment.

You should provide a small chain collar, a leash, and a crate (the size of which is designed to be large enough for comfort when he is grown) .

203

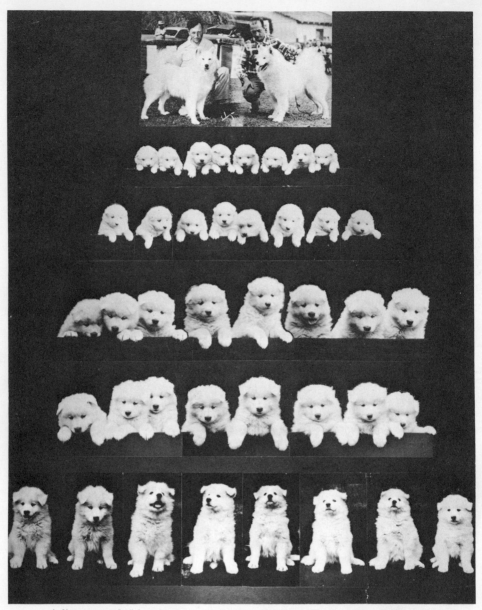

A litter recorded in pictures. (At top are the dam, Ch. Suzanne of White Way, and the sire, Ch. Rainier. Breeders were Mr. and Mrs. Edwin Adams.)

Row 1—At three weeks.
Row 2—At four weeks.
Row 3—At five weeks.
Row 4—At six weeks.
Row 5—At seven weeks.

THE following chart, showing an average increase in weight of puppies through their first eight weeks, is based on statistics compiled by the authors over a 25-year span:

Age	Average Weight
At birth	14 oz. to 18 oz.
One week	1½ lbs. to 2 lbs.
Two weeks	2 lbs. to 3 lbs.
Three weeks	3 lbs. to 4 lbs.
Four weeks	4 lbs. to 5 lbs.
Five weeks	5 lbs. to 8 lbs.
Six weeks	7¾ lbs. to 8¾ lbs.
Seven weeks	9 lbs. to 12 lbs.
Eight weeks	11 lbs. to 14 lbs.

The darkening of the black points, such as eyes, nose and lips varies greatly with the bloodlines, but generally will follow this pattern:

1. Rarely a few spotted noses at birth
2. On the fourth day, a few eye-rims will begin darkening.
3. On the fifth day, at least half of the litter will have black eye-rims and noses will appear smoky.
4. At one week, all eye-rims appear dark and all noses are spotted with black. Now dark spots are showing on lips.
5. By the ninth day all eyes appear darker and ready to open, but will probably not open until the 13th or 14th day.

At the age of eight weeks, the following characteristics should be enough established to determine what they will be in the adult dog:

1. Shape and set of eyes, color
2. Biscuit shadings (which fade about ears with age)
3. Size of ears and placement
4. Set and carriage of tail
5. Disposition (outgoing to timid)
6. Bone—large knuckles for proper size
7. Gait

Pictured with her litter at one day of age is Ch. Samtara's Sugay N' Spice (by Ch. Frostar's Taza Kibiriak ex Ch. Samtara's Snow Gay Fantasy). Sire of the litter was Noatak's Nik O'Saturn. Breeders, Louis and Joyce Cain, Ripon, Wisconsin.

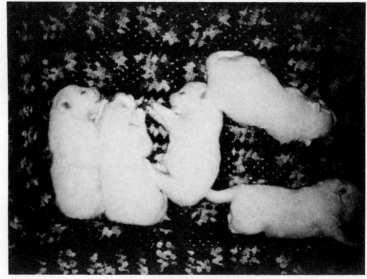

Two weeks old—sacked out.

Four and one half weeks old.

Seven weeks old—some ears beginning to come up. Adventurous.

Eight weeks old—stacking with confidence. This is Samtara Suga Daddi, now co-owned by Curtis Ubinger and Joyce Cain.

207

Seven months after whelping her litter, Ch. Samtara's Sugay N' Spice returns to the ring and scores Best of Breed, with one of her puppies—Samtara's Suga Daddi going Best Opposite. Samtara Kennels are owned by Joyce and Louis Cain, Wisconsin.

And now it is Champion Samtara's Suga Daddi, the first of the litter to finish championship. So we have thus seen a puppy from whelp to title.

On Raising Puppies

Author's Note: This article is by Mrs. Susan North, a noted Poodle breeder, and is from a lecture delivered by her (under title of "Will Your Dog Need a Psychiatrist?") at a recent breeders' seminar. We consider it one of the finest presentations on its subject we have encountered, and every bit as applicable for Samoyeds as it is for Poodles. We include it here with Mrs. North's permission.

THE breeder's responsibility for raising puppies on a sound psychological foundation is just as great as his responsibility for raising puppies that are free from parasites and innoculated against distemper. Emotional health is actually more precarious: a worm infestation can be treated, but a puppy that has not received socialization before the age of three months will be permanently crippled emotionally and can never realize his potential in forming a responsive relationship with a human being.

Based upon the research of Drs. Scott and Fuller at Jackson Laboratory (I highly recommend their book, *Genetics and The Social Behavior of the Dog*) and the practical application of their conclusions at Guide Dogs for The Blind as described in Clarence Pfaffenberger's most interesting book, *The New Knowledge of Dog Behavior*, it is now possible for breeders to give their puppies the best possible head start by some simple training and experience at a very early age.

When you breed a litter, you are bringing lives into this world and must, I believe, accept the responsibility for them. Your pet puppies have just as much right to the time and attention as that show prospect that you think is going to do all that winning for you. If you don't have time for the pet puppies, you really don't

Eight weeks.

Three months.

Seven months.

Two years old.

Chum exemplified the most influential lines in the United States, whose combinations have been behind virtually every bloodline that has excelled in show and reproduction. Bred by Aljean Mason in 1939, his sire was Ch. Petrov Lebanof (Czar Nicholas Lebanov—Dasha of Laika), and his dam was Ch. Nianya of Snowland (Ch. Siberian Nasen of Farningham of Snowland—Ch. Vida of Snowland). Nansen was by the immortal Ch. Kara Sea ex Pinky of Farningham, and Vida was by Ch. Storm Cloud ex Morina of Taimir.

have time for the litter! Breeders too often assess their litters, picking out the show prospects and then ignoring the pets who are sold as quickly as possible with a minimum investment of time and money. Nothing could be more foolish or detrimental to the breed as a whole.The real public relations job in dogs is done by these pet puppies who in their daily lives contact many, many people, leaving an impression for better or for worse. By investing a modicum of time you can build a firm emotional base for each and every one of your puppies and help to assure dispositions that will be a credit to you in or out of the ring.

Now how does one go about preparing these puppies—and just what kind of temperament are we really after? I think one could find some difference of opinion among breeders as to just what ideal temperament was—just as breeders differ in their ideas about head proportion and sound movement.

I personally feel that the one hundred percent extrovert that sells himself so well to puppy buyers and judges alike is not completely desirable. A totally fearless dog, a dog without caution or reserve who is indiscriminately friendly with every passing stranger, a dog without nerves or sensitivity may be the handler's delight, but frankly he is not my idea of an intelligent animal. It is possible, I think, to have a dog that shows himself off proudly, a dog that is polite, manageable and sensible, but still a dog that has his dignity and maintains his natural cautions about new people and new situations.

If you have a dog that is self-confident and secure and that knows he can trust you, you can ask him to do certain things. You can ask him to stand still in the ring while some stranger goes over him from top to bottom—and this dog will do it because he has learned to trust your judgment, not because he is necessarily delighted with attentions from a total stranger.

Friendship with an intelligent and aware animal must be earned. So I permit some reserve in my dogs; I welcome some selectivity in their friendships—and this is because I have great respect for each of my puppies as individuals and feel they are entitled to develop their own unique personalities. The training program that I follow with my puppies is not designed to turn out robots or totally uniform dispositions.

The idea, rather, is to take some time to explore with each puppy his own personality, to cultivate his particular potential at that so very critical early time when it is possible to do so very much.

211

Begin to prepare this ideal emotional climate with your bitch in whelp. She is all important—and if she is the right type of bitch (and the others should NOT be bred), then she can give you a great deal of assistance with these puppies. She should be loved; she must be happy; she should have extra, tender attentions as well as extra calcium. She must be made to feel very, very special—and when it is time for her to whelp, you MUST be there for this is a joint venture.

You begin with the puppies at birth, not waiting until that almost magical twenty-first day when the puppies first find the world opening up to all their senses. Touch, taste, and smell are somewhat operational at birth although most neo-natal behavior is a matter of reflex response. The newborn puppy is certainly concerned, however, with food and warmth—and so I supplement all my puppies with a bottle even when this is not indicated by the size of the litter or the condition of the bitch—feeling that by this bottle feeding you begin a regular, pleasurable human contact.

The tactile sensitivity of the tiny puppy is quite developed, and I like to handle my puppies constantly, beginning immediately to turn them gently on their backs. To lie on one's back is to be utterly defenseless and by making this a routine exercise pleasurable from the beginning, you start the bond that will become absolute trust. One can spot at this time the puppies that resist—and these will invariably be the same puppies who will have an initial freeze reaction to a new situation, the puppies with an additional emotional vulnerability that will need a bit more work along the way.

Do not, however, confuse sensitivity with shyness and instability. A sensitive and aware intelligence, a curiosity and a certain wariness are necessary for survival. A dog totally without caution or insensitive to his surroundings is not equipped to care for himself in any kind of living situation. The path from the crate to the exercise pen three times a day is NOT a living situation—and NO dog should be so impoverished as to think it is!

Up to the fourth week the routine is just daily contact and handling. I do the first haircut at three weeks—and every two weeks thereafter and never have any grooming problems. Raw meat is first fed from the fingers—and what a treat that is, again supporting the concept in that tiny head about pleasurable human contact. As the babies begin to eat out of a pan, I accustom them to my "puppy call"—I prefer a clucking noise with lots of "puppies, come"—and

212

within a few days this call brings them instantly and eagerly to their feet and you've gotten still another lesson across.

At four weeks I take the babies one by one and put them in a strange place. I leave them in the position they automatically assume—usually a sit—and move two feet away, coaxing with my puppy call. Up to this time the puppies have known only the place in which they were born and it is very interesting to see their reactions to totally new surroundings. Some puppies will vocalize immediately and constantly and, in my experience, these are the puppies that will continue to have a great deal to say throughout their lives. Some puppies back up rapidly in an escape reaction. Others, the more dependent types, come directly to the one familiar object: my shoes—and refuse to budge, while others pick themselves up and march off in a show of great independence.

I NEVER allow any of the puppies to become fearful. For the first time in their lives they are consciously faced with a totally new problem, and the experience that I want them to have is NOT fear but rather that of conquering their first anxiety and being reassured by human contact.

Even the simple training that I do with my puppies involves problem-solving behavior on their part; from a number of responses that they could make, they learn to select the one which most quickly brings them praise. At four weeks I start with light puppy collars and brief times in a crate—always in groups of two or more as isolation at this stage is very frightening. Between six and twelve weeks the real training begins. This training period establishes for the puppy a time when he is removed from the dominance of his mother and the interaction with his brothers and sisters and is taken off to be your very special dog, the center of your attention. I snap a light lead on the collar, under the chin, and the puppies usually trot right along. You never run into the resistance that you encounter if you put off lead training until three or four months. You support the puppy with your clucking noise or whatever sound you prefer—and because that sound has always meant "On your feet and good things coming," the puppy will be happy and willing to follow you. Once in a while you run into someone that is not going to cooperate and sits down solidly, refusing to budge. LET HIM SIT—he'll soon be bored with that! And when he moves, go right along with him. Soon enough he'll be going along with you.

Introduce the sit, the stand, the stay—always briefly and without force. When the puppy is headed for me anyway, I introduce the

CH. STARCHAK, C.D. GROWS UP:

"Chatter" at seven months.

At 14 months.

Three years old.

When the authors were novices at shows, no one ever told us to "call the show photographer." So all we have are snapshots to show our beloved Starchak.

"Come"—again no forcing, no dragging, no corrections—just suggestions about what the puppy was about to do anyway. At this point you will get the feeling that this baby is training you.

Now if all this sounds like I'm suggesting you make a lot of spoiled little darlings who get praised for doing exactly what they wanted to do anyway, let me correct that impression. I do indeed believe in discipline. An undisciplined dog is not a secure dog because he does not know what you want and constantly has to face your displeasure. Moreover, an undisciplined dog is a danger to himself. There are several stern corrections that I do impress upon these baby minds and there is no nonsense about it.

One of the most critical of these lessons is that regarding electric cords. I lay an inviting length of cord on the living room rug and bring the puppies in one by one. Invariably they go for the cord, and when they do, POW—a loud NO and a good shaking by the back of the neck. (This shaking by the back of the neck is instant canine communication for "Don't try that again.") I make this lesson a harsh one, knowing it must be effective once and for all. I also allow puppies to almost dash out the door on their own impulse—and quickly and firmly close the door right on them, holding them there for a few struggling seconds—and the babies generally wait for an invitation from then on.

We also give a lesson in cars—the puppies are allowed to wander in front of a car whose motor is running, and when the puppy gets to the critical spot, a loud blast on the horn is usually enough to convince him to avoid the front ends of cars whose motors are running.

If I had a swimming pool, I would also include a lesson on how to swim and how to find the steps; as it is, I can only warn new owners that this is their responsibility.

The word NO is completely eliminated from *teaching*. If the puppy is wiggling and refusing to stand, just keep repeating the Stand command, telling the puppy *what* you want, NOT telling him that he's not doing what you want. The NO is reserved for specific crimes like chewing on the couch, puddles on the rug, or biting ankles. The gnawing and biting that reaches a peak in the seven or eight week old puppy can be stopped quickly by returning the pressure on the jaw when the puppy takes your hand in his mouth. Immediately the puppy will only be interested in spitting you out, and if you hang on for another few seconds, he'll be so

Kahneetah of Whitecliff, by Ch. King Frost IV ex Schozophea of Whitecliff, pictured at left at 8 weeks of age, and at right at 18 months, scoring Winners Bitch at the State Fair in Dallas, Texas. Owned by Nancy Foster.

Children love dogs, and Samoyeds love children.

delighted to get you finally out of his mouth, that he will not be apt to chew on you again.

Once the puppy is going well on the lead, he is exposed to different kinds of terrain, flapping canvas, lawn mowers, and bicycles. He learns to go OVER small obstacles, go around others; he goes under ladders, in and out of doors, and up and down stairs. Inside the house he meets the vacuum cleaner, noisy pots and pans, electric trains, and assorted household confusions.

By this time he is lying happily and quietly on his back for a tummy rub, and it is a simple matter to teach him to lie on the grooming table with which he is already familar from his regular brushings. He has had his mouth examined constantly and been given his calcium pills regularly so that medication need never be a problem.

In the sixth week I teach the "Carry"—and it doesn't matter to me what object the puppy likes to walk around with—a ball, a glove, a stick—anything that delights a particular puppy enough to make him hold his head proudly and trot around on the lead showing off. You are building neck and head carriage control in the best possible way with this exercise and laying the groundwork for the retrieve which is the next lesson.

The retrieve is a most important exercise psychologically. It involves the puppy going away from you, off on his own towards an object he likes, and then returning with his treasure to share it and please you. Some puppies make an immediate and instinctive retrieve. The puppies that at four weeks reacted to the new surroundings by clutching your shoes will now be the puppies that love you so much they can't bear to leave you long enough to run after the ball. But they will learn—make the task as simple as possible. Run with them and pick the ball up and give it to them and praise them profusely for carrying it around. By the ninth or tenth week you will see a dramatic grasp of this exercise and should have a whole litter of willing retrievers.

Like any pack oriented animal, like man and like monkeys, dogs learn by example and imitation. In your kennel you probably have older dogs whose behavior is exemplary in one way or another; use these aunts and uncles to help you educate the babies. An older steady dog on a grooming table will quickly teach a youngster about "sitting out" and you reenforce the example by the already familiar "Stay" command. Take the puppy in the car with a calm

217

rider so the puppy learns to sit quietly and will wait patiently while you go into the store.

I also accustom the puppies to going around with me off leash. At this age they are still very dependent and will naturally follow. If the first freedom off leash doesn't occur until they are older, you will run into the smart alecs that run off to be chased and you've allowed an unnecessary bad habit to begin.

At ten weeks I separate the puppies into single crates for a nap every day, giving each an incredibly succulent round bone, trying to make the isolation as pleasant as possible. By three months all the puppies are happily sleeping alone at night in crates and naturally housebroken.

I keep mothers with puppies much longer than the general practice because I feel a good mother is such a good influence. Of course by six weeks, mothers do not care to be with their babies ALL the time, nor is it good for the puppies; but I do arrange it so that mothers and children spend some time together every day.

As for coat, I sacrifice it—on both mothers and puppies. Coat can always be grown, but puppyhood is a matter of weeks, at the most months, and this should be a time for playing and running and exercise emotionally and mentally as well as physically. The show puppy that is isolated at three months for the sake of coat is cheated out of a very important part of his life and you can't ever make it up to him. The business of showing comes soon enough, and I won't have my puppies robbed of their childhood just to make them into hairy child stars.

As the interaction between the puppies themselves increases, the order of dominance in the litter will become apparent. I try to minimize the competition and minimize the dominance. I keep more toys available than there are puppies. Dry food is available at all times and when the meat meals are served, I feed singly or in amiable groups of two. If fighting does occur, I shake both puppies by the scruff of the neck and insist on immediate friendly contact. I am not interested in terrier spirit and I do not want the fighting pattern to begin.

If one puppy is noticeably subordinate to all the others and becoming timid, I remove him before he comes to view defeat as inevitable. Often an older, outgoing puppy won't compete with him but take care of him instead and pass on some of his already established confidence. It is most important to avoid any sense of failure. One of the most interesting discoveries made at Jackson Laboratory

218

was that once a puppy has learned to fail, he becomes reluctant to try even a simple problem. Success seems to breed success, and what you want to accomplish is to convince the puppy that he is self-reliant and can handle the world around him.

My approach to all this is admittedly unscientific. I have no test cases; I don't withhold socialization from a control puppy to prove a point. These are not dogs in a laboratory, these are my babies—and I want the very best for every one of them. With every new litter I find different things that are helpful, a refinement of technique here and there, a new lesson that has come to mind.

It is not possible, of course, to foresee or simulate most of the new situations that your puppies will encounter in their new homes. But what you can do is give them a framework of reference: they will know they have encountered new situations in the past and been able to cope with them. You will have built their self-confidence to a point that they can adjust and take things in their stride. Because you protected them from failure during those sensitive weeks, they will not be imprisoned by doubt and anxiety but instead eager to tackle new things with confidence and assurance.

Shorewood's Teina Louise, "Teenie Bear," with her sire, Am. and Can. Ch. Sno-Bilt's Play Boy, "Little Bear," sled dogs owned by Lillian and Irving D. Slusser.

219

Nutrition

by Eileen Whitlock

(Mrs. Whitlock, a professor in Home Economics at the University of Tulsa, has been a breeder and owner of Samoyeds for many years.)

IN both the Arctic and the Antarctic, especially where the terrain is variable, unknown, or treacherous, the dog-drawn sledge still provides a valuable means of transport. Although these lands support a varied wild life, it is often necessary to travel long distances with no resources other than those that can be depoted or carried.

Fresh meat in the form of white whale, walrus, seal, or bear have always formed the basis of the northern dog's diet. Perry stressed that the dog's food was meat and meat alone. Croft suggested six pounds of fresh meat, with extra blubber if necessary, as the ideal daily diet during cold conditions. Lindsay emphasized the importance of feeding fresh meat before starting on long sledge journeys.

Dried fish, especially cod or halibut, has been widely used. Hawden estimated that two pounds of dried fish represented six pounds of fresh fish (which he felt was an adequate daily ration). Thomas recommended two or three pounds of dried fish with two pound cubes of blubber, though he felt that a full diet of seal meat is preferable.

Pemmican as a sledging ration is prepared both locally and commercially. It contains 66% protein and 33% fat and its preparation consists of lean beef, dried and pounded, mixed with fat. Although it is considered one of the best rations available, all authorities agree that it should be supplemented with fresh meat as frequently as possible. A diet of 100% pemmican usually results in persistent diarrhea.

On the trail the usual practice is to live off the land except for depoted rations. Fresh meat under those conditions can become a precarious luxury. Many explorers who have relied on game found themselves and their dogs in very short supply. Nansen, who used Samoyeds, was reduced to feeding dog to dog until he was forced to consume the remaining dogs himself.

Some authorities, however, maintain that no matter what he is fed, the husky dog appears to thrive. Some of the early explorers gave little thought to the problems of feeding their sledge animals which resulted directly in the failure of several of the expeditions. Scott, for example, who also used Samoyeds, admittedly was not an expert on the subject of dog handling. Food for the dogs on his Discovery expedition was a ration of 1½ pounds of deteriorating stock fish daily. For the later Terra Nova expedition the ration was ⅔ pound biscuit. When the dogs became "quarrelsome and fickle" he finally realized that they were underfed. After much soul searching, he decided to feed dog to dog. According to his reports, the "dogs never pulled their own weight and left each member of the party with an unconquerable aversion to the employment of the dogs in this ruthless fashion."

When Amundsen compared the unhappy experience of Scott's expeditions to his own, he determined that it was the master who had not understood the dogs. On his own expedition he provided seal meat and dried fish in addition to the pemmican, and all this was supplemented with fresh dog meat. Twenty-one of the fifty-two dogs returned from his expedition "bursting with health and putting on flesh."

Subsequent expeditions included those of Mawson, Shackleton, and Byrd, the British Grahamland Expedition, the Norwegian, British, and Swedish Expedition, and the Commonwealth Transantarctic Expedition, all stressed the importance of supplanting the diet with fresh seal meat and blubber whenever possible.

More detailed works on the nutritional requirements of sledge dogs began with the building of a permanent population of Antarctic sledge dogs in 1945. It is now estimated that adult working sledge dogs require between 3,000 and 8,000 kilocalories per day, dependent largely on the extent of their activity. Seal meat, although it is composed almost entirely of protein (33%) and fat (66%), still appears to be the ideal diet for sledge dogs.

However, in the United States today the typical Samoyed is not a sledge animal. His role is that of family caretaker, companion, and

221

member of the family. Therefore, his needs are not identical to those of the working sledge animal.

Comparatively few direct investigations of nutritional requirements of dogs under normal household conditions have been made. However, it is felt that for certain breeds of dogs the requirements are known with some precision because dogs have often been used in experiments designed to study the nutritional needs of man.

Most good quality dry type dog foods sold today meet the requirements for vitamins or exceed them. Since experimental animals have been reared on these diets through several generations with no ill effects, it would seem that most good quality commercial dry type foods are totally adequate to maintain optimal growth, reproduction performance, and resistance to the usual environmental stresses.

Most commercial dog foods are manufactured from a wide variety of ingredients. The average commercial dry type dog food is palatable to the Samoyed over extended periods and is adequate nutritionally. If the owner feels that supplementation is necessary, the addition of 100% meat and most by-products or fat is recommended. This supplementation does not necessarily add to the nutritive value of the food but it may improve palatability for some Samoyeds.

The fat content of most dry type dog foods is kept low by the manufacturer to increase the shelf life of the product. Therefore many Samoyed breeders add fat to the food in the form of bacon drippings or other meat drippings, particularly during periods of cold weather or heavy work. Too much fat can result in reduced food intake and therefore decreased intake of necessary nutrients. Vegetable oils as a supplement are not recommended as animal fats are more palatable to the dog and are more readily usable by him.

Beef, chicken, turkey, veal, lamb, and their by-products are excellent supplements. Horse meat may give chronic intestinal upsets to some Samoyeds or may result in persistent allergic reactions. Cooked liver in large quantities will cause diarrhea, as will pasteurized, homogenized cows milk. If eggs are added to the dog's diet, they should be cooked. The avidin in the uncooked egg white combines with the biotin in the dog's other foods, thus making the biotin unavailable and creating a biotin deficiency over a period of time. The dog's biotin requirement is much higher than man's.

Feeding the Samoyed is always a topic of much discussion. Probably as many methods exist as there are breeders. The Samoyed coat and boning seem to be the subject of many special diets designed specifically to grow coat or induce heavier boning. It is well to remember that genetics will determine the potential for your Samoyed. Feeding can only determine how near to the full potential he will reach. Food cannot improve any dog beyond his genetic capacity. The use of supplements in excess of the dog's needs and tolerance can actually be dangerous by upsetting the delicate metabolic balance of the dog's body. Some nutrients such as Vitamins A and D and the trace elements become toxic at high dosage levels. Therefore it is recommended that *diet supplementation be approached with caution.*

Another fallacy that is so popular with novice owners is that the dog is a carnivore, a meat eating animal. This does not refer to muscle meat alone such as hamburgers, steaks, and roasts. The dog in the wild, as the sledge animal in the Arctic and Antarctic, consumes the entire carcass, thus insuring himself of a well-balanced diet which cannot be obtained from muscle meat alone. Any dog fed only on hamburgers, steaks, or chops will not thrive.

Canned commercial dog foods usually vary quite widely in composition and nutritive value. Some are 100% meat and meat by-products while others contain very high percentages of cereals and water. Their content may be identical to dry type dog food with only water added.

Table scraps or food fed from the table will not harm the Samoyed. However, they may create a feeding problem when the Samoyed decides that human food is more to his liking than dog food. Also, table foods can add excessive amounts of carbohydrate to the diet, which may upset the balance of the body.

Vitamins and other supplements are recommended only during periods of rapid growth, during pregnancy and lactation, and during illness upon the advice of a veterinarian. At all times give only the recommended dosage. If more than one supplement is given at a time, do not duplicate a given nutrient.

Some Samoyeds easily become problem eaters. For their own sake it is important to deal quickly and at times harshly with them. First make sure that the failure to eat a certain food is not due to illness. Then offer your Samoyed only the food you want him to eat. Offer nothing else until he eats. He may refuse to eat for a few days but this will not hurt him. Dogs live in the wild for days without eating. Occasionally you will find a certain food your Sam simply does not like, but this is rare. Most Sams who have not been allowed to become problem eaters will eat most anything.

Special Care for Samoyeds

START from his puppyhood with daily observations. Look at his eyes. Open his mouth to look down his throat. Examine his teeth. This is training for both master and dog.

Periodically take his temperature with a rectal thermometer. Grease the bulb end with vasoline before inserting it gently and hold about 2 minutes. Normal is about 101°.

If you are with the dog daily, you are more able to observe abnormalities of appetite, energy, dull eyes, a funny cough, or indications that could be the forerunner of serious problems and may require a visit to his friend, your veterinarian.

With sound nutrition already described and adherence to cleanliness and definitely your attention, your Samoyed will thrive. Keep the dog clean through grooming and care and through careful attention to the cleanliness of his living quarters.

Fleas

As Jan Kauzlarich says, "Purebred dogs get them—the disgrace is keeping them."

"The flea hops on your dog and bites him, causing all sorts of unpleasant skin irritations and eczemas. After feasting on blood, the female drops off and lays her eggs in the dog's bedding, in the ground and kennels, and in the house. The larvae hatch, develop into adult fleas, and hop back on your dog to start the cycle again.

"Fleas on a dog can be killed by a pet flea spray or a bath using a flea soap. Many of the commercial flea soaps are too harsh for Samoyed skins, but Thionium Shampoo or Purina Shampoo are gentle, effective, and aid the skin to heal bites.

"The best tactic is to kill adult fleas and larvae *before* they get on your dog by spraying the yard and pens with an insecticide. Malathion or commercial sheep dip once a week is effective and non-irritating to the skin on dogs paws. A weak solution of Chlorox is good for saturating gravel, cement, and Dichondra as it is about the only thing, short of a blow torch, that will kill the tough flea egg."

Some General Hints

We are not the first to recommend that you depend on your veterinarian for proper diagnosis and treatment of your Samoyed. But there are a few helpful hints about home care that, with common sense, might save you a trip to your Samoyed's doctor; even your veterinarian would appreciate it. First, take the temperature, and with any rise or fall call your veterinarian. Otherwise—

Margaret Schlichting advises the following:

For upset stomachs: Charcoal biscuits—and keep the milk of magnesia handy.

For simple diarrhea: Use cooked rice instead of kibble.

For eye care: Boric acid solution and an opthalmic ointment such as sulfathiazole.

For cuts or wounds: Hydrogenperoxide followed by Terracortril spray (Pfizer). To stimulate hair growth and prevent scars apply castor oil once a day.

For ear trouble: Treat with Furacin powder or Terracortril spray after cleaning with alcohol on cotton swabs (gently). Others recommend Panalog Ointment, which is fine for any skin irritation.

For nerves from thunderstorms: An aspirin.

For an ounce of prevention: On returning home from a show, it is a good practice to wipe off feet with Lysol solution.

For a fussy eater: Cooked (boiled) tripe and rice are a good combination to help put on weight. Some use a tablespoon of clear gelatin to the drinking water each day.

For baths: Stuff ears with cotton and put a drop of olive oil in each eye to prevent irritation from soap, which should always be Ivory.

Doris McLaughlin adds:

For calloused elbows or hocks: Apply sulfathiazole cream, a baby oil, or Panalog Ointment.

For dogs that continually bite or chew: Mix equal parts of water and Tincture of Capsium and spray once a day. OR, try one capsule (five grains) powdered quinine with cold water or face cream and apply twice daily.

Summer Care

Regarding special care of Samoyeds during the hot summer months, *William H. Ivens, Jr., DVM,* writes: "In my opinion it is not essential to change the diet to any extent; a good, well balanced diet should do in hot as well as cold weather. However, the addition of any of the sour milk products to the daily schedule is sometimes wise. Sour milk, buttermilk, or cottage cheese will do; the most effective is acidophilus milk, which has merely a greater concentration of the active organisms than the former have. Tomato juice, about one half cup per day, is also good. Merely mix it in with other foods. In the average dog, a diet of straight meat is sometimes conducive to moist eczema in hot weather. One might also use a variety of basic meats, such as lamb, or fish, in place of the more widely used beef or horsemeat. With the occurrence of eczema, any dietary change may bring improvement."

During the fly season keep dogs in during the hot part of the day. Use insect repellant *on* the ear tips if necessary. The best treatment is prevention of flies biting the ear tips.

Drop Ears

Ears usually come up, but if you are impatient and want to help, wait until after their teething, about four months. *Barbara Hayward* of San Antonio suggests the following method, recommended by her veterinarian: Buy Kire-felt at your druggist. A brand name is Dr. Scholl. Cut it to the desired shape of the ear. Peel the plastic off the adhesive back and tape it into the insides of the ear or ears. Then tape the entire ear around with adhesive tape and leave it on

What'll you have—Samoyeds stand ready to serve.

Ch. Happi's story has Princess Penni rolling with laughter.—Courtesy, C. P. Tiers, Tulsa, Okla.

for five to ten days. It's important that the ear be held absolutely erect. Repeat the "bandaging" if necessary until the muscle is strengthened so the pup will hold it up by himself.

If the drop ear is prevalent in the whole litter or in several litters of the same stock, one had better look to a change of bloodlines to eliminate this serious fault, for although the standard does not say a drop ear is a disqualification, it does say the ears shall be erect. Ears should be erect before the dog is shown. It is not a universal problem, but breeders must be aware and eliminate the fault by selection of stock throwing no soft or drop ears.

227

Inspired by the photo above, of a Samoyed playing on a Sherman Clay piano and singing on the radio some thirty years ago, 6-months-old Tsiulikagta Kara Sun lifts his head in song for owner Nancy Foster in Texas.

Dogs In Cars

Traveling in automobiles or planes requires precaution for the safety of your Samoyed. Adequate ventilation is a necessity, of course. Dogs left in cars without enough air, or with insufficient air, have perished—as they have in planes from incorrect loading or whatever.

Crates

A crate is a prerequisite to safety. In the car your dog is comfortable and windows may be opened wider for he won't be jumping out to follow you. A crate is indispensable for the Samoyed bathed, groomed, and ready for the show. It is HIS place, and he likes it. It does help to keep him clean. If his crate is left on the floor with the door ajar, you will find your dog will walk in to lie down for a catnap. We like wire crates, not solid metal ones.

Worming

Recommended times for having stools checked by the vet: Four weeks, eight weeks, twelve weeks, six months, and one year. A twice yearly check for the adult Samoyed is adequate under normal conditions. Either have your veterinarian worm your dog or use *only* the medication he prescribes for the type of worms and the dosage he prescribes.

Immunization

Veterinarians vary on this subject, but suffice it to say your Samoyed must have shots for Distemper, Hepatitis, Leptospirosis, and Rabies at the proper times your vet advises.

Serum at 4 weeks and eight weeks.
Trivalent Vaccine at 12 weeks and one year.
Adult boosters at 6 months intervals for show or breeding stock, or once a year for pets.

Hip Dysplasia
by Joan Turkus Sheets, M.D.

> *(Dr. Sheets, together with her husband, James, is owner of the Best in Show winning Samoyed, Ch. Sam O'Khan's Chingis Khan.)*

There is a significant incidence of hip dysplasia in the Samoyed, as in other large breeds, and as breeders it behooves us to be aware

229

of this hereditary disease whose incidence can be decreased by selection.

Hip dysplasia is a hereditary malformation of the hip joint in which the normal relationship of the ball (femoral head) and socket (acetabulum) is disturbed. There is a poor fit between the two, and the joint is "loose." As a result of this joint instability, degenerative joint disease (osteoarthritis) usually develops.

The diagnosis of hip dysplasia can only be made radiographically, not on the basis of physical examination or gait. Affected animals may move quite well, particularly those with mild degrees of dysplasia. The hip joints are normal in all puppies at birth; the abnormalities appear with subsequent growth and development. A seriously affected animal may show radiographic changes at 10–12 weeks. In 90% of cases, the diagnosis may be confirmed at 6 months (many breeders do a screening film at this age). But a final diagnosis of normality cannot be made until skeletal maturity at approximately one year of age. Even at one year, there will be an occasional animal whose x-ray is inconclusive, requiring a repeat-radiograph 6–8 months later. It is most unfortunate that the diagnosis of hip dysplasia cannot be made earlier.

Hip dysplasia is an inherited, polygenic (the interaction of multiple genes) trait or disease involving both bone and muscle development. Because multiple genes are involved, its inheritance pattern is complex and not well worked out. No line is completely clear, and probably all Samoyeds are genetic carriers. Some lines do better than others; these are the ones whose breeders have been conscientiously x-raying and selecting dogs for a number of generations. At the present time, the breeding of a normal sire and dam still yields up to a 35% incidence of dysplasia in the offspring. (One normal parent and one near-normal: 41%. One normal parent and one dysplastic: 55–60%. Both parents dysplastic: 85–90%). And keep in mind that statistics are based on a large number, say 100 pups. Statistics are skewed in a numerically small litter—a 3 or 4 puppy litter may be all clear or all dysplastic. Genetics is a game of chance.

Although hip dysplasia is an inherited trait, the influence of environmental factors is not ruled out. There is still much room for research here. Meanwhile, we can practice some preventive medicine, which is important in pediatrics, be it human or canine. Pups should receive a good, nutritious diet, yet not be permitted to get fat and roly-poly. They should romp and play and go for walks on lead, but a forced exercise program (e.g. roadwork) should be

230

avoided until development has stabilized at about 6 months. puppies need good footing, so keep them off slippery surfaces and trim nails and pad hair. All this just makes good common sense.

Samoyed breeders are being encouraged to x-ray their breeding stock and submit the films to the Orthopedic Foundation for Animals (O.F.A.) for examination and certification. O.F.A. is a nonprofit research and teaching institution which was established to promote the control and eventual elimination of musculoskeletal diseases. Its first project is a hip dysplasia control program. An owner who wishes to have a dog certified as free of hip disease may obtain application form and instructions for submitting a pelvic radiograph from the Orthopedic Foundation for Animals. The radiograph is sent to O.F.A. with a ten dollar fee for examination. The x-ray is screened for diagnostic quality, then reviewed by a panel of three Board-certified veterinary radiologists, each of whom gives an independent opinion. A concensus opinion is prepared, and a report sent both to the owner and his veterinarian. A certificate of approval is issued if the dog has no rediographic evidence of hip disease. For those that do not qualify, a letter of explanation is sent.

Hip dysplasia is not a problem to be solved in one or two generations, and it is this fact that is so discouraging to novice breeders. From studies in other breeds, I can tell you that it takes from four to five generations of breeding normal dogs ("pedigree depth") to significantly decrease the incidence of hip dysplasia. Then we will start coming up with more "all clear" litters. In the meantime, the overall quality of the hip joints will increase. We will still have dysplasia, 1 or 2 or even 3 pups per litter, but it will be of the milder form. And these dogs who are usually "serviceably sound" can live out comfortable lives as pets.

It takes an objective and philosophical viewpoint to be a breeder, and we must take particular care to keep the hip dysplasia problem in proper perspective. One cannot breed for clear hips alone and throw away breed type, conformation, and temperament. Wouldn't that be ridiculous? Nor are normal hip joints the only aspect of soundness to consider in a breeding program. There are certainly dogs certified by O.F.A. that have poor rear ends (just clear hips) or who are poor specimens of the breed otherwise.

I applaud the efforts of our pioneer breeders who attacked the problem with the assistance of their local veterinarians—they have paved the way. If we pool our resources, we will, with O.F.A.'s help, solve the hip dysplasia problem faster and more efficiently.

231

Grooming

SAMOYEDS have *no doggy odor,* it's true, but they must be groomed for health and beauty. They do not need a bath to be clean. Dry baths are possible using only brushing and cornstarch, powdered magnesia or commercial powdered preparations which are rubbed through the coat and brushed out again. Some owners bathe their pets once a year for the Christmas season. The "show Samoyed" is bathed for shows and the treatment rivals any Poodle parlor.

Years ago, Hazel Dawes brought out the first aids to the ultimate in show grooming in the West. Lucile Miller, in Albuquerque, had a few tricks up her sleeve for putting down a Samoyed. In the East, Bernice Ashdown Samoyeds were never presented except in superb condition.

In the 1950s, the late *Helene Spathold* shared her knowledge graciously with her competitors and wrote up basic grooming instructions for friends and club bulletins. Samoyed Fanciers in Northern California have carried on her banner and mimeographed a collection of her worthwhile articles of instruction. We present some of them here to benefit all Samoyed owners, as Samoyed owners like to help each other. *LaVera Morgan* has added additional aids to grooming and so we combined them all and give you this potpourri:

Equipment needed: Grooming table, natural bristle or nylon brush, a long pin brush set in rubber (Hinds or St. Aubrey), coarse toothed comb, fine tooth comb (Resco or Twinco), Miller Forge pet nail clipper or Dremel electric nail trimmer outfit, scissors, and thinning shears.

Daily grooming is the ideal, but that is not often achieved, so we'll settle for every other day as a realistic goal. This may not mean you do a complete all over brushing. It would be better to do an area with thorough combing from the skin out than to skim the complete surface.

The purpose of brushing every other day is to maintain cleanliness and remove the loose and dead hair; to prevent matting and knotting of the silky hair, expecially behind the ears; and to tone the skin and stimulate new hair growth.

The method: With your left hand, part the coat as you move up the leg briskly combing small sections from the skin out. Develop your own pattern of reaching every part of the Sam on one side, then turn him over and repeat the same pattern. You may need an assistant to comb him underneath, and he may appreciate your using the bristle or nylon brush around his sensitive parts, and inside the legs.

Particular attention should be paid to the heavy ruff under his neck. It helps to train him to hang his head over the table, enabling you to get at the thick hair from his chin down the neck and front. Use a fine tooth comb to meticulously comb the head, elbows, and short hair on the legs and hocks, which need special attention.

After proceeding in one direction, you may find more loose hair by grooming in a different direction.

Be especially gentle on the tail. He does not like this part at all. "Sweet-talk" him and use a bristle brush, starting at the base and going around the tail, before you try the comb. Never yank the tail. Fold the tail over the back and brush the hair at the undertail base down into the pants. That is the last polish for the hindquarters.

Finally, use the pin brush vigorously, brushing against the grain of direction of the growth; then polish with the bristle brush, creating static electricity to help each hair stand up on end.

Exhibitors who are most proficient in putting down the show Sam recommend a complete grooming twice before the bath.

The Bath

Equipment needed: Ivory soap or any non-detergent base and biodegradable soap, opthalmic ointment, olive or mineral oil to put in eyes, cotton to to plug the ears, towels and wash cloth, the sun or a forced warm air dryer (human or special dog dryer), bathtub or large stall shower, and a spray attachment with a sturdy fastener for the outlet. On a hot day you may bathe him on a table in the yard if you are able to attach a hose to warm water.

Method: Lift Samoyed into tub on rubber mat footing. Place cotton in ears and ointment in eyes for their protection. Thoroughly wet the coat with lukewarm water with spray attachment.

First soaping: Apply shampoo in a line from the head to tip of tail, and in an X at the shoulders and hips. Scrub, scrub, scrub with fingers, especially on the elbows, hips, and feet. Rinse and rinse.

Second Sudsing: Same, with special care in rinsing. Watch especially the following difficult spots, which are mostly underneath: under the chin; underside of tail; inside the back legs; underside of tail down the pants; and the bottom of the feet. Use wash cloth on face and ears. Scrub teeth with brush and cleanser. Scale, if needed.

Drying: Use your hands to squeeze and slick down the body to remove the excess water from the coat. Remove Samoyed to area where he can shake himself well. Towel dry with many towels, rubbing briskly back and forth. The dog will normally shake often.

Place on grooming table for blower drying with hot air. It takes from 36 to 48 hours to dry an adult Samoyed in full coat, so provide some clean, draft free quarters, preferably in the house. We consider the crate indispensable at this time.

When thoroughly dry, comb as you did before the bath. It will be easier now. Before he steps out for his showing, whether it be a family reunion or a dog show, polish with the following: Comb with the fine tooth comb on the thick furred head. Brush with pin or bristle *up* and *out* on the ruff, chest, shoulders, and leg featherings; brush *down* and *out* on the belly fringes, thighs, pants, shoulders to elbow, and inside legs. Fluff the tail by holding tip and brush away from you starting at the base and working up to tip.

Trimming

Hocks: Use thinning shears to cut the excess hair on the back sides of the hocks to look natural and uncut.

Around feet: Do not overtrim, just neaten the foot. Do not make it appear catfooted or your Sam may appear unbalanced without sufficient underpinnings.

Whiskers: A personal preference whether to trim or not. Same

Grooming—before and after. Sayan's Chuckataw Tymba (by Ch. Sayan of Woodland) with owner Steve Skrobiszewski.

with scissor trimming the edge of the lip line. This may improve the smile and show more contrast.

Cut nails: Use clippers. Long nails will cause arched toes to become splayed and spoil otherwise good feet.

PUPPIES should not be bathed until they are six months old. Brushing or dry cleaning methods with brushing are sufficient. We recommend using powdered magnesia on six-week-old puppies instead of any boric acid product, which sometimes includes baby powders. Boric acid is poisonous.

For extreme stains on older Samoyeds you may try this *with caution:* First thoroughly groom, bathe, and dry Samoyed. Prepare equal parts of carbonate precipitated merck (powdered chalk) or cornstarch and twenty volume peroxide (or 4 oz. Miss Clairol Creme Developer) into paste consistency. CAUTION: KEEP BOTH PREPARATION AND FUMES AWAY FROM OPEN ORIFICES SUCH AS EYES, EARS, NOSE, MOUTH, AND CUTS. Wear rubber gloves and apply with small brush or sponge to the outer edges of the coat only. Never touch his skin. Leave on three or four hours or until dry and powdered and brush and vacuum out every bit! Do not let him lick the paste or powder. You may prefer to take your Samoyed to a grooming shop. Just make sure they know about Samoyeds, and caution them not to overtrim, as they often want to do.

After all these instructions, we might add that nothing takes the place of consistency in care, good health, and daily brushing. Excuse us while we groom a couple of Samoyeds.

Show Handling

by Bernice Helinski

THE time to prepare you and your Samoyed for that first show should begin shortly after his arrival in your home. Allow an adequate period for the puppy to adjust to the new surroundings. The novice handler can use this brief period to begin his education on dog shows.

1. Write the American Kennel Club, 51 Madison Avenue, New York, New York 10010 for the free booklet "Rules Applying to Registration and Dog Shows." Read it thoroughly at least once and then study particular sections. Keep it for reference. Amendments appear in the *AKC Gazette*.
2. Study the Breed Standard. This will enable you to evaluate your dog. Learn not only about your dog's virtues, but also the faults according to the Standard. Each dog does have faults. Knowing these will be of value to you in the show ring so you may avoid calling attention to the faults by poor handling.
3. Attend Sanctioned Matches and dog shows as a spectator; observe handlers and ask questions.
4. Inquire about Handling Classes in your area and attend. These classes will give your dog exposure to noise, other dogs, strange surroundings, and people. You will learn the basic principles of show handling.
5. Enter your dog in Match shows for practice. Classes will be the same but there is no "winners class" as there is in a point show. Point shows award points to the Winners Dog and Winners Bitch toward championships.

Ch. Samovar of the Igloo, C. D., by Silver Sean of Arctic Isle ex Countess Neenana of the Igloo. Bred by Verla Davis and owned by Mr. and Mrs. Alan Stevenson. Best of Breed over 71 entries at the first Specialty of the Samoyed Club of Los Angeles held with the California Associated Specialty Clubs in 1968. Judge, Mrs. Alstasia MacBain.

Ch. Tsiulikagta's Lady Barchenok, at right, owned by Nancy Foster, is Best of Breed at Austin, Texas 1968, while two of her offspring take puppy honors. Left, Silver Storm del Sol, owned by Anne and Archie Peil, First in Puppy Dogs, and (center) Kobi del Sol, owned by Norma and Barry Boecker, First in Puppy Bitches.

Conditioning and training your Samoyed for the show ring takes time and work on your part. Too often exhibitors overlook conditioning for health and beauty. Conditioning means a proper, well-balanced diet; maintaining a dog in good health and correct weight; proper care of teeth and toe nails; plenty of proper exercise to maintain good muscle tone. Consistent care of your dog's coat by frequent grooming is his beauty conditioning.

Training Your Dog
for Show

When beginning training, plan to spend a minimum of fifteen minutes a day, and with puppies it is preferable to have several five-minute periods of training per day. Then allow a few more minutes to *play* with your dog after the lesson period as a reward. Don't expect your dog to walk into a perfect show position automatically. You must teach him and he learns by *repetition*. Hands and voice play an important part in training your show dog. (Author's note: Also patience and consistency.)

Just how important are hands and what do they mean to your dog? He will learn *to stay* by hand signal. Your hand will hold the bait, either food or a squeaky toy, that aids in bringing out the alert, happy expression that your dog needs in the ring. With your hands you will place the dog's feet or legs into correct positions. (See illustrated charts for proper stance.) Accustom your dog to the feeling of hands examining each part of his body, especially around his muzzle and to showing his bite (how his teeth meet) ; and in the males be sure to have them accustomed to hands touching the testicles. Your dog will have the judges' hands going over him for examination. Last and most important, your hands are used to caress and pat him in praise.

With your voice, tell your Samoyed what you want him to do. Use one or two words only such as "Stand", "Stay", "Heel", or "Forward" when gaiting. Use praise such as "Good Boy", "Good Girl", to let him know he is pleasing you. (The use of the dog's name in the ring is taboo except in Obedience Trials.)

The TONE of your voice has great meaning to your Samoyed. He can detect when you are pleased, impatient, angry, or uncertain with him.

Debbie Seavers supervises roadwork for Ch. Karasea's Golden Girl and Ch. Samtara's Karion Frost. Roadwork is fine for adult Sams, but is not recommended for pups under one year. —*Photo, West Allis Star Newspaper, Wisconsin.*

Northwest stars. Left, Steffi Luna's Shanna Tsinuk, wh. 1967, by Am. and Can. Ch. Joli Tsinuk ex Steffi Luna's Kira Too. Owned by Ethel Stefanik. Right, Am. and Can. Ch. Steffi Luna's Troika of Sea Sun, wh. 1966, by Ch. Joli White Knight ex Bel-Ora's Kira-Vam. Owners, Rosemary and Melodee Jones.

239

A Few Do's and Don'ts at the Dog Show:

1. Before the judging of your breed, observe the judging of the breeds ahead of you by the judge who will be judging your breed. Note his ring procedure and you will know what is expected of you and your dog when your dog is judged.
2. Before entering the ring, be sure your armband obtained from the ring steward is on your left arm so the number is clearly visible to the judge.
3. As you enter the ring, have your dog under control on your left side and looking alert. The first impression the judge gets of your exhibit is important.
4. Remember you and your dog are working as a unit to bring out the best in the dog. ALL attention is to be on the dog, not on you, the handler. You will detract from your dog if you bend over him or allow too long leads to drape over him. By standing too closely to his side or allowing him to lean on you, you do not present him well. Hold the bait unobtrusively.
5. When gaiting, moving your dog at a trot, keeping him at an arms length on a *loose lead*.
6. Be sure to follow the judge's instructions. If you do not understand them or do not hear the judge, just ask him to repeat or clarify.
7. Last but not least, if you must correct your dog's behavior in the ring, do so inconspicuously.

Keep one eye on your dog and one eye on the judge. The finer points of handling come with experience.

Dress for the Ring

This is an active sport, if you are the handler. Dress appropriately. Heels are taboo. Never wear white shoes. In a picture (after that win) too many white feet show up, almost six. If the weather is unpredictable, you may need a selection of choices, for heat, sun, cold, and rain. That "the show goes on" is never more true in the theater than it is in the Dog Show.

240

CH. SILVER DUKE OF THE ROCKIES, wh. 1960 (in Denver), by Blizzard of the Rockies ex Tonya of Broken Bow. The first Samoyed to win a Group in the South, Ch. Silver Duke scored 43 Bests of Breed and 8 Group placements. Owned and shown by Mrs. Kathryn Tagliaferria, of Baton Rouge, La., now a licensed judge of the breed.

Mrs. Donna Yocom and her son, Mike, of Albuquerque, New Mexico, shown handling Sams to honors at Colorado in 1964 under judge Albert E. Van Court. At left, Ch. Chu San's Silver Folly (1959–1968) and right, Ch. Chu San's Princess Ghajar (1961–1966). Ghajar finished her championship at 9 months with all BOBs, all major points, and a Group placement.

And here's a switch—a dog handling a junior. May Day's Lil' Rascal (by Ch. White Krystal's Balalika ex May Day, C.D.) with two-months-old Lance Cowell.

Mardee Ward handling Helen King's Ch. Tilka's Tinka to win at Ventura, 1960.

242

Junior Handling

Many children go along for the ride while their parents engage in the sport of dogs, whether it be conformation showing or Obedience training and/or sledding. Many children will exhibit an interest in participating when they are *ready*. Some parents will push their children into dog activities. No matter how they arrive, the children may benefit in manifold ways.

Sportsmanship. If it is manifested in a good light by the parents, it will be learned in that light by the youth. If the reverse is true, it is unfortunate. This is the pattern of learning, though it may have its exceptions. Therefore, the adults in the dog game must teach the younger set the right way. That can be a challenge.

Often childless couples will find their young ones to love and teach in the dogs themselves. That very Samoyed may be the substitute for the wanted child. What a lucky Samoyed to be adopted into such a home!

The junior handlers (who used to be called to "children's handling" competition) learn to win and lose gracefully, we hope. They learn the proper care of canine life and how to communicate with a dumb animal who is often not so dumb. They meet nice people connected with animals. Instead of getting into trouble because they have nothing to relate to, nothing to be superior to, nothing to love, they may be found grooming and training their "show dog."

Professional Handlers

There may be a need for a professional handler. Not all people are able to handle animals. They will differ as much as you or I because we are all individuals. The Professional Handlers Association has high standards of ethics and they are what they are titled, "professional" in this field. They may be found through superintendents and dog magazines. Some may not be a member of the PHA but may be licensed for certain breeds by the American Kennel Club. That is like the seal of "Good Housekeeping." You may still want to talk to them, to size them up for yourselves, to see them handle dogs, to see their kennels or facilities. Fine, reputable handlers will welcome such an investigation.

Club Matches and Shows

Some people are joiners and some are not. What you do depends on what kind of a person you are fundamentally. Even if you have never liked social clubs or Church groups particularily, you might try a dog club. You can get a liberal education there. All of man's never liked social clubs or Church groups particularly, you might human relationships found in any group may be found there. You have to deal with people if you are in a club. It is no place for a hermit! There are few hermits, if any, who go to dog shows or join clubs even if they own a dog.

Would you believe that dog clubs are not just for dogs? Well, it is true and those who say "This is a dog club, let's keep the people out" are unrealistic. Constitutions, which are the rules of the game, are read and debated by people, not their dogs, even though the club is formed because of the interest in the breed or all breeds.

All activities relating to purebred dogs are supervised by the American Kennel Club. Know their rules and regulations and abide by them. A copy of the rules may be obtained by writing to the Secretary, American Kennel Club, 51 Madison Ave., New York, N.Y. 10010.

Specialty clubs are formed for the breed on the local scene. Parent clubs are formed for the breed on the national scope. Parent clubs work with the AKC for the protection of the breed, guarding the Standard and the activities influencing the breed.

All breed clubs are formed to hold AKC sanctioned events, which include one or two dog shows a year, usually on the same weekend of each year. This is when the breeders bring out the best they have planned and produced in their breed. This is when the novice dog owner attends his first show unless his Specialty club has been actively holding fun matches and sanctioned matches for his breed alone. This is when the club people put forth their best efforts to put "on a really big show." This is when the social activities may be combined with the competitive sport.

Samoyed people are beginning to become a part of this broader aspect of the dog game. Usually "Sammy people" stay within their own group, hardly casting an eye to any splendors of another breed not of their choice. While this may be considered meritorious and faithful, it is a type of tunnel vision we are glad to see waning as more Sammy people begin to join all breed clubs and look at breeds other than Samoyeds at a show or event. We do not fear that Samoyed people will choose any other breed because of "integration."

At her first match, Sassillie's Ursula, not yet 4-months-old, goes Best of Breed over 37 Sammies, and places in Group at Santa Ana Valley KC sanctioned match, January 1969. Ursula repeated a month later over 25 Sams (and a Group placing) at Hemet match. By Ch. Star's Boloff of Altai ex Ch. Williwaw's Frost River, bred by Carol Barnum, owned and handled by Joe Goss.

Do not hesitate to locate your local groups formed for education about dogs in general and your breed in particular. There is as much of a hobby to be had in clubs and their work as there is in enjoying your Samoyed.

Matches are of several kinds. Fun matches are for fun and are practices for more formal matches called Sanctioned matches.

Sanctioned matches are held to give the puppies and young dogs training in a ring situation; the owner-handlers practice in managing their dogs; club members practice in the various facets of putting on the show; apprenticing judges and stewards an opportunity to put their book learning into the live laboratory of actually judging the dogs and dealing with the people who are learning everything from handling to good sportsmanship. Seek out such advertised events and attend them, first as a spectator and then as a participant. There is growing trend to assess more weight to the importance of matches. We believe America is developing the dog sport to the level of the English, who provide Open shows (our matches without points) and Championship shows (our Point shows, awarding points toward championships) .

The sport of dog shows has so many parts to it, you will never learn them all to perfection. But just think—you can try for a lifetime. Shows give you a destination for travel and something to do when you get there. Condition your Samoyed, love your Samoyed, train and show your Samoyed, and take him to shows and it can make a whole life for you and your family. The most wonderful people in the world have become our friends through the "dog game" activities, which are all-inclusive.

245

Samoyed drill team under direction of Warren Stephens (at extreme left), Bea Large (3rd in line) and Vera Kroman (12th).

Obedience
(as related to the Samoyed)

by Warren Stephens

(Samoyed owner, AKC-licensed Obedience and breed judge)

O BEDIENCE as defined is the state or fact of being obedient. Obedient is "obeying," or the willingness to obey.

Today, the word *obedience* is more often associated with the training that the dog has received for purpose of precision necessary for competition. In reality, obedience is the simple training that dates back to man's first association with the canine family (dog) — the simple training that was so necessary to develop the companionship that both man and dog have enjoyed down through the ages.

Many books have been written on the procedures and/or arts necessary to follow in the training of the dog, but when they all have been reviewed, they all revert to the basic rules:

(1) To show
(2) To demand response
(3) To praise

To show and to demand response becomes more or less one act and may involve a degree of force on the trainer's part to attain results. Continuous repetition will, however, eliminate eventually the necessity for any force. Praising from the beginning, following any reaction by the dog is the most important part. The repetition of showing soon develops into an automatic reaction by the dog. The praise becomes the reward the dog expects and it becomes his pleasure to please. In all animals, and the Samoyed is no exception, there is a certain amount of obedience bred into the animal. Many

247

other acts of obedience are taught by the parent from the day of birth, and many other acts of obedience are within the capabilities of the animal, but require man's direction in developing. I might add that these directions are for man's personal purposes, such as for protection, herding, retrieving, hunting, etc., and probably more important than all other, as a companion for man.

Today's society demands that the dog must have a certain degree of training in obedience to make him acceptable to society and to be able to live in the confines of our cities, in the close association with people and other animals to which man subjects them.

As I have read many times, and have been told by many people "I have yet to find the dog that will make any attempt to bring man down to his level." All of them seek, to the best of their ability, to attain the level we, as men, have reached.

It is very true of the dog, as it is of men, that there are some that learn more easily and more rapidly; there are some that are capable of displaying more perfection. The physical conformation of some breeds make precision difficult, but all, given the opportunity, have the desire to learn.

The Samoyed is not one of the easiest breeds to train, nor can it be classed as the hardest. The Samoyed does have a mind of its own and is slanted toward being a very independent individual—not in the sense of being mean, but more in the sense of being reserved (or, for lack of better words, just stubborn) in his first reactions to accepting directions from man.

All dogs do not respond to training in identical ways, just as all children do not respond to their schooling alike. Consequently each Samoyed must be considered individually, and the methods of training varied in order to produce the desired results. To some, the training is a game and a delightful pleasure; consequently, results are obtained with little or no difficulties. There are others, however, that display a degree of resentment (the degree may vary considerably) and training may become a challenge, and the basic methods must be altered from asking to demanding in order to obtain acceptable results.

The Samoyed is not a breed whose spirit can easily be broken by the implementation of some force on the part of the trainer to attain results; however, bear in mind that, as mentioned before, all animals to a certain extent are individualists. Therefore, a method acceptable and successful in the training of one may be rejected and very unsuccessful in the training of another. Professional advice should always be sought in resolving problems.

Ch. Snowline's Joli Shashan, C.D.X., first winner of the annual trophy for the outstanding Obedience Samoyed (for 1969), donated by the Juliet T. Goodrich Trust Fund, and awarded by the Samoyed Club of America. By Ch. Joli White Knight ex Ch. Lady Sasha of Kazan, C.D., Shashan was bred by Nancy and Laurel Alexander, and is owned by Mr. and Mrs. Thomas Mayfield of North Hollywood, California. Below Shashan is seen in the "Long Sit" exercise at an Obedience trial.

Utility Samoyed heads for tracking with tractor. Ch. White Barks Chief Snow Cloud, U.D. (kennelmate of Ch. White Bark's Misty Snow Maid, U.D.), owned and trained by Daniel J. Winn of New York.

Ch. Ivan Belaya of Taymylyr, C.D., by Ch. Kazan of Kentwood ex Ch. Trina of Taymylyr. Bred by Mr. and Mrs. Tuttle, and owned by Mr. and Mrs. John Chittum. Handled by Carol Chittum.

Ch. Joza of Mar-Vin-Lou, with Mrs. Virginia Belikoff of Indiana, visits a kindergarten to give a demonstration in Obedience.

Kobe's Nicole of Encino, C.D. completes her Obedience title, trained and shown by junior handler, Ann Marie Wheelock of Canoga Park, California.

Ken-Dor's Twilight of Saroma, U.D. By Ch. Ken-Dor's Sky Komish ex Ch. Ken-Dor's Princess Kim. Bred by Kenneth and Dorothy Kolb, and owned by Valerie Robbins of Renton, Washington.

Ch. Samoyland's Vojak, U.D. (1945–1952), the first Samoyed on the West Coast to win dual championship (Obedience and conformation). Trained by his owner, AKC-licensed professional handler, Tom Witcher of San Francisco, Vojak performed on TV and in benefit programs for handicapped children, service organizations, etc.

Companion dogs are companionable outside of the ring, too. Am. and Can. Ch. Kombo's Silver Prince, C.D., by Am. and Can. Ch. Tod-Acres Fang ex Can. Ch. Snow Ridge's Sonya. Bred and owned by Mr. and Mrs. Louis Weltzin, of Canada.

Ch. Major Bee, C.D.X. Dual champion, placed with the Top Ten Samoyeds (Phillips System) in 1965. Owned by Charles and Marjorie Van Ornum of Cincinnati.

The breeding of the Samoyed through the past years has developed the breed with an intelligence greater than the average breed and a good, sound, strong body, and, most important, made him a great companion for man. On the average, he is only too anxious to improve his abilities through obedience training. The Samoyed in his services to man asks only for companionship, good food, a little praise, and a lot of good loving care as his reward.

Daniel Winn of New York writes: "Samoyeds adapt readily to Obedience training when handled with love and understanding. Each Samoyed has a distinct personality and when being trained is to be approached in a manner peculiar to him alone. Some you have to command, some request, some plead with and some have to be worked with a mixture of firmness and gentleness to get the best results.

"The real secret to training is knowing your Samoyed. Most of them are full of tricks, and when you think you have everything figured out, they'll floor you with something entirely different. This is what makes training them so fascinating and rewarding. No matter how exasperated you may become while training, you always finish the session with a little more respect for the Sam, and a feeling of amusement at his antics."

Valerie Robbins says, "Like all dogs, the Samoyed loves to work for praise, but he is far more sensitive to correction than most other dogs. A correction when he does not realize he is wrong will produce sulkiness and an unwillingness to work. On no account should he be put grudgingly through his paces in such a situation. Better to cut the lesson short and end on a positive note."

253

Bob Ward drives a happy bunch: "Chatter," King, Witan, Raini and Skippy.

The Samoyed
as a Working Dog

J UST as the Morgan horses that we ride for pleasure are known
as the all-purpose horse, so are the Samoyeds admired as the all-
purpose dog. Beverly Ward of New York writes,

> The Morgan was equally at home pulling the plow on weekdays,
> taking the family to church by buggy, giving the little children
> rides on Sunday afternoon, participating in the races of yesteryear
> and was still a beautiful, proud horse with spirit, under the saddle. A
> majestic, noble animal, with the dependability to adapt himself to
> any task.
>
> Our Samoyed can and will pull a cart or a sled. He will be a
> hunter; sometimes, unfortunately, it is the neighbor's cat. He will
> herd, again, perhaps the neighbor's cat. He will do himself proud in
> Obedience, in his more serious moments. He will guard, although
> he prefers you do his biting for him. He will step into the show ring
> with all the spirit and beauty that anyone could want. He will be
> your companion, give you his coat off his back to keep you warm
> and all the while he will never allow life to become dull. Given a
> chance, most Samoyeds will do all these things, some better in some
> things, but they all excel in the last category.

If the Samoyed has a definite place outside the home or show
ring, it is as a multi-purpose sled dog somewhere between the
Siberian Husky and the Alaskan Malamute. The Samoyed is just a
bit larger than the Siberian and a bit smaller than the Malamute.
The Samoyed pulls just a bit more per day in freighting than the
Siberian; and while smaller than the Alaskan Malamute and not his
equal in heavy freighting, the Samoyed will travel faster and eat

less. The ability to eat like a Siberian means less food need be carried. This is borne out by their use by the Canadian Forest Ranger and Park Service. Until about 1961, the Canadian Rangers used St. Bernards to haul heavy loads into their snow-bound stations. *The Complete Saint Bernard* has a picture with the Saints and refers to the Samoyeds being used as point and lead dogs to break trail. Improved trucks and track-laying vehicles now carry bigger loads into the stations in the summer and fall, and the Samoyed has thus become the team dog for medium loads and messenger work.

Sledding

Activities outside the show ring bring many pleasant moments with people, and the insight you can gain about your dogs may be even more rewarding. The second Samoyed which owned us was named Ch. Starchak C.D. We called him Chatter because of the way he talked in the morning. While Chatter was successful in the show ring, it really was in other fields that he was most enjoyed. As a lead dog, he acquired the knack of judging the length of his team. Before making a turn, he would seem to look back and gauge the width needed to swing the team around a corner or tree. We actually believe that he did not like the sudden jerk and abrupt halt that came with wrapping the sled against a tree. Whatever his reason, it was amazing to watch him. This talent did not come to him at an early age, but at about five years. When you consider that he was in harness and competition at the age of twelve as a lead dog, there were many years of learning for us. This ability is not unusual for lead dogs. Lloyd Van Sickle had several, as did Bob Richardson with Siberians.

Once bitten by the hobby bug of sledding, you become a romanticist. It helps to also become an athlete. You meet people and see places you never knew existed, and begin to know your dogs in a different light and understand the structure, length of leg and grit that make such teamwork possible.

Some people maintain that dogs do not think, but are creatures of habit. Consider this incident. During a mail run from Ashton, Idaho to West Yellowstone Ranger Station, a distance of 64 miles, Lloyd Van Sickle lost the trail in a blizzard. After many attempts to find the road in eight feet of snow, Lloyd told Rex, the lead dog of

Rex of White Way.

his all-Samoyed team, to "Go home." Several near disastrous turns and stops later, Rex took off through the forest. (These sudden stops really create tangles in the lines when one is driving a hook-up of 15 dogs.) Rex began threading his way through the National Forest, leading the team with only a slight pause and cocking of his head now and then as if listening, and the team and Lloyd eventually reached Ashton, Idaho. But they came into town from the South instead of the North as would be usual from Yellowstone. We went out with Lloyd several times to look at the path which Rex had followed into town, but it just didn't make much sense to us. Determined to find out what Rex knew that we didn't, we took him out on a leash and tried the same thing over again. Finally, when

Picking up air mail in Idaho for fast delivery by dog team. Driver, Lloyd Van Sickle, trainer for Mason White Way Samoyed team. In lead, Rex of White Way.

257

"Here they come!" The Mason team in 1948. Rex of White Way in lead of fifteen.

off the main traveled path and with repeated commands, "Go home," he finally cocked his head, listened, and took off at a trot in the still deep snow. Thankfully, as we were running behind in deep snow, he stopped and cocked his head as if listening again. This time we listened. We heard the humming and crackling of tiny voices, and realized that the noise was coming from the Forestry Telephone lines laid through the trees, rather than on regular telephone poles. We were convinced that Rex associated the humming of the lines with people, and by following the sound of the telephone lines into town we duplicated the "new" trail which he created that day.

This same Rex and his kennelmates were removed from the show bench of the Golden Gate Kennel Club in 1949 for a rescue mission. They were taken to the Donner Pass Area of the High Sierras, where a plane had been forced down in a heavy snow storm. Lloyd Van Sickle hooked two teams together to drag the small plane down to where a tracklaying jeep could attach to it.

At the San Mateo Kennel Club show in 1952, at the Bay Meadows Race Track, there was a race between five teams of dogs taken off the show bench following the breed judging. We became so confident that we hooked up all five teams into a twenty-five dog hook-up. A great problem arose when we neglected to take into account the fact that some of the ganglines and tug ropes were made of nylon. The fact that nylon stretches when under stress created difficulties as the dogs are hooked both by the neck lines and the rear tug lines. When the lines stretched we had to quickly lengthen lines to give the dogs space to work. The load that we were attempting to pull was a full-sized Ford automobile. It seemed as though we would have had no problem in moving it if the man made lines had been as strong as the dogs.

A complete summation of the activities of Rex of White Way with his trainer and driver Lloyd Van Sickle further shows the versatility and endurance of a trained dog. The itemized list does not list the three exhibitions a day at the Sportsman's Show, nor the three-a-day with the team pulling a calliope through the grounds at the San Diego Exposition, or the fact that this calliope had been pulled with four ponies and that nine dogs handled it very well. In his "off-time" Lloyd actually hauled mail for the United States Post Office between Ashton, Idaho, and West Yellowstone.

The longest dog team hook up of Samoyeds in the United States, with 24 dogs taken off the bench after the Specialty at San Mateo in 1952. At lead, Rex of White Way.

Rex was a first generation breeding of English imports through his imported father, Ch. White Way of Kobe, and his dam, Ch. Herdsman's Faith, sired by imported Spark of the Arctic. Rex was bred by Agnes Mason, and his plaque is inscribed:

1948 Winner of Childrens Race; Leader of Freight Race; Lead on U.S. Mail team; Leader of exhibition at the California State Fair.

1949 Leader of winning team at the Truckee Races; Led rescue team to plane crash at Truckee, California, pulling out 3 drowned planes; The Cedars rescue; Leader of team into Ever Valley snow removal rescue.

1950 Hollywood Sportsman's Show Exhibition; Nevada Day Parade, Carson City; March of Dimes Exhibit, San Francisco; Homecoming Parade University of California; Leader of runner-up team at the Truckee Races.

1951 Leader of Winning team at San Mateo Show and leader of 25-dog team pictured here.

1952 Removed from bench of Golden Gate Kennel Club Show to take doctors to snowbound train in the Sierra Mountains.

1953 Led a team of Targhee hounds to win the West Yellowstone Dog Derby; Broke the world record weight pulling contest with 1870 pounds. Worked as leader in team pulling 600 pound loads to repair Donner Lake piers in winter emergency; Movie work and guard duty for John Wayne on location for *Islands in the Sky* motion picture.

1956 Winner of several events at the Big Bear Valley Sled Races; won several show points and one major.

1957 Died in August

The real mushing ability of the Samoyeds was demonstrated February 1948 in the All-American Dog Derby at Ashton, Idaho.

Two of the drivers at the Idaho Derby were Bob Van Sickle and Lewis Price, who had been in the Sled Dog Section of the United States Army in World War II, under the command of Captain Major Godsol, the well-known all-breed dog show judge.

Six thousand spectators from thirty-three states cheered a team of five white beauties. Lou Price parachuted from an airplane over the starting line with the team and sled. The sled and team of Samoyeds came floating down from a 1400-foot altitude, and was then hooked up and driven in the race. This was a practical demonstration that airplanes can drop rescue crews in remote areas during winter.

During a sled dog team exhibition at the Harbor Cities Kennel Club in 1950, the "Sourdoughs" (a group of Alaskan veterans who get together to re-live the days of the Klondike) were having a convention in Long Beach, California. One, a small, wiry man approached the team with great interest and introduced himself as Leonhard Seppala. He was probably the greatest and best known of all sled dog drivers in the history of sledding. He organized the Race to Nome with the badly needed serum for a raging diphtheria epidemic, and a statue of his lead dog Balto, built with pennies collected by school children in America, stands in Central Park in New York City. Seppala related that Balto really was not his regular lead dog. Togo was his favorite lead dog, and with him he had won so many races. Balto belonged to Leonhard Seppala, but was a freighting dog who usually ran at point which is behind the lead dog. The serum run was really made with a series of six teams and drivers which Seppala helped to set up, and many of his stable of 122 dogs were the ones used in the various teams. Used as the lead dog on the last relay with the serum, Balto thereby received the total credit. To us the most interesting fact of Seppala was his devotion to purebred dogs in his teams. He used Siberian Huskies, and had a preference for white ones when he could manage it.

Coincidentally, Seppala was in partnership with Mrs. Margaret Ricker with a kennel of Samoyeds and Siberians in New Hampshire in the 1920s. Mrs. Ricker married the son of Fridtjof Nansen, the man who first really brought the Samoyed dog to the notice of the explorers in the 1890s.

Leonhard Seppala continued his interest in Northern Dogs until his death in 1967. He officiated at Sled Dog Races in and near Mt. Rainier, Washington, where he lived. His Bow Lake Kennels were well-known to all Northern Dog owners.

Training a Sled Dog

To train your dog to harness, you first need a lead dog or "pilot." If you are to work only one dog he needs to be a lead dog. When the final goal is a complete team, you must have a good lead dog for safety and your own physical comfort. An accompolished leader will eliminate much running in the snow by the driver to straighten harnesses. A well trained leader requires fewer commands, and there is less confusion in crowded or noisy situations.

Start with a fifteen or twenty foot training lead, and permit the dog to walk out in front of you. Use either the training harness as illustrated or the pulling harness of the Siwash type. Do not use a choke chain collar, but do use a leather or solid no-slip type. You do not want to confuse this training with show or obedience.

Make the work pleasant, for you want to develop a willing worker. Once your dog begins to start out on his own in front of you, encourage him with commands of "Hi, Hi," or "All right, All right." The command of "Mush" is largely one of fiction. It is not a sharp enough command—probably as it started with the French word "Marche" it was guttural enough, but not as "Mush." Many drivers begin to add their own variations in commands, which is a great aid if one later participates in sled races with other teams. By using different words your team will not then respond to commands of other drivers.

Traditionally sled dogs have been trained by other sled dogs. Lead dogs have been trained by other lead dogs. Today that is not feasible for most owners. Because of the speed with which a dog moves, a bicycle is an excellent aid to the training of a lead dog. Command "Hi" and whistle to start. At the beginning, it is a good idea to give a command whenever the dog begins to do something, for this will associate the action with the command. The one independent action which you must not permit is stopping. Always stop a dog or a team before they get tired and stop of their own will.

Assuming that you now have a dog which will lead while you are riding a bicycle, permit him to go ahead on the lead until he is pulling you. Maintain a steady pace by the use of the brake to create just enough pull to keep your tug line taut. Take advantage of every fork or turn in the road which your dog comes to, to begin the commands, "Gee" for right, and "Haw" for left. Many times you will have to jerk the dog to the right or left while giving the commands. Always give praise to him for success even if you had to

"There they go!" Notice rear gait, and tree bar of harness attached to tug line making the gear comfortable.

Racing in the East. Al Riese of Golden, N.Y. and R. H. Ward
of Gasport, N.Y. combine sons of Kobe's Oni-Agra Chief of
Encino and Elkenglo's Plumber.

Kobe's Oni-Agra Chief of Encino, a lead dog at the
Oni-Agra Kennels of Ralph and Beverly Ward, Gasport, N.Y. (we regret, no relation to the authors).
Chief, a double great grandson of Rex of White Way,
was bred by Mrs. Margaret Tucker.

do all of the turning. This system of jerking for right and left becomes valuable if you can settle for one jerk for right or "Gee" and two jerks for left or "Haw." This, along with the whistling to start, will be a help when you have many dogs and the leader cannot hear your commands. Do not rush your dog by placing other dogs behind him as soon as he begins to obey commands. Work the dog for several seeks by himself and then only add one or two dogs if he is strong enough to drag them around upon command.

To add the "Turn-a-bout," use the command "Gee" followed by another "Gee" when the dog has moved a few feet in the new direction. This creates a wide swinging turn which is necessary to avoid injuring or running over the dogs in the team with the sled as it spins. Some drivers do command "Gee, Come Here," or "Haw, Come Here," but this does create quite a sharp about turn and often trouble. An about turn at a high speed or running is also dangerous.

You will find that your dog prefers to stand when you halt for a rest. This is a good habit to foster. Tell him "Stand Stay." If your halt is a long one, the command "Down" is necessary, for later when you are working a team, run-a-way teams are avoided if the team is trained to "Down." Your lead dog must be particularly good at the "Stand Stay," for you shall expand this to the command, "Hold It," when you are harnessing up the team. When you tell him to "Hold It," pull on his tug line and make him stay in position.

The command to "Whoa" and the reining in are the same as those used to stop a horse. A series of short jerks to throw the dogs off balance becomes their signal when voice commands cannot be heard in the wind and snow.

Once you have trained a lead dog he becomes the trainer for all successive leaders. Your point dogs which run behind the leaders most often learn the commands in one season's work. When a point dog shows promise of leading, merely lengthen the tug line until he is running alongside the leader. Gradual lengthening of the line will place the novice lead dog out in front. Many drivers have been successful with a double lead dog hook-up.

While most dogs may be trained for simple work as lead dogs, remember that a great one is rare. Sex is no determiner. A lead dog must be able to resist temptations of chasing other animals or being distracted. He must be able to outrun the majority of the team. He must be trainable to commands. Above all, the lead dog must like to work and run.

Lee Fishback's team working at Zima. At lead is Zima Shubah ("Shu"), with son Scotty at point position. Shu, pictured at left, was whelped in December, 1956. In working condition he was 62 pounds, 23¾ inches. From 1958 until 1962, Shu was leader of the best Arctic team at Big Bear. First over all-breeds racing. Shu is the only Samoyed lead dog to head a Husky team in all-breed competition, placing in the top four of almost every race he ran. First in lead dog competition at Big Bear, Ebbetts Pass and Tahoe (over entries from five Western states). And with it all, a dog of exceptional disposition. Owned by Lee and Mel Fishback of Nevada City, California.

Lloyd Bristol driving a Startinda team with Ch. Starchak's Witangemote at lead. Wintangamote and Ch. Princess Startinda, formed the foundation stock of Startinda Kennels, Reg. which has achieved the goal of an all-champion team.

Thus far we have been discussing the training of the lead dog, not really dog team driving. To drive a team we must know that, as in obedience work, the voice and manner of command is all important. A few suggestions which seem to help:

Limit each command to one word and as few syllables as possible.

Gather the team in readiness to start by calling the dogs' names sharply. Some drivers call "Hupp-Hupp" or "Now-Now." These must have a tone of eagerness or anticipation.

Command "All right" or "Hi" to start the team forward.

Reprimand an individual dog by calling his name sharply. Do not use a word that would reprimand the entire team.

Stop the team with a long drawn out "Whoa."

Animate your voice to each need. Remember that the dog responds to sounds and inflections rather than specific words. (Try your dog with his name spoken gruffly, then kindly.)

Major Rodman, of West Yellowstone, Montana, drove a team of Malamutes using a whistle and never a voice command. The team was gathered with a long whistle with a rising inflection. The dogs started with a series of short, sharp whistles. A right turn was signalled with one long blast and a jerk on the gangline, a left turn with two distinct blasts and two jerks on the gangline. Increased speed or rallying were accomplished with short sharp blasts repeated with enthusiasm.

Your training has begun with the lead dog. Then one or two dogs have been added to your beginning team. From this point on you will find that most of your effort and direction will be in training new dogs to add to your existing team. We have pictured here the tandem hook-up or double-line of two abreast with a single lead dog. This method of harnessing is most satisfactory as you will have a shorter over-all length of the team and it will thus be easier to handle in wooded or mountain areas, or amidst the crowds, parades, and traffic of our modern life.

Equipment for training is basically a harness and various types of lines and collars. The most versatile harness is the Siwash type as it may be used for training and working. There are many other types for racing but they do not give the control needed for newly trained dogs. The Siwash harness which you see pictured in this book may easily be made of webbing and sewn by hand or riveted. Approximately sixteen feet of webbing material is adequate for one dog.

Remember to fit an individual harness for each dog. Make all strain and pressure rest upon the shoulders, neck, and chest of the dog. Never permit pressure upon the throat or back. Allow the utmost freedom to both the forelegs and hindquarters. The use of the ring in the rear of the harness prevents tangles and the pulling sideways of the harness in action.

In training your new additions to the team, do not expect too much at first. Place your new dogs next to and behind an experienced dog if possible. Maintain a slow pace with new dogs in the team and stop immediately if a new dog is dragged or thrown off his feet. A dog once frightened is very difficult to train. Do not punish the new dog in harness, as he does not know what is expected. Beginners rarely pull their share of the load, so be content if they run freely along.

The question of: "How young may we start?" will vary from breed to breed and according to size within the breed. Generally puppies are started at the age of six to eight months. Do not expect him to pull. In fact, many drivers do not hook puppies in with a tug line, but just with the neck line. If possible, avoid placing puppies in the wheel position, just in front of the sled, as a wheel dog must be strong and stolid. Simple maneuvers are best when puppies and new dogs are in the team. Puppies will limit your length of training time to a few hours until they are at least ten months old.

While the dogs are important, the driver will create the happy team. By making the sled work fun and not allowing bad habits to develop, one trainer will be more successful than another. Most tangles and hurt dogs occur when a driver permits the sled to run up on the team, as the main gangline then becomes slack and even the best lead dog cannot maintain a straight team line. A good driver will move dogs around in a team, as some prefer or work better in one spot than another. The successful trainer does not punish a dog in the team, but only when the dog is out of it. Perhaps the one thing that distinguishes the good driver from the inept is that he drives his team from the rear without someone leading them.

Betty Allen drives Drifting Snow of Snow Ridge at lead, Polaris and Nodka at wheel. Son John drives two Sams at wheel, two Siberians at swing, and Irish Setter, Bing, at lead. John later won the Long Distance Sled Race at Big Bear Sled Dog Derby.

Tom Witt driving combined team from southern California at Ebbetts Pass race. Notice bend of stifle, reach of front legs, and use of tails in action (not tightly curled).

If your sled team training progresses beyond the pastime stage you may be working by yourself in isolated areas, and a few words of caution are needed.

Harnessing and unharnessing are times when great problems may occur unless you have a consistent system which the dogs understand. A good method is to fasten the main gangline to the sled and stretch it out upon the ground. Anchor your gee line to a post or stake in the ground. The gee line runs from the tug line ring to the driver, usually under the sled, and trails loosely. With the sled thus

Author's team pictured above, carried letter below in world championship race at Truckee, California, March 1949. Each driver carried similar envelope.

THE HUSKY AND MALEMUTE
They herald the growth of the Snowland
And progress is marked by their trail;
A railroad now goes where they brought out
The Truckee, Sacramento and Frisco mail.
He's first in the growth of the Northland
And without him this land would be lost,
For there's never a stream in this country
That the Husky and Malemute trail has not crossed
—Pat O'Cotter.

DOG TEAM COVER

This Letter Carried by Dog Team
During World Championship Race at Truckee, California

BOB WARD
DOG SLED DERBY
TRUCKEE, CAL

Sheriff on duty. Harry Johannson at Lake Tahoe, with Pretty Katrina at lead.

secured a runaway team is prevented. Now the leader is hitched
with the command "Stay," or "Hold It." This keeps the tug line
taut and prevents the remaining dogs from becoming tangled. With
all dogs harnessed, place the steadier dogs in the team first and
command, "Down" to each as they are hitched in place. Do not
hitch up a team too long before you intend to start, as the dogs'
natural eagerness to go will be lost.

In unharnessing a team, the sled must be again anchored from
the rear by fastening the gee line to a post or tree. It is interesting to
note that Leonhard Seppala carried a metal rod which he drove
through a hole in his brake lever, deep into the snow to hold his
team on every halt. Many drivers merely turn the sled on its side.
Unharnessing usually begins with the swing and point dogs, as the
wheel dogs cannot be very easily entangled with others as they are
fastened to the sled, and thus cannot go very far sideways or back-
wards. This is an excellent time to check pads of the feet and bodies
for chaffing from the harness.

271

Jiandi's Winds of Nepachee, bred by Mrs. Betty McHugh and owned by J. Jeffrey Bragg, of Toronto. The owners report: "Windy frequently accompanies us on jaunts in the Southern Ontario forest, and will carry 20 pounds or more of photographic equipment, lunch, rocks, or what have you for hours at a time. He enjoys packing, loves his pack (made from two Army surplus knapsacks) and jumps for joy when the pack is taken from its place in the closet. He is a true example of the Samoyed's willingness to work and his love of humanity."

Packing

Dog packing is as old as sledge team driving. Many of the natives of the north use their dogs to carry belongings over terrain which is too rough for sledding. There is practically no place a pack dog cannot go with a load.

Loads by the natives generally average one-half of the dog's weight. For week-end excursions to the mountains the hiking clubs of the Samoyed owners limit the weight to one-third of the dog's weight.

Training consists of learning to follow behind the hiker. A dog that has been taught to "Heel" is at a definite disadvantage upon a narrow trail. The command here is "Back," and the dog is taken out on a lead and tapped gently upon the nose until he remains in back. "Down," "Stay," and "Come," are of course very necessary for the protection of the small packs which the dogs carry.

The pack consists of two pouches, one on each side of the dog, held on by a breast strap and a belly strap. A dog is a loose skinned animal, and thus cannot be packed on the same principle as a horse. The pack must be balanced and stablized upon his back. For serious and heavy work a breeching strap is advisable to keep the pack from slipping forward.

When the pack is first used it is usual to load it with bulky and light loads such as straw, to accustom the dog to the art of missing trees and rocks with the projecting pack.

Everyone does not wish to work their dogs in harness and mush through the snow, and something should be said for other activities. There have been only two experiences known to us personally of using the Samoyed for hunting—once for ducks and the other for deer when it was legal to use dogs on a leash.

The dog that was used for retrieving ducks was purchased by the woman in the family because she wanted a dog at home when her husband went hunting with his Labrador Retriever. These people lived near Fresno, California, a great area for water fowl. The Samoyed was taken along first because there was no dog-sitter at home. He romped and played until a duck was brought down. In he plunged with the Labrador to get the duck, but the bird was carried downstream by the current. Jack, the Samoyed, didn't get

Diane Reise, junior driver with three Sams, the progeny of Elkenglo's Plumer and Mac's Snow Queen. First at Glenwood, N.Y. and at Buffalo Winter Carnival, 1964.

the duck. On the second downed bird, this two-year-old Samoyed took one look at the duck floating downstream, ran ahead down river, jumped in and retrieved the duck. Quite a time was had by all to get that first duck away from him, but by mid-morning Jack was bringing them in like a retriever. When Blackie, the Labrador, passed on, our duck hunting friend used a Samoyed to retrieve for the next seven years.

While the use of dogs on deer is forbidden in most states, a few states permit it with restrictions. Others permit it if the dog is on leash. Samoyeds make most unusual sounds when they "hit the trail." The sound is almost a baying, much like the singing of Norwegian Elkhounds.

The Samoyed's versatility extends to Seeing-Eye work. Mrs. Verla Davis of the Igloo Kennels donated a Samoyed dog to Hazel Hurst, of the Pasadena Seeing Eye Foundation. The dog not only passed through the entire course but was graduated and trained with a blind boy. He performed his work with great skill and lived out his life as a worker. Many Samoyeds were not used for this type of work because it was felt that the grooming was too much for the sightless handlers.

In the film industry, the Samoyed has had a limited career. In 1949 we were approached for a team by a large movie company, to be used for the film *Two Years in the North*. After five months of intense training, we had a team that worked very well. They did not require any leading nor cables to run them past the cameras. Lo and behold, when production was changed from color to black and white, it was found that the white dogs did not have sufficient contrast against the snow to show up well. It looked like ghosts pulling the sled. We tried dyes, but only the undercoat or wool took the dye and the white guard hair gave them an ethereal or frosted look. Needless to say we lost out to the Siberian Huskies with their color contrast.

Perhaps the only successful Samoyed film career was that of a puppy owned by Mr. and Mrs. Doug Lovegrove of California. In the Television Series *The Monroes,* a Great Pyrenees is used as the family dog. When the script called for a puppy to be introduced, it was found that a Great Pyrenees puppy was too large to look like a puppy. Mr. Carl Spitz, the well-known dean of all Hollywood animal trainers, called us for a Samoyed puppy. Teri's Teddy of Starchak, an eight-week-old Samoyed puppy was used as the stand-in. Teddy lasted until his ears began to stand erect. Then finis to a career, for who ever saw a Great Pyrenees with erect ears?

On television, the Samoyeds have occasionally been featured on Betty White's TV show, "Pet Set."

Sams have at least one notable sports star, as revealed in this story told us by Jean Baer, Baerstone Kennels.

When Don Snodgrass (son of Bill and Lucille Snodgrass, Mt. Morris, Ill., who have had Samoyeds since 1956 when they purchased Frostar's Samantha Queen from Estalene Beckman of Clayton, Ill.) went off to college, he took Lu Sam's Frosty Boy Bopper along with him. Bopper became an integral part of fraternity life at the Alpha Tau Omega house. When Don graduated, and was to take Bopper with him, he left behind as a successor, one of Bop's eight-weeks-old puppies—White Paws of Baerstone, or "Kusang."

During the football game between Purdue and the University of Illinois, with the cheers from the stadium wafting afar to the ATO house, "Kusang" decided he was missing out on something. His 23 inches, 65 pounds and high intelligence enabled him to free himself and head for the sounds. Through the streets, past the guards, into the stadium, and onto the field he sped—completely unnoticed until he dived at the ball, knocking it from the hands of the Illini. Purdue recovered, and went on to win the game.

Newspaper accounts hailed "Kusang" as "Purdue's Secret Weapon." He attended all the Big Ten games (on the sidelines, of course) and went on with the team to the Rose Bowl in 1964. He was adopted by Homer Cole, who upon graduation took him to Macon, Ill. to live, where "Kusang" still romps with his football in the yard.

When, with their family raised and away, Wade Hill—Staff Commodore of the California Yacht Club—and his wife, Robin, took to year-round adventurous living aboard their Cal 45, they found the Samoyed a bit large for this new environs. They turned to the boat dog, the Schipperke, upon the advice of the authors—who loyally rationalized that at least the Schip was a descendant of the Sam.

Really the only field in which the Samoyeds have failed is as attack dogs. During his army career the author visited the San Carlos Dog Training Center in California. Here he saw the Samoyeds being sent away to Camp Rimini, Montana, for use as sled dogs. Too few of them made worthwhile attack dogs.

Frank Bauer's Samoyeds assist newsboy delivering papers for Akron Beacon Journal.

Ch. Beta Sigma's Mufti, mascot of the Beta Sigma Chapter of Alpha Sigma Pgu at the University of Cinncinnati.

Movie star, Ch. Kazan of Kentwood ("Clancy the Clown"), wh. 1959, bred by Laura and Elva Edwards. With Lloyd Bristol's Startinda Samoyeds, "Clancy" was in the movie, "Lad, A Dog," in which all-breed judge Vincent Perry played—what else, a dog judge.

The sweater starts with the combings. Mrs. Agnes Mason combing the loose hair from Ch. Herdsman's Chattigan.

Bel-Ora's Maverik models finished cap made of Samoyed hair. The ornament was made from the long tail feathers by his owner, Ethel Stefanik.

Spinning Samoyed Wool

by Ethel Stefanik

S PINNING is one of the oldest handicrafts known to man. The spinning of Samoyed wool is a fascinating, rewarding and useful hobby. Strong and virtually weatherproof, it can be either knitted or woven, and many lovely garments can be made of it.

Since we want the spun wool to be as soft and fine as possible, it is best to use only the undercoat. If it happens to be a year that the dog sheds a lot of his guard hair, that should not be saved. It is too coarse, and makes the wool scratchy, though a little of it adds strength to the wool. The short hair from the legs should not be saved, as the fibers are too short in the staple. Very soiled wool is unpleasant to spin, though it can be washed before spinning if great care and many hours of working are taken with it. When the dog first begins to "blow" coat, he should be bathed, then the undercoat combed out and packed loosely in plastic bags or kept in a covered container.

In order to spin the wool, it must be carded, so any mats have to be thrown out. If the wool cannot be carded it cannot be spun. The wool is taken from the cards in what is called a "roleg" and it is in this state that it is spun. The small electric spinner is easier to use than the wheel, and for the novice spinner is the best type to get. After the wool is spun, it is taken off the bobbin to what is called a "swift." This should be of hardwood, and makes the "skein". It is then tied in four or five places to keep it from tangling, and is washed in a good mild soap. It will shrink a bit with the first washing, but will only shrink the once. It can be washed in quite hot water without harm.

279

A blue-ribbon winning sweater, spun of Samoyed hair by Mrs. Marion Seavers of West Allis, Wisconsin.

"It never shows dog hair," says Mrs. Vincent Duffy, pictured with her Samoyeds, Dondianes Siberian Ranook and Dondianes Czaruke, on the 8 × 10 foot rug she made of their hair. "After saving 10 pounds of the wooly combings from the undercoat of my dogs, I sent it to Martha Humphriss to be spun into 4-ply yarn. I had an awning company saw three strips of white canvas together. Since the rug is made for my octagonal dining room, I cut the edge to the shape of the room. This I bound with white tape.

When the yarn came I started tufting. Every ½ inch, I sewed through the canvas, and tied three 3-inch strands with each knot. At the finish, I brushed liquid rubber on the back, and placed the rug on a mat. It cleans well with detergent or dog cleaner, and seldom needs the vacuum."

Though many breeds of dogs have wool that can be spun, the advantage of wool from the Samoyed is that it has no color, and can then be dyed if one wishes to do so. Before being dyed, the wool has to be put through a process called "mordanting." When this is finished, it can be dyed with either natural dyes or any good commercial type dye. Many people prefer it in the natural white, however, and when made up it looks like no other wool.

Many of the Samoyed owners and fanciers spin the combings from their own dogs, while others may spin wool sent to them for you.

The present day spinning device is the fly spindle with an electric sewing machine motor and foot treadle which, although it is fast, still takes one hour to do one ounce (including carding and washing time too). It is said this is not a fast hobby or a money maker, but more like a labor of love.

The wool is put in an old nylon stocking and washed in a bathtub full of suds in warm water. The cards (pictured) for straightening out the fibers so they all go in one direction may be obtained from the American Wool Growers Association. When a large box is carded, the spinning may begin.

After three ounces or so are spun it is taken off the spindle bottom and put into a skein with tying in a couple of places. Then it is washed the second time when in the skein. This is called *scouring*.

Samoyed wool has only a small amount of oil in it. It can be dyed by using "Rit" or a natural dye such as black walnut, dandelion, or berries. Some set better if one ounce of alum is added to the dye bath of boiling water and about two pounds of the color.

Vera Messier, Candia Station, New Hampshire 03034, Lenora Sprock, Steamboat Springs, Nevada and Dean Turner of San Diego still spin raw Samoyed wool or hair. They prefer the wooly undercoat, which ought to be free from matts, burrs, and soil.

At best the process is slow and tedious. The price of the finished yarn is five dollars per ounce including postage and insurance. A pound of raw fiber may not yield a pound of finished yarn, for there is bound to be a certain amount of waste.

A finished sweater would average from fifty to seventy-five dollars. A coat would be about $150.00 from the woven material.

Contact any of our spinners direct. To send the Samoyed wool or combings, ship in a well constructed container such as a corrugated cardboard box or heavy bag.

Ch. Karasea's Silver Kim, by Am. and Can. Ch. Noatak of Silver Moon ex Can. Ch. Kamchatka's Princess Tamara. Bred by Mrs. Vera Johnson Gowdyk, and owned by Mr. and Mrs. Louis F. Bishop, III of New York City. Best in Show at Green Mountain KC 1966 under Mrs. G. B. St. George, with Bob Forsyth handling.

Ch. Star Nika Altai of Silver Moon, by Ch. Joli Knika ex Ch. Silver Moon. Bred by Mr. and Mrs. Robert Bowles, and owned by Lucile Miller of Albuquerque, N.M. Best in Show winner and sire of outstanding champions. Pictured in win under judge Albert E. VanCourt with Sally Terroux handling.

Appendix

Best in Show Winners

The following is a list of the Samoyeds that have won Best in Show at an AKC-licensed all-breed show. The name following the identification of the dog is that of the owner.

SWEET MISSY OF SAMMAR (Marshall)
 Toledo KC 1949
CH. PRINCESS SILVERTIPS OF KOBE (Ashdown)
 Central Maine KC 1951
 Green Mountain KC 1953
CH. VERLA'S PRINCE COMET (Hill)
 San Gabriel KC 1951
CH. SILVER SPRAY OF WYCHWOOD (Ashdown)
 Troy KC 1952
 Brooklyn KC 1952
 First Co. Governor's Foot Guard Assn. 1953
 Eastern DC 1953
 Worcester KC 1954
CH. SILVERTIPS SCION OF WYCHWOOD (Ashdown)
 Tuxedo KC 1953
 South Shore KC 1954
 Rhode Island KC 1955
CH. VRAI OF LUCKY DEE (Dawes)
 Seattle KC 1954
 Santa Kruz KC 1954
CH. AMERIC OF KOBE (Ashdown)
 Tonawanda Valley KC 1957
 South Jersey KC 1957
 Chester Valley KC 1958
 Elm City KC 1959
CH. SNOWSHOE III (Dawson)
 Portland KC 1957
MINISHKA, CDX (Dyer)
 Intermountain KC 1959

CH. YUROK OF WHITECLIFF (Blank-Matheron)
  Inland Empire KA 1959
  Idaho Capital City KC 1959
  Harbor Cities KC 1959
  Vancouver KC 1959
  Oakland KC 1960
CH. WINTERLAND'S KIM (Heagy)
  Sioux Valley KC 1960
CH. JOLI KNIKA (Cabe)
  Colorado KC 1963
CH. BAUZUHL OF CARIBOU (Ralphs-Dyer)
  Mt. Ogden KC 1964
CH. SAROMA'S POLAR PRINCE (Beal)
  Longview-Kelso KC 1964
CH. KARASEA'S SILVER NIKKI (Gowdywk)
  Whidbey Island KC 1964
  Longview-Kelso KC 1965
  Peninsula DFC 1965
CH. KARASEA'S SILVER KIM (Bishop)
  Green Mountain DC 1966
CH. SAM O'KHAN'S CHINGIS KHAN (Sheets)
  Lackawanna KC 1966
  Perkiomen Valley KC 1966
  Elm City KC 1967
  Bronx County KC 1967
  Blennerhassett KC 1968
CH. STAR NIKA ALTAI OF SILVER MOON (Miller)
  Heart of the Plains KC 1967
CH. LULHAVEN'S NUNATAT (Lutham)
  Lewis-Clark KC 1969
CH. LULHAVEN'S SNOWMIST ENSIGN (Hyatt-White)
  Polouse Hills KC 1970
  Inland Empire KC 1970
  Yakima Valley KC 1971
  Olympic KC 1971
CH. MAUR-MIK'S KIM (Alred)
  Grand Rapids KC 1970

284

Ch. Muushka, C.D.X. By Ch. Williwaw, C.D.X. ex Lace, C.D. Bred by Tom Ralphs, and owned by Joe and Mabel Dyer, Caribou Kennels, Idaho. Best in Show at Intermountain KC, 1960.

Am. Can. Berm. and Bahamian Ch. Karasea's Silver Nikki, full litter brother to Ch. Karasea's Silver Kim. Best in Show winner, and winner of the 1965 A. E. Mason Trophy. Nikki acquired all four championships in one year, plus a record of many group wins. Bred and owned by Mrs. Vera Johnson Gowdyk, and handled by Pat Tripp.

Am. and Can. Ch. Saroma's Polar Prince, by Am. and Can. Ch. Tod-Acres Fang ex Ch. Leordan's Taku Glacier. Best in Show Samoyed and 1964 winner of the A. E. Mason Trophy. Owned by Mr. and Mrs. Richard Beal, of Mercer Island, Washington.

Ch. Vrai of Lucky Dee, wh. 1950, by Ch. Lucky Labon Nahum ex Ch. Faustina Fauna. A litter sister to Ch. Modoc of Lucky Dee. Ch. Vrai had two 1954 Bests in Show and was the 1967 Tucker Brood Bitch Trophy winner. Owned by Bill and Hazel Dawes, Cupertino, California, and handled by Jack Carson.

Ch. Bauzuhl of Caribou, son of BIS winner Ch. Muushka, C.D.X. ex Ch. Shondra of Drayalene. Best in Show at 7 months of age under judge Vincent Perry. Sire of five champions. Owned by Mr. and Mrs. Joe Dyer.

Am. and Can. Ch. Lulhaven's Nunatat, Best in Show winning son of BIS winner Ch. Saroma's Polar Prince. Owned by Clyde N. Lulham and Sybil R. Spaugh of Yakima, Washington.

Samoyed Club of America Specialty Winners

NOTE: First line of listing identifies date, show at which held, number of entries and judge. Name of owner is in parentheses following the dog's name.

1. Sept. 14, 1929—Tuxedo KC—40—Louis Smirnow
   BOB—Ch. Tiger Boy of Norka (Mr. and Mrs. H. Reid)
2. Sept. 13, 1930—Tuxedo KC—12—Mrs. F. Romer
   BOB—Ch. Storm Cloud (Mrs. E. Hudson)
3. May 29, 1937—Morris & Essex KC—19—Louis Smirnow
   BOB—Krasan (Msgr. R. F. Keegan)
4. May 28, 1938—Morris & Essex KC—43—Msgr. Keegan
   BOB—Ch. Norka's Moguiski (A. V. W. Foster)
5. May 27, 1939—Morris & Essex KC—31—Enno Meyer
   BOB—Ch. Prince Kofski (B. M. Ruick)
6. May 25, 1940—Morris & Essex KC—20—Ruth Stillman
   BOB—Ch. Prince Igor II (Msgr. Keegan)
7. May 31, 1941—Morris & Essex KC—29—C. H. Chamberlain
   BOB—Ch. Alastasia's Rukavitza (A. L. McBain)
8. March 28, 1943—International KC of Chicago
   Cancelled because of war regulations.
9. Oct. 19, 1946—International KC of Chicago—46—A. Rosenberg
   BOB—Ch. Frolnick of Sammar (J. J. Marshall) —on to GR1
10. June 8, 1947—Pasadena KC—47—Dr. Richard Walt
    BOB—Ch. Staryvna of Snowland (Mr. and Mrs. R. H. Ward)
11. Apr. 25, 1948—Los Angeles KC—35—Dr. Wm. H. Ivens
    BOB—Ch. Gay of White Way (Agnes and Aljean Mason)
12. June 25, 1940—Harbor Cities KC—110—Chris Knudsen
    BOB—Ch. Verla's Prince Comet (Shirley Hill) —on to GR4
13. Aug. 3, 1952—San Mateo KC—78—J. W. Cross
    BOB—Ch. Verla's Prince Comet (Shirley Hill)
14. Sept. 11, 1953—Westchester KC—40—Ruth Stillman
    BOB—Ch. Zor of Altai (A. V. Ruth)
15. Apr. 13, 1954—International KC of Chicago—51—E. D. McQuown
    BOB—Ch. King of Wal-Lynn (E. M. Smith)
16. Sept. 11, 1955—Westchester KC—16—C. H. Chamberlain
    BOB—Ch. Tazson's Snow Flicka (A. E. Ulfeng)
17. Nov. 26, 1955—Los Angeles KC—83—Alf Loveridge
    BOB—Ch. Polaris Pan (G. Klein and M. Mueller)
18. Feb. 25, 1956—Seattle KC—35—A. E. Van Court
    BOB—Ch. Bunky Jr. of Lucky Dee (Mr. and Mrs. B. P. Dawes) —GR2
19. Sept. 9, 1956—Mason & Dixon KC—22—Mrs. M. B. Meyer
    BOB—Ch. Nordly's Sammy (J. M. Doyle) —GR2
20. May 25, 1957—Monmouth KC—39—Chas. A. Swartz
    BOB—Ch. Nordly's Sammy (J. M. Doyle) —GR1, Best Am-bred in Show
21. Feb. 29, 1958—International KC of Chicago—49—W. H. Reeves
    BOB—Ch. Nordly's Sammy (J. M. Doyle)

Ch. Nordly's Sammy, winner of four national Specialties, in four parts of the country. By Am. and Can. Ch. Tazson ex Bluecrest Karenia. Owned by Mr. and Mrs. John Doyle, Doylestown, Pa.

Ch. Sayan of Woodland, three-time Specialty winner. Wh. 1964, by Ch. Kazan of Wentwood ex Snow Heather Radandt. Bred by J. M. and A. H. Radant, and owned by Joseph and Evelyn Kite, of California. Handled by Jack Dexter.

Am. and Can. Ch. Tazson's Snow Flicka, 1948–1963, by Am. and Can. Ch. Tazson ex Snowbelle. Specialty winner, 1965. Often BOS to her sire, "Snowsy" had two Group Firsts. Bred and owned by Ashbjorn and Borghild Ulfeng.

Am. and Can. Ch. Venturer of Kobe, 1967 Specialty winner —from the classes. Wh. 1965, by Silver Gleam of Kobe ex Koscena of Kobe. Imported and owned by Don and Arlene Jordan, Massachusetts.

Ch. Wynterkloud of Silver Moon, 1965 Specialty winner. Wh. 1962, by Am. and Can. Ch. Noatak of Silver Moon ex Winter's Windy of Ga-Les. Owned by John and Bernice Helinski, Colorado.

Am. and Can. Ch. Shaloon of Drayalene, 1965 Specialty winner. By Barceia's Shondi of Drayalene ex Silver Dede O'Snowridge. Bred by Elliot Colburn. Owned by Pinehill Kennels, Lee and Sandra Wacenske, of Spokane, Washington.

Ch. Snowpack Silver Melody of Kobe, 1965 Specialty winner at Ox Ridge under judge Alva Rosenberg. Undefeated in 20 breed showings, and winner of two Groups. Owned by Mrs. Bernice Ashdown, Wychwood Kennels.

Ch. Shondra of Drayalene, 1964 Specialty winner, litter sister of Am. and Can. Ch. Shaloon of Drayalene, and BOS to him at 1965 Specialty. Owners, Joe and Mabel Dyer of Idaho.

291

Ch. Zor of Altai, 1953 Specialty winner. Wh. 1949, by Zanik of Altai ex Zareena of Altai. Owned by Alta and Leroy Ruth.

Ch. Park-Cliffe Snowpack Sanorka, C.D., 1966 Specialty winner. Wh. 1962, by Ch. Park-Cliffe Snowpack Frost ex. Ch. Park-Cliffe Princess Maruca. Bred by Mildred S. Davis, and owned by James and Janice McGoldrick. (Pictured with bench chain, necessary equipment at a benched show.)

22. Feb. 22, 1959—Santa Clara KC—71—Major B. Godsol
    BOB—Ch. Nordly's Sammy (J. M. Doyle)
23. Oct. 2, 1960—Maria-Obispo KC—38—O. C. Harriman
    BOB—Ch. Shoshone of Whitecliff (Mrs. J. Blank)
24. Sept. 9, 1962—Westchester KC—32—C. H. Chamberlain
    BOB—Ch. Elkenglo's Dash O' Silver (E. L. Miller)
25. Apr. 6, 1963—International KC of Chicago—34—V. D. Johnson
    BOB—Ch. Winterland's Kim (Heagy)
26. May 31, 1964—Framingham DC—35—Mrs. N. Demidoff
    BOB—Ch. Sarges Silver Frost (R. N. and W. C. Parry)
27. 1st parent Samoyed Club of America separately-held Specialty
    July 24, 1964—Miramar Hotel, Montecito, Calif.—92—A. E. Van Court
    BOB—Ch. Shondra of Draylene (J. M. Dyer)
    BOS—Ch. Noatak of Silver Moon (R. J. Bowles)
28. Apr. 3, 1965—Western Pa. KA—22—Theodore Wurmser
    BOB—Ch. Winter Kloud of Silver Moon (J. A. Helinski)
29. 2nd separately-held SCA Specialty
    Aug. 20, 1965—Bellevue, Wash.—83—Virginia Keckler
    BOB—Ch. Shaloon of Draylene (L. R. Wacenske)
    BOS—Ch. Shondra of Draylene (J. M. Dyer)
30. Sept. 20, 1965—Colorado KC—34—Robert H. Ward
    BOB—Ch. Kenny's Blazer Boy of Caribou, CDX (D. Yocum)
31. Sept. 25, 1965—Ox Ridge KC—28—Alva Rosenberg
    BOB—Ch. Snowpack Silver Melody of Kobe (Ashdown)
32. Oct. 24, 1965—San Fernando KC—60—Forest N. Hall
    BOB—Ch. Danlyn's Silver Comet (L. L. Torres)
33. Mar. 6, 1966—Natl. Capitol KC—50—Mrs. L. W. Bonney
    BOB—Ch. Park-Cliffe Snowpack Sanorka, CD (McGoldrick)
34. 3rd separately-held SCA Specialty
    Sept. 24, 1966—Inglewood, Calif.—92—N. L. Kay
    BOB—Ch. Sayan of Woodland (J. and E. Kite)
    BOS—Ch. Tsarina of Lassen View (E. J. Burns)
    Puppy Sweepstakes (29) —Karshan
35. May 7, 1967—Trenton KC—28—Mrs. Eve Seeley
    BOB—Ch. Venturer of Kobe (Donald Jordan)
36. 4th separately-held SCA Specialty
    June 30, 1967—Madison, Wisconsin—47—Robert H. Ward
    BOB—Ch. Star Nika of Altai (Lucile Miller)
    BOS—Ch. Bradley's Powder Puff (C. and B. Bradley)
    Puppy Sweepstakes (9) —Baerstone's Kasij
37. 5th separately-held SCA Specialty
    Sept. 23, 1967—Inglewood, Calif.—71—Mrs. Helen Wittrig
    BOB—Ch. Sayan of Woodland (J. and E. Kite)
    BOS—Ch. Tei Juana Cayenne of Virburnum (L. L. Bill)
    Puppy Sweepstakes (19) —Almost Xmas Chatter

38. 6th separately-held SCA Specialty
   Sept. 13, 1969—Thousand Oaks, Calif.—94—Mrs. Joyce E. Cain
   BOB—Ch. Sayan of Woodland (J. and E. Kite)
   BOS—Ch. Hoti-Ami of Starchak (Mr. and Mrs. R. H. Ward)

39. 7th separately-held SCA Specialty
   Aug. 14, 1970—Renton, Wash.—150—Joseph Faigel
   BOB—Ch. Darius Karlak Cheetal (LaVera Morgan)
   BOS—Ch. Tsonoqua of Snow Ridge (Margo Gervostad)
40. Sept. 11, 1971—Somerset Hills KC—149—J. M. Cresap
   BOB—Ch. Elrond Czar of Rivendell, C.D. (E. and M. Gaffey)
   BOS—Ch. Babe's Gypsy Magic of Gro-Wil (H. E. and S. L. Dewey)

Ch. Darius Karlak Cheetal, by Ch. Darius King of Snow
Ridge ex Drayalene's Bunky. Winner of the 1970 Specialty
at Renton, Washington. Owned and handled by LaVera
and Dan Morgan.

294

Ch. Modoc of Lucky Dee receives special award from actress Lucille Ball for being the initial winner of the Charles Tucker Brood Bitch Trophy in 1954. Bred by Mr. and Mrs. B. P. Dawes, and owned by Mr. and Mrs. Roy Long.

The Trophy Winners

Until 1969 there had been four perpetual trophies offered annually to promote nationwide recognition of outstanding producers and show winners.

The trophies honoring top producers were the Charles Tucker Memorial Trophy for brood bitches and the Wimundstrev Trophy (offered by Miss Elizabeth Wyman) for stud dogs. Both trophies were awarded on the basis of points won toward championship by their get during the year, with added points for Group placings (4 for 1st, 3 for 2nd, 2 for 3rd and 1 for 4th), and a bonus 5 points for Best in Show. An extra ten points were added for each championship completed by the get.

The perpetual trophies offered to top winners were the A. E. Mason Memorial Trophy and the Champion Suzanne of White Way Memorial Trophy. The Mason Trophy was offered by a group of his friends, and was awarded to the top winning Samoyed, regardless of sex. The Ch. Suzanne Trophy was limited to bitches, and offered a 9-generation pedigree that included over 500 ancestors. The trophies were awarded to eligible dogs scoring the greatest number of points at AKC shows under a special scale. The Best of Breed winner acquired the points awarded for the day, provided there were at least three Samoyeds owned by three different owners in competition. If there were no points in the classes, at least one of the dogs defeated must have been a champion. Additional points were awarded for Group placements and Best in Show.

Ch. Silver Moon, with a puppy. At left is the A. E. Mason Trophy, won by her son Noatak (below), and at right, the Charles Tucker Brood Bitch Trophy, which Silver Moon won for 1963, 1964 and 1965. Owned by Robert and Bonita Bowles, Renton, Washington.

Am. and Can. Ch. Noatak of Silver Moon, wh. 1960 by Can. Ch. Polar Star's Nika Tillicum ex Ch. Silver Moon. Noatak, winner of the A. E. Mason Trophy for top winning Samoyed in 1963, was the Wimundstrev Stud Dog Trophy winner for four successive years—1965, 1966, 1967 and 1968. Bred and owned by Mr. and Mrs. Robert Bowles.

Tundra Princess Starya, 1960 and 1962 Tucker Brood Bitch Trophy Winner. By Ch. Frolnick of Sammar ex Tundra Princess Vicki. Owned by Estalene Beckman, of Illinois.

Tucker Brood Bitch Trophy Winners:

1953 Ch. Modoc of Lucky Dee (Mr. and Mrs. R. Long)
1954 Ch. Faustina Fauna (Mr. and Mrs. B. P. Dawes)
1955 Ch. Sparkle Plenty of Arbee (Mrs. Ruth B. Young)
1956 Ch. Frola of Snowland (Mr. and Mrs. J. J. Marshall)
1957 Ch. Vrai of Lucky Dee (Mr. and Mrs. B. P. Dawes)
1958 Ch. Lt's Lulo Luloto (Mr. and Mrs. T. Schneider)
1959 Ch. Sparkle Plenty of Arbee (Mrs. Ruth B. Young)
1960 Tundra Princess Starya (Estalene Beckman)
1961 Am. & Can. Ch. Kobe's Nan-nuk of Encino
      (Mr. and Mrs. John Weir)
1962 Tundra Princess Starya (Estalene Beckman)
1963 Ch. Silver Moon (Bob and Bonnie Bowles)
1964 Ch. Silver Moon
1965 Ch. Silver Moon
1966 Ch. Sam O'Khan's Tsari of Khan (Mr. and Mrs. G. Fitzpatrick)
1967 Ch. Sam O'Khan's Tsari of Khan
1968 Ch. Sam O'Khan's Tsari of Khan

Wimundstrev Trophy Winners (Top Stud Dog):

1954 Ch. Martingate Snowland Taz (imported by Dr. Wm. H. Ivens and
      acquired in 1950 by Elma Miller)
1955 Ch. Martingate Snowland Taz
1956 Ch. Starchak, CD (Bob and Dolly Ward)
1957 Ch. Omak (Mr. and Mrs. Percy Matheron)
1958 Ch. Stormy Weather of Betty Blue (Mr. and Mrs. Martin Gleason)
1959 Ch. Elkenglo's Jola (Lucy Schneider)
1960 Ch. Elkenglo's Jola
1961 Ch. Yurok of Whitecliff (Mr. and Mrs. Percy Matheron and Jean
      Blank)
1962 Am. & Can. Ch. Tod-Acres Fang (John and Lila Weir)
1963 Ch. Elkenglo's Jola
1964 Am. & Can. Ch. Tod-Acres Fang
1965 Am. & Can. Ch. Noatak of Silver Moon
      (Bob and Bonnie Bowles)
1966 Am. & Can. Ch. Noatak of Silver Moon
1967 Am. & Can. Ch. Noatak of Silver Moon
1968 Am. & Can. Ch. Noatak of Silver Moon

A. E. Mason Trophy Winners (Top Winning Samoyed):

1956 Ch. King of Wal-Lyn (Mrs. Ethel Smith)
1957 Ch. King of Wal-Lyn
1958 Ch. Yurok of Whitecliff (Mr. and Mrs. Percy Matheron and Jean Blank)
1959 Ch. Yurok of Whitecliff
1960 Ch. Yurok of Whitecliff
1961 Ch. Shoshone of Whitecliff (Jean Blank)
1962 Ch. Winterland's Kim (Bernice Heagy)
1963 Ch. Noatak of Silver Moon (Robert and Bonnie Bowles)
1964 Ch. Saroma's Polar Prince (Richard and Martha Beal)

Ch. Dudinka's Diva, wh. 1964 by Ch. Barceia's Shondi of Drayalene ex Ch. Patrice of Snow Ridge. Winner of the Ch. Suzanne of White Way Memorial Trophy for 1966. Bred by Elliot Colburn and owned by Mary Nolan and Irene Eaton of Colorado.

1965 Ch. Kara Sea's Silver Nikki (Vera Johnson Gowdyk)
1966 Ch. Sam O'Khan's Chingis Khan (Mr. and Mrs. James Sheets)
1967 Ch. Sam O'Khan's Chingis Khan
1968 Ch. Sam O'Khan's Chingis Khan

Ch. Suzanne of White Way Memorial (Top Winning Bitch):
1959 Ch. Ell-Tee Roxanne (Mr. and Mrs. T. Schneider)
1960 Ch. Ell-Tee Roxanne
1961 Ch. Frostar's Tundra Starfrost (Louis and Joyce Cain)
1962 Ch. Frostar's Tundra Starfrost
1963 Ch. Frostar's Princess Snowball (Mr. and Mrs. S. Lawton)
1964 Ch. Chu-San's Mei Ling O'Yeniseisk (Nelda Dendinger)
1965 Ch. Samtara's Sugay'N Spice (Joyce Cain)
1966 Ch. Dudinka's Diva (Mary Noland and Irene Eaton)
1967 Ch. Ka-Tag's Memory in Silver (Kathryn Tagliaferri and Nelda Dendinger)
1968 Ch. Ka-Tag's Memory in Silver

Ch. Chu San's Mei Ling O'Yeniseisk, wh. 1963, by Ch. Chu San's Silver Folly ex Elbur's Mitzie of Yeniseisk. Winner of the Ch. Suzanne of White Way award for 1964. Bred by Gary Gray, and owned by Kathryn Tagliaferri of Baton Rouge.

Ch. Ka-Tag's Memory In Silver, wh. 1966, by Ch. Silver Duke of the Rockies ex Ch. Chu San's Mei Ling O'Yeniseisk. Winner of the Ch. Suzanne of White Way award for 1967 and 1968. Bred by N. and K. Tagliaferri, and owned by Nelda and T. J. Dendinger.

Ch. Elkenglo's Jola, wh. 1952, by Ch. Martingate Snowland Taz ex Frona of Blakewood. Winner of the Wimundstrev Stud Dog Trophy for 1959, 1960 and 1963. Bred by Elma Miller, and owned by Lucy Schneider of Indianapolis.

Ch. Sparkle Plenty of Arbee, by Ch. Zoveek of Snowland ex Nimreena of Snowland. Tucker Brood Bitch Trophy winner for 1955 and 1959. Owned by Ruth Bates Young, Ohio.

Ch. Honey Babe of Gro-Wil, wh. 1968, by Ch. Muushka Silva-Ranger ex Honey Bear-Stone. Winner of the Juliet T. Goodrich Fund Trophy, Top Winning Samoyed Bitch of 1969. Owned by Mr. and Mrs. Grover C. Walls of Iowa.

299

Ch. Nachalnik of Drayalene, wh. 1962, by Ch. Rokandi of Drayalene ex Drayalene's Clarisse. Winner of the Juliet T. Goodrich Fund Trophy, Top Producing Stud of 1970. Owners, Harold and Doris McLaughlin of Colorado.

Beginning in 1969, awards were instituted in cooperation with the Juliet Goodrich Trust Fund, to be made to the Top Winning Dog, the Top Winning Bitch, the Top Stud Dog, the Top Brood Bitch, and the Top Obedience Winner.

A listing of all winners follows:

1969   Top Winning Dog—Ch. Sam O'Khan's Chingis Khan (Sheets)
        Top Winning Bitch—Ch. Honey Babe of Gro-Wil (Walls)
        Top Producing Stud—Am. & Can. Ch. Saroma's Polar Prince (Beal)
        Top Producing Bitch—Ch. Tempest of Misty Way (McCarthy)
        Top Obedience Samoyed—Ch. Snowline's Joli Shashan, CDX (Mayfield)
1970   Top Winning Dog—Ch. Sam O'Khan's Chingis Khan
        Top Winning Bitch—Ch. Orion's Mishka of Marcomar (Eggiman)
        Top Producing Stud—Ch. Nachalnik of Drayalene (McLoughlin)
        Top Producing Bitch—Can. & Am. Ch. Sam O'Khan's Tsari of Khan (Fitzpatrick)
        Top Obedience Samoyed—Ell-Tee's Square Do Tasha, UD (Gormley)

Ch. Sam O'Khan's Tsari of Khan, by Am. and Can. Ch. Zaysan of Krisland, C.D. ex Ch. Whitecliff's Polar Dawn. Winner of the Tucker Brood Bitch Trophy for 1966, 1967 and 1968, and of the Juliet T. Goodrich Fund Trophy for Top Producing Bitch of 1970. Owned by George and Frances Fitzpatrick.

The early AKC champion Samoyeds (1907–1929):

1907   deWitte of Argenteau, by Moustan ex Sora of Argenteau
1908   Siberia of Argenteau, parentage unknown
1914   Zuroff, by Szarevitch ex Tamara
1915   Tamara, imported, by Pedro ex Countess Thora
1917   Greenacres Kieff, by Szarevitch ex Tamara
1918   Malschick, by Czarevitch ex Wiemur
1919   Shut Balackeror, litter brother of Malschick
1921   Leedy, particulars unknown
       Ivan, by Malschick ex Bee Bee
       Tobolsk, imported, by Fang ex Vilna
       Zanosa, by Shut Balackeror ex Sunny Ridge Pavlova
1922   Donerna's Barin, imported, by Kieff ex Ivanofna
       Draga, litter sister to Tobolsk
       Kazan of Yurak, by Tobolsk ex Sunny Ridge Pavlova
       Olga of Farningham, imported, by Antarctic Bru ex Oka
       Vilna of Yurak, by Shut Balackeror ex Draga
1923   Alba of Oakham House, by Fang of Yurak ex Oka of Oakham House
       Nico of Farningham, imported, by Antarctic Nico ex Kama of
           Farningham
       Yurak's Nansen, by Polar Sea ex Olga of Farningham
1924   Czar of Arctic, by Malschick ex Yansei
       Nanook II, by Tobolsk ex Otiska
       Donerna's Tsilma, imported, litter sister to Donerna's Barin
       Ishma of Oakham House, litter sister to Alba of Oakham House
       Donerna's Kolya of Farningham, imported, by Russki of Orton ex Roda
       Donerna's Ilinishna, imported, by Zahra ex Donerna's Tsilma
1925   Toby of Yurak II, litter sister of Nanook II
       Nanook of Donerna, by Tobolsk ex Petrova of Yurak
       Dowd's Nansen, by Prince of Arctic ex Yansei
       Alexy, by Yurak's Nansen ex Kritelka of Yurak
1926   Yukon Mit, imported, by Husky of Winkworth ex Polga of Winkworth
       Grover Cleveland, ancestry unknown
       Fang of Yurak, litter brother of Kazan of Yurak
1927   Bomba of Winkworth, imported, by Antarctic Bru ex Louva of
           Farningham
       Snyeg, by Nanook II ex Kar
       Kleptovsky, by Snyeg ex Yurak's Nadya
       Kritelka of Yurak, by Shut Balackeror ex Drga
       Yuratado of Snowview, by Yurak's Trip of Farningham
           ex Yrak's Bjelkaske of Coronado (California)
1928   Yrak's Trip of Farningham, imported, by Antarctic Bru ex Muffit
       Brunoff, by Donerna's Barin ex Princess Veta
       Stara of Farningham, imported, by Starsun Bru of Farningham
           ex Ice Floe of Farningham
       Lash's Lyof, by Nanook II ex Alexy
       Laika's Natiya, by Yurak's Nansen ex Zelkina

1929 Jascha, by Bondarchuk of Rurik ex Zulieka of Yurak
Zanato of the Snows, by Tobolsk ex Yurak's Zanada
Mushinsk, full brother of Yukon Mit
Darya of Donerna, by Nanook of Donerna ex Donerna's Tsilma
Bakou, imported from France (had to make his championship to become
    registered)

A rare picture of
Antarctic Buck.

```
                         ( Sire: ANTARCTIC BUCK, from
                         ( Borchgrevink Expedition, 1908
All male litter:

SOUTH POLE               (               ( MUSTI, imported dog
SOUTHERN CROSS           (               ( from Siberia
FANG                     (        NANSEN
MEZENIT                  (               ( WHITY PETCHORA, imported
OLAF                     (               ( bitch from Siberia
                         ( Dam:: KVIKLENE
                         (               ( RUSS, purchased by
                         (               ( Trontheim
                         (        PEARLENE
                         (               ( KVIK, from Jackson-
                         (               ( Harmsworth Expedition
```

An historic early litter